Lost Intimacy in American Thought

Lost Intimacy in American Thought

Recovering Personal Philosophy from
Thoreau to Cavell

Edward F. Mooney

continuum

NEW YORK • LONDON

The Continuum International Publishing Group Inc
80 Maiden Lane, New York, NY 10038

The Continuum International Publishing Group Ltd
The Tower Building, 11 York Road, London SE1 7NX

www.continuumbooks.com

Copyright © 2009 by Edward F. Mooney

Library of Congress Cataloging-in-Publication Data
A catalog record for this book is available from the Library of Congress.

ISBN: 978-1-4411-8166-4 (hardcover)
ISBN: 978-1-4411-6858-0 (paperback)

Typeset by Newgen Imaging Systems Pvt Ltd, Chennai, India
Printed in the United States of America

a mountain shelter or a hut in the moor become seeds for words,
a way to become intimate with wind and cloud.
Listen recklessly.
—Basho, *Knapsack Notebook,* 9

[Without] the intimacy of touch, nothing is truly known.
No intimacy, no revelation.
—Henry Bugbee, *The Inward Morning,* 130

. . . ours is the long journey of the Saturday,
between suffering, aloneness, unutterable waste, on the one hand
and the dream of liberation, or rebirth, on the other.
In the face of the torture of a child, of the love which is Friday,
even the greatest art and poetry are almost helpless.
The apprehensions and figurations in the play of metaphysical imagining,
in the poem and the music, which tell of pain and hope,
of the flesh that is said to taste of ash
and of the spirit which is said to have the savour of fire, are always Sabbatarian.
They have risen out of an immensity of waiting which is that of man.
Without them, how could we be patient?
—George Steiner, *Real Presences,* 231

For
Steve, Gary,
Clark, Gordon,
Herb and Jack

CONTENTS

Contents

PREFACE

These essays on the loss of intimacy in American thought were not written with a book-length argument in mind. Each was composed from an immediate yet lasting impulse to celebrate the impact on my reading and thinking life of a philosopher or writer, or of a fragment of thoughts tendered. Recovering personal philosophy is recovering the transfiguring impacts of writing addressed intimately that may well resonate not just with me, but with an indefinitely large circle of hearers—call it an infinite but intimate universal. Some aspect of the words or sentences of these writers would catch me off-guard, seem to resonate with my deepest interests in ways it was up to me to work out. A number of crisscrossing themes and the return of certain passages that seem to have become iconic for me hold these efforts together, culminating in my lengthy excursion with Thoreau. Each can be read independently.

One of my early efforts focuses on Henry Bugbee's *The Inward Morning,* a philosophical journal that explores somewhat autobiographically the writer's earliest sense of what tied the world together—or opened it up—for him. After two decades reading in and around this book, by the mid-1990s it seemed time to acknowledge it, recount its impact over the years—difficult as that might turn out to be. And it seemed time to make my reflections known to its author, a man well into retirement and of uncertain longevity. His journal was written while on a George Santayana Fellowship in his last year as an assistant professor at Harvard. To my ear, his entries registered a genius for instilling an intimacy with what led him to think philosophically, and how that thinking continued, in and out of books, in ever-surprising directions. I was touched—and it turned out many others were, too—by his candor and eloquence as he made his way through what seemed a wondrous and sometimes treacherous venture of coming into philosophy and keeping it close to the marrow of life. He figured it as a path in wilderness.

When I encountered Stanley Cavell's "autobiographical exercises," collected in *A Pitch of Philosophy*, I knew the intimacy of autobiographical revelation was not an accomplishment of *The Inward Morning* alone. Each exploration, with its themes of exposure and revelation, could be illuminated by the light of the other. Now after weaving that story, it's evident that Cavell and Bugbee belong to a neglected tradition that includes Rousseau's *Reveries of a Solitary Walker*, Kierkegaard's *The Point of View of my Work as an Author*, and Thoreau's *Week on the Concord and Merrimack*. It seems equally clear that the many who admired *Inward Morning*, including myself, had remained academically silent because of being professionally embarrassed by its autobiographical, even literary cast—and that this suffering was unnecessary. There was no need for philosophy, as I now saw it, to exclude the personal and intimately revelatory. *A Pitch of Philosophy* and *Inward Morning* were good for more than weekend reading in a mood of informal reminiscence.

The essay on Bugbee and Cavell soon led (with a push from Dan Conway and others) to a collection of essays, later published as *Wilderness and the Heart*, presented to Henry in Missoula Montana at a banquet celebrating his teaching life and the haunting power of his "philosophical explorations in journal form." Those efforts were followed some years later by a chance to record my excitement over Bob Pippin's book on Henry James. This was an account of a moral life as forming in the intimate place of conversation in the thick of love, envy, betrayal, greed, and all the subtle dimensions of reciprocally formed tenors of selves. Tracing the unfolding contours of moral consciousness of characters in the novels of Henry James was, if anything, an exploration of the philosophical significance of personal revelations. The theme of lost intimacy was beginning to take hold as I began to measure the distance between the fine-grained and evocative explorations of Cavell, Pippin, and Bugbee and the cool, disengaged, and quite abstract arguments so common in the profession. A bit later I had an opportunity to write on Glenn Gray's *The Warriors*, an account of war and relationships laced with his memories of his time at the front during World War II. Then to buttress my sense of philosophy's self-imposed alienations from the personal, I was intercepted by Bruce Wilshire's lamentations that American philosophy had lost touch with the earth as a locus of spirit and instruction, and with what we should be able, without blushing, to call the soul.

Preface xi

One could hear the whispers in the hallways, "*It's all a bit muddled and self-indulgent, don't you think?*" But muddle or no, the soul and an intimate touch with the world (and why do we make these *distinct?*) are well worth preserving.

I can't neglect my late rediscovery that Thoreau is so much more than an endearing tramper and outspoken defender of civil resistance. In an adventure rich beyond my wildest dreams, I've found a subtle and penetrating philosopher who can hold his own, in range and depth, with Schiller or Schopenhauer—and as Cavell had argued in the early 1970s (to little avail), who can converse with Kant and Wittgenstein. This makes a full circle. Both Bugbee and Cavell learned from and leaned on Thoreau, with whom they worked out their conviction that exposing one's intimacy with place and one's friends and others can be worthy philosophy.

Recognitions belated are better than never. These essays are late appreciations that are tendered to a circle of writers who testify to the intimate side of reflective philosophical life. These writers deliver works of remarkable accomplishment despite the dispiriting power of professionalization, and despite the deep pressures in philosophy to disown all intimate exposure in pursuit of a broad dispassionate view from the top. I attempt here a measure of appreciation and a gesture of resistance and transformation, a small step down toward recovery of the personal.

February 25, 2009
Syracuse, New York

ACKNOWLEDGMENTS

Thanks to Dan Conway for his support and initiative in bringing Henry Bugbee into the open; to Bruce Wilshire for knowing Montana gold when he saw it; to Rick Furtak for bringing to Santa Fe philosophers who see Thoreau as a philosopher; to Steve Webb for his sustained devotion to good writing and his marvelous mind; to Anthony Rudd and John Davenport for seeing that philosophy is written in a variety of ways; to William Day for helping focus the intimate dimension of Cavell's writing; to Marcia Robinson, my wife, for reminding me to see love and the political as interwoven, and much else; to Tyler Roberts for urging me to write on Cavell as a religious-continental thinker; to Lyman Mower for bringing Levinas so close to Thoreau; to Clark West for planting the seeds for bringing Thoreau's politics and "nature writing" together; to Herbert Fingarette for teaching me not to look over my shoulder; to Phil and Judy Temko for their love of fragile birds, neglected peoples, and poetry; to Kailen and my new family for showing that biological research and poetic attachment are companions; to Jack Caputo for seeing the person beneath polemics; to Gary Whited for brotherly love; to Gordon Marino, Sally Moore, Alastair Hannay, Dirk, Karen, Joe, George, Haaris (at *Continuum*), Carson, and to so many others who know well who they are.

Dean Cathy Newton of Syracuse University has supported my writing financially and collegially, as did the Religion Department under the gentle leadership of Dick Pilgrim. A number of these chapters first appeared in journals, having subsequently undergone varying degrees of revision: chapter two first appeared as the introduction to Henry Bugbee's *The Inward Morning, Philosophical Explorations in Journal Form,* reissue by University of Georgia Press, 1999; chapter three, in *Wilderness and the Heart,* ed. Edward F. Mooney, University of Georgia Press, 1999; chapter five, in *Prayer and Post-Modernism,* ed. Bruce Benson and

Norman Wirzba, Fordham University Press, 2005; chapter six, in *The Journal of Speculative Philosophy* 2003; chapter seven, in *Soundings, an Interdisciplinary Journal,* Summer 2005; chapter eight, in *Human Studies,* December, 2001; chapter nine, in *Inquiry,* 2002. I thank Laura Dassow Walls, editor of the *Concord Saunterer* for her encouragement as chapter twelve worked its way toward inclusion in that Journal, vol. 16, 2008. I thank these for permission to recycle.

Part I

_____

INTRODUCTION

Chapter 1

THOREAU AND OTHERS:
Thinking from Imagination and the Heart

Ortega calls his *Meditations on Quixote* "essays in intellectual love." As he puts it, "[these essays] . . . have no informative value whatever; they are not summaries, either — they are rather what a humanist of the seventeenth century would have called 'salvations.'"[1] But what can we, of the twenty-first century, make of the idea that essays can be *salvations?* Ortega writes that a salvation—for example, his salvations of *Don Quixote*—will take up "a man, a book, a picture, a landscape, an error, a sorrow" and then seek "to carry it by the shortest route to its fullest significance."

We should expect, then, that some essays are expressions of love, a kind of preservative love, a love that cares for persons and things and gives them life. Such essays can carry out a generous, even pious criticism or elaboration that brings a theme or person or object to its next and fuller meaning. Without such attentive care, fields of significance we now take for granted fall into disuse, decay. Like ill-treated living things, they slowly die, or stay fallow, awaiting summer's rain and seeding. Texts or paintings, trees or figures from our past, can carry undiscovered plenitudes. The artful critic, like the curator of invaluable archives or someone husbanding objects of great cultural worth, can bring that plenitude out and into life, saving it from extinction or from an only paltry half-life.

We wish to be spared the painful eventualities that may beset us, saved from the worst that life can hold in store, and saved, too, from the less visible hurt of indifference or neglect. Mediocrities and

---

[1] José Ortega y Gassett, *Meditations on Quixote,* trans. Evelyn Rugg and Diego Marín, Urbana: University of Illinois Press, 2000, 3f. Thanks to Steve Webb for bringing me to Ortega.

mechanical routines can be killing, too. Ortega doesn't speak autobio-graphically of calamities or lesser horrors or discomforts, but he thinks of things a writer can face in opening toward the world. He speaks, for example, of writing an "essay in intellectual love" that attends to an "error" or a "sorrow." We are to imagine, I think, that the writer's atten-tion might rescue that error or sorrow, whatever it might specifically be, from a kind of disgrace or neglect. We want neither to be neglected in our sorrow nor disgraced by our errors.

A writer might consider a man or a woman in the expanse of life. The person attended to might be real or fictional, alive or dead. A preservative care or love might revive a person whose life would otherwise slip into anonymity. A fantastic yet luminous life might await its detailed imaginative articulation, its birth through the writer's art. Cervantes brings a man alive we otherwise might think a fool best to be forgotten. Don Quixote's days are laced with sorrow and mistake, as he travels a bizarre, fanciful, and violent landscape. Yet he's saved in his glory, to our glory, by the novelist's deft hand. And Ortega in his *Meditations on Quixote* once again saves that bygone road and woeful traveler from desuetude and death.[2]

Of course, the world holds enough affliction and decline to occupy all the doctors, mayors, parents, and other helpers that we could ever hope to muster. They are rightly among our valued first responders. But novelists and artists, essayists and poets, singers and painters also have a powerful, saving role to play. Care and love for the waiting-to-be-revived (like the good Quixote, or like a cruelly abandoned child) can come from priests or good-willed politicians or responsive passersby and also from devoted speakers, writers, teachers who curate the past, revive the present, and project paths into the future. They are transmitters and restorers of spirit sufficient for at least a sip of healing, a breath of life, a touch of resurrection.

Now the work of helping and healing, as Ortega has it, can take up not just the "error" or "sorrow" of a person or a way of life but also the presence of "a book, a picture, or a landscape." And the writer can administer a preservative care for the things and objects of the world that despite their potential radiance are forgotten or declining.

Those "things of the world" that a writer or artist might glimpse through imaginative gift and then catch creatively in words or paint

---

[2] Miguel de Unamuno has Quixote resurrected as Christ in his 1905 essay, *Our Lord Don Quixote: The Life of Don Quixote and Sancho*, Princeton: Princeton University Press, Bollingen, 1976. Ortega's *Meditations on Quixote* appears in Spanish in 1914.

are not, or not only, bits of lifeless Newtonian matter fit for a chemist's or physicist's analysis. They are often living things, or animated things like great storms, or things resonant with serenity, like great reclining rocks. To deny that thunder speaks or rocks recline is an instance of "the *apathetic* fallacy." This is denying feeling or stance to all but human life. It is acceding to a "disenchantment of the world." Living things one and all and some nonliving ones, like rocks or thunderheads, call out our intellectual love; they're vehicles of their own surpassing worth. As Ortega puts it, "We want to place the objects of all kinds which life, in its perpetual surge, throws at our feet like the useless remains of a shipwreck, in such a position that the sun as it strikes them may give off innumerable reflections."[3] He thinks here of Rembrandt. The painter can take something almost forgotten that nevertheless has "an indication of a possible plenitude." This possible plenitude (or meaning) is what the painter brings to birth. Rembrandt finds "a coarse household utensil," for instance, and through his painterly attention lets it be "wrapped in a luminous and radiant atmosphere, with which other painters surround only the heads of saints." He continues, "It is as if [the painter] said to us in gentle admonition: 'Blessed be things! Love them, love them!'"[4]

Now the mood that Ortega instills in this evocation is distinctive, and cannot be generalized without exception. It's a mood appropriate to things that can be loved, and not everything in this life can be met with that sort of loving gaze. Some things might be better scorned, forgotten, or peeled away from life. We might wish to pulverize a weapon rather than ring it with lovely radiance. There is a gamut of things we properly meet with rejection or revulsion. And on the other hand, along the gamut of things we greet with care or love, there is variation in the tenor of our greetings or receptions.

Love or care brings us to sites of death and mourning, and we might find ourselves attending there to things of the world—lilies, clumps of damp earth. In that mourning circle we'd wish, it seems, not to love or bless them in the voice Ortega offers. Instead, we might bring out the darkness of the earth, the fragility of the lily. We might abide in tears and resignation with wet earth and funereal blossom.

There can be "an essay in intellectual love" that *mourns*, that greets worth or plenitude in its absence, or loss, or desolation. Rembrandt's love of a utensil is a fresh acclamation, even consecration. But love in

---

[3] Ortega, *Meditations*, 31.
[4] Ibid.

its mourning attire weeps and loves things that are memorials to trauma, loss, or devastation. That love may become a lasting memorial, outlasting what is lost, the song or poem or stone that lingers even as the body's buried. In *Cape Cod*, Thoreau writes out salvation at a site of mourning. He lifts to our gaze what seems at first to be but an object the size of Rembrandt's spoon. It's a small thing apparently forgotten on a beach. He lifts it to let it speak.

Here is Thoreau approaching Ortega's "remains of a shipwreck," remains that "life, in its perpetual surge, throws at our feet." The difference is that Thoreau approaches a *specific* shipwreck, not the generalized wreck existence can so easily present. He walks on Fire Island. The offshore storm-splintered hulk is what remains of the ship in which Margaret Fuller and her family, returning from Italy, were drowned. It's not merely a hulk just off the beach. It's a disaster. We're far from a painter's ordinary flower or utensil or sweet meadowlark. He walks the beach, and preserves the approach in words.

> I expected that I should have to look very narrowly at the sand to find so small an object, but so completely smooth and bare was the beach . . . that when I was half a mile distant the insignificant stick or sliver which marked the spot looked like a broken spar in the sand. There lay the relics in a certain state, rendered perfectly inoffensive to both bodily and spiritual eye by the surrounding scenery, a slight inequality in the sweep of the shore . . . It was as conspicuous on that sandy plain as if a generation had labored to pile up a cairn there . . . It reigned over the shore. That dead body possessed the shore as no living one could.[5]

Emerson and others had asked Thoreau to travel south from Concord to recover Fuller's body and to save what might be found of her writing and personal effects. She had been a star among the transcendentalists, and was sent by the *New York Tribune* to cover the Italian Revolution. A number of local onlookers had seen her offshore 250 yards or so clinging helplessly as the ship broke up. By the time Thoreau arrived, a week later, they remembered where on the beach her shallow grave had been clumsily dug out and marked with that simple stick.

Thoreau, as we see, feared he would not notice so small an object, yet as it came into view it captured his lyrical eyes "like a broken spar." Then he finds himself by "the relics" of a saint, saved by his eye from the offensive stench of a corpse. She is held by "the sweep of the shore,"

---

[5] Henry David Thoreau, *Cape Cod*, New York: Thomas Crowell, 1961, 123; worked up from *Journal*, vol. 3, 1848–51 ed. R. Sattelmeyer, M.R. Patterson, W. Rossi, Princeton, 1990, 127.

gently, it seems, leaving the "bodily and spiritual eye" serene. Thoreau writes her salvation. She is not a forgotten casualty of a wreck, not a remnant, not a rotting disturber of our dreams or of the equanimity of the sands. His eye and then his words raise her to the height of a cairn or monument, built over decades, tribute to her reign. "That dead body possessed the shore as no living one could." She has been saved from the dead through Thoreau's "essay in intellectual love," a "salvation" that brings every "indication of her plenitude" vividly before us.

* * *

If we take the spirit of Thoreau's work to be the retrieval of "indications of plenitude," the work of another American philosophical writer wonderfully revives that spirit. To my ear, Henry Bugbee, writing one hundred years later, brings us a Thoreau-like capacity to see those diminutive splinters and larger aspects of landscape (and we who traverse them) as markers of plenitudes. They become plenitudes that move him—and then move us—to elevate and praise the life so marked. Thoreau and Bugbee write "salvations" that raise life from decline; they are philosophers who write intimately, personally, for love of the world.

Bugbee's journal speaks of Socrates and Kant and also of Marcel, Eckhart, Tillich, and Melville, and it harbors mysterious reflections on wilderness and war in the Pacific. Harvard called him to teach philosophy in the 1950s, a fact that gives his philosophical explorations some authority, although his conception of the field can sound eccentric today as it no doubt did then. He proposed that philosophy was "a walking meditation of the place."[6] Decades later I linked this revelation to Thoreau's essay, "Walking," but on first reading it I was completely bewildered.[7] But I knew in my bones that his was a philosophy that brings life to things, a lyrical philosophy that finds plenitudes in them.

* * *

---

[6] Henry Bugbee, *The Inward Morning, A Philosophical Exploration in Journal Form*, foreword Gabriel Marcel, intro. Edward F. Mooney, Athens, GA: University of Georgia Press, 1999, first published State College, PA: Bald Eagle Press, 1958, p. 139.

[7] See *The Collected Essays of Henry D Thoreau*, ed. Lewis Hyde, San Francisco: North Point Press, 2002.

Walking can bring us into intimate contact with a place and with our stride and balance and breathing within and through a place. But still we might ask how walking meditations are relevant to philosophical self-understanding or to a theoretical grasp of the world. There is a clue in the ancient Greek understanding of *theoria*, the word from which we moderns get our word, "theory."

The venerable sense of *theoria* is a transformative walk or journey to behold foreign sights.[8] Not exactly the nineteenth-century Grand Tour of European capitols, museums, and natural sights, but not that far off, either. Thoreau might endorse this notion of traveling-to-behold, so long as the walking was not through a *city's* festivals or sights but toward wondrous rural or wild sites. For the Greeks, a sacred shrine or festival was often the sight to see, to behold, as it were. To behold is to be present to revelation—to a revelation of worth or power or terror as these might accost us as an appearance of the divine, or stop us in our tracks in attendance to the arts, or stop us under distant stars, or before striking deeds, or startling flocks in flight. This premodern sense of *theoria* as astonished or frightened *beholding* gets displaced in the modern world.

For moderns, *theoria* comes to mean "theory," something abstract that's indispensable to scientific or critical understanding. We test theory against objects (or against actions or institutions that are taken as objects of attention and interest). We hold the object or field of objects to be theorized at arm's length. To test a world by theory, we retreat from the world-to-be-theorized and size it up in terms of that theory. Thus the detachment of theory is the detachment of the *theorizer* from an intimate immersion in the world.

A theory's capacity to grip the world incapacitates and defeats intimate self-knowledge, of necessity. If I turn my interest or attention to myself in a theoretical vein, I try to hold up *my own self* as something to be explained. I try to become a theorist with regard to myself. And that leaves the active "me" who does the holding up, explaining, or examining volatized, out of the picture, not in the midst of the world-to-be-theorized.

The theorizer organizes her field of data; she will always be already outside that field, and hence can't know herself by means of her theory; she can know (parts of) the world but not herself. Furthermore, this stance of "looking at" (rather than beholding) destroys the

---

[8] See Andrea Wilson Nightingale, *Spectacles of Truth in Classical Greek Philosophy*, Cambridge: Cambridge University Press, 2004.

wider intimacy that a religious sensibility seeks and sometimes finds. If we want to know the world as a place that can portend the sacred or the holy, or a place that just *matters*, we can't detachedly *stare at it*; and if we want to know ourselves as centers of vibrant life, we can't just examine the world (inner or outer or neither) unattached, expecting to find ourselves. To know a sunset intimately is in part to bask in its presence, which is to find ourselves basking—not theorizing.

Thoreau links walking to sauntering.[9] To saunter, he suggests, is linked to medieval wandering *á la Sainte Terre*, wandering to the holy land in search of the site where one's soul can be refreshed. Henry Bugbee inherits this tradition. As he puts it, philosophy is not a theoretical venture but, as we've mentioned, a walking meditation of the place.[10] It is a reflective journey toward astonishing instructive sights to behold, a pilgrimage that includes the venture out and one's journey home as a person now transformed. Thoreau walks to the wild, returns to his cabin, and then sets out again. He walks to Maine's Ktaadn or tramps Cape Cod, and returns. His walking is an exercise in weaving the world, weaving the self, weaving contacts that occur as revelations of the world as a place overflowing with meaning—even holy, so deep is its significance.

* * *

Plato is a pivot in our understanding of theory, and of philosophy. The *Republic* opens with Socrates on a road leading to a wondrous festival. But he also features the philosopher as an onlooker, a spectator somewhat detached from the everyday or the wondrous. Plato begins to bend *theoria* toward what becomes the modern meaning: a formal, abstract intellectual grasp of the widest expanse of things. To grasp the intellectual form of things, one leaves local landscapes and city squares and places of rest and sleep. One elevates to become a spectator of all time and eternity, peering *down* at the meager imperfections of a mutable world from a site of conceptual perfections.[11] Thus begins a powerful and familiar tradition stretching from Aristotle through

---

[9] "Walking," in Hyde, *Collected Essays*, 149.

[10] Bugbee, *Inward Morning*, 139.

[11] The *Symposium*, often cited as leading us up out of the world of particulars, also shows Socrates relaxed in his love for flesh-and-blood friends. So the lover of beauty might ascend, but then descend to the world of particular beauties, much as Socrates' wise man returns to the cave.

St Thomas and on through Descartes, in which philosophy becomes identified less with a saving journey, and more with cognitive grasp attained through abstract products—explanatory or critical schemes. Thinkers in the style of Descartes, Leibniz, or Hume are pictured writing metaphysics (or anti-metaphysics, or physics-based systems), many steps *away* from the first-personal everyday world of Rousseau's *Reveries of a Solitary Walker* (for example). Thinking theoretically vaults one above or outside the fray in an aspiration to motionless onlooking that freezes that onlooker in a narrow slice of the significant range of life's wider plenitudes. To cut back from the immersions and submersions, passional and practical, that are the tissue of life is to cut adrift from opportunities for self-knowledge.[12] A knowing contact with oneself cannot come about through distancing oneself from vital contacts.

Taking the neglected path of ancient *theoria* is banking on encountering one's aliveness in encountering things and places in the mode of beholding.[13] One becomes aware of oneself as an offshoot of an outer-directed attention, manifested, for instance, as a physiological shudder. It attains a kind of certitude: one can't argue with goosebumps. One travels, with baggage, passions, and commitments. Sometimes the wondrous is not in the remote valley or mountain top, or distant heavens but in the local. One finds the astonishing as one moves with and around parochial passions, promises, and practices. Then philosophy can become a quasi-religious journey toward intimate knowledge of the ins and outs of family or neighborhood life, of rock-climbing and cooking, of the ups and downs of walking a friend through cancer, or of swimming away from catastrophe.[14]

Walkers are mobile bodies and also a concomitant presence to things worthy to behold. A moment basking in the shade of a tree (or in the delightful sounds of children at play) can leave one open to a subtle normative "call" folded into this basking absorption. We are gripped by, and so beholden to, things that can take our breath

---

[12] Descartes famously detaches himself from his moral, political, and religious engagements as he begins his fireside meditations. Hume finds that even writing *against* metaphysics left him detached; he reconnects through a good game of billiards.

[13] There is nothing esoteric about a non-intellectualistic contact with myself; it's how I know I'm about to slip. Neither Kant's image of grasping ourselves as free agents nor as observers of natural objects helps; we need Kant's image of ourselves in non-intellectual contact with ourselves when accosted by the sublime, open to the wonders and terrors of existence.

[14] See Alphonso Lingis, *The Community of those who have Nothing in Common*, Bloomington: University of Indiana Press, 1994.

away—*that* shaft of light or laughing child. In such absorption, I find myself in resonance *with* the place, *in* the place. If our place lacks life, is drowned in routine, peppered with sleepwalking, suffused by a "normal nihilism" of numbness, distraction, and indifference, then the prescription is evident: a journey *out* of that hard or soft tyranny in a venture toward transformative sights.[15] Walking meditation (philosophy) brings one to *behold* the world and come alive *as and within* a place that's alive. We behold the place, and the place holds us.

A foreign or sacred place puts one's shape, mood, and contour, one's strengths and fragilities, in finely etched relief. We are then a subtle openness to the world and what it might portend. Presence to the wondrous or holy opens us to the possibility that our attachments can be owned or disowned. As I behold "foreign" ways, I sense that my differences, differences that suddenly stand out contrastively, mark ways in which I am already formed. I am beholden to loves, aversions, and habits whose grip is inherited, not chosen. They become salient as *especially mine*—even as I find them, on reflection, amenable to *renewal, alteration, or rejection.* It's also true that the beholding self can be overwhelmed. Explicit awareness of a self that is ready to form or to own its attachments can seem to disappear. The self is emptied; in awe, it melts away.

Walking attentiveness would be only one phase of a life—perhaps a pause in focused attention to scientific theory, or in irritable unloving attention to fixing the car. But that pause is not to be swapped for the illusory security of the uninterrupted "eternal" standpoint of theory, or for the benefits of impersonal theory-production, a detached stalling that occludes our particular immersions in local pains and delights, family ties and occupational demands. For these are—are they not?—the lively weave of all which we might call our unfolding reality or existence.

Bugbee finds the world "consolidated in taking steps."[16] He finds the vulnerabilities and opacities of his condition clarified, not by argument or theory but by moving ever deeper *into* his condition, altering his place, or returning to it—with luck, beholding that deep and vibrant place that *grips* him, *is* him, even as he wonders at its provenance. What *grips*, for the moment, we trust, *is* us; and we trust

---

[15] See James Edwards on malls and mindless work as "normal nihilism." See *The Plain Sense of Things: The Fate of Religion in an Age of Normal Nihilism*, College Park: Penn State University Press, 1997.

[16] Bugbee, *Inward Morning*, 139.

perforce that there is something like what we are and will become, something beyond despair and detachment, that *will* grip—to which we can be beholden. The last word is neither numb routines of pre-reflective sociality, nor elegant moves within the "safety" of theorizing, nor a flight to distraction (with Hume) through a game of billiards.

* * *

The essays that follow are less a sustained theoretical argument, or series of them, than a set of somewhat independent and necessarily incomplete evocations and invitations—meditations or "salvations," as Ortega would call them. Such writing is for and from imagination and the heart, and witness to both. Lyrical philosophy witnesses to inhabitation of a lively, intimate place. We *are* place, as Emerson says, the place we alertly traverse.[17] And so I try to evoke the writer's place, and my place with that writer, with whom, even if only intermittently, I travel intimately, whose words touch me, often in ways I can barely comprehend.

The Inward Morning tells us, "No intimacy, no revelation," and "[Without] the intimacy of touch, [nothing] is . . . truly '*known*.'"[18] To "know" wilderness, love, or terror, we must contact each in turn—from one angle and evocation to another—and let *it* contact *us*. Many of the passages that I return to again and again in these essays take on an iconic status. They are words that look back at *us*, interrogate us, or give us blessing. Finding words that contact us at this level of intimacy, words to which we can return, over and over for instruction, words that, like icons, will continually pierce our souls in looking at us, calling on us, touching us—these are vehicles of a premodern, old-style sort of knowing that we still possess but that we culturally and academically disavow.

To think of reading as approaching passages that have become iconic for us, or that might become iconic, is to think of passages that look into our souls (rather than directing us exclusively outward to see something that representations represent, something elsewhere). But passages that look into our souls also afford us new contact with the place, the place where we move and have our being. To prize that contact is to acknowledge and prize *Old Testament* tactile knowledge,

---

[17] Robert H. Richardson, Jr. in *Emerson, The Mind on Fire*, Berkeley: University of California, 1995, 312, quotes Emerson as saying, concisely, "he *is* place."
[18] Bugbee, *Inward Morning*, 130.

revealed in fleshly embrace, or in wrestling God, or in being over-whelmed, as Job was, by creation sung out in language of intimate address that silences, thrills, and frightens. To know through the soul is to behold, to be held, to be shaken, head to toe.[19]

* * *

Chapter two serves as an overture to the essays on Bugbee that comprise Part Two. Therein I consider Bugbee's evocations of Eckhart and Tillich, of war in the Pacific, of Melville's seas, and of autumn snow far into the Canadian Rockies. This links philosophy to wilderness. His prose delivers wonder and danger, the nearness of death and meditation of the place issuing a call to abide close to the wild. Bugbee's words tilt backward toward Thoreau and forward to Cavell, a writer who in the last few decades has brought Thoreau and Emerson into their full philosophical stature. Bugbee gives us lyrical philosophy (chapter three) that sings the life and elusiveness of things, even as Ortega's "salvations" do; Thoreau's tribute to the sand-held remains of Margaret Fuller achieves this, as well.

Chapter four introduces Bugbee's 1936 undergraduate thesis, a remarkable document that evokes a Kantian sublime as the fitting way to highlight the enigmas of persons in their worlds, facing death, yet in full affirmation of the world. He takes our mobile settings to be scored by tragic conflict and affliction, even as he keeps faith in deep renewals. Although modern philosophers are not known for their attention to prayer, Bugbee is an exception. In chapter five, I trace his scattered but crucial testimony. He figures prayer as meditation or reflection in a phase of passion's transformation. Its tempering passions modulate more violent ones. For Bugbee, prayer is a quiet articulation of a compassion that might answer such moral suffering as befalls us. Henry Bugbee composes *The Inward Morning* one hundred years after Thoreau's *Walden*; Stanley Cavell writes "salvations" from the 1960s to the present. In the last excursion of part two (chapter six), I pair Bugbee's search for philosophical voice with Cavell's search in the autobiographical sections of *A Pitch of Philosophy*. Cavell sounds the voice that brings Thoreau and others back to life, unraveling and reweaving the play of plenitude and aspiration in which each searches for their next and better self.

---

[19] I discuss tactile knowledge in *On Søren Kierkegaard: Dialogue, Polemic, Lost Intimacy, and Time*, Aldershot: Ashgate, 2007.

As we've seen, Thoreau gives us an aftermath of shipwreck that brings the transcendentalist editor of *The Dial,* Margaret Fuller, up from the dead, a scene not unlike Cavell's citation of St Joan's spirit rising in the Dreyer film *Jeanne d'Arc.* As she awaits a martyr's death, her eye follows the flight of wheeling birds, sun in their wings, lifting up as would her soul. And in its way, her lyrical eye, as Dreyer saves it for us, betokens a love of the world. Opening part three, chapter seven, sketches the rich trajectory of Cavell's writing since the 1950s, tracing its weave through my experience of it as it unfolds. He often writes a kind of Midrash, taking texts as scripture open to a kind of religious interpretative meditation, replete with benedictions and offerings of gratitude. Thoreau's rescue of a corpse has affinities with Bugbee's excruciating descriptions of Kamikazes descending on his ship, discussed in part two, and both compare favorably with Cavell's citation of Jeanne d'Arc finding her soul rising amidst fire.

Disaster permeates Bruce Wilshire's diagnosis of contemporary life, but for him it wears the face of drawn-out enervation; lives and worlds are drained of enchantment and vitality. In chapter eight, I consider his delineation of our uprooting through millennia from a tribal intimate contact with the world, ourselves, and others. In chapter nine, the moral vision of Henry James emerges. The disaster at issue is less visible and lacks a broad solution. If Wilshire sees our salvation residing in closer proximity to primal rhythms, sights, smells, and ceremonies of natural life, epitomized in lost tribal ways, Henry James sees salvation from enervation arrive in moments of intimate conversation, in a mutual dance of listening and revelations.

The classroom is where many of us first encounter what can be essays (and lectures) in intellectual love, words that might verge on salvations. There can be a drama there of passion, imagination, and insight that can overtake a classroom to lift spirits. Why do we hear so little of this drama? Is it a mistake to think of teaching as a theater for remembrance, refinement, and awakening of imagination and the heart? These are questions for chapter ten.

No doubt there is fear that teachers can misuse their power. We don't want universities or colleges to be sites of religious, political, or moral harangues or indoctrination, but the alternative isn't a retreat to a flawed picture of the supremacy of neutral knowledge and unbounded critique—the sort of thing that gets published in respected biological or social scientific journals. Words like "wonder," "behold," "unrequited love," or "mourning the world" then seem inept, out of place, if not romantic or old fashioned.

To speak in the same breath of moral formation and classroom teaching brings up the quaint image of a nineteenth-century college president teaching the senior course in ethics. To endorse Ortega's "essays in intellectual love" that "have no informative value," that awaken "indications of a potential plenitude," creates a dissonance easily satirized or critiqued. His aims violate the definition of a university as an institution devoted to the acquisition and dissemination of value-neutral knowledge. To alums or incoming freshmen a university or college can be described in upbeat terms; it's a place that promotes self-realization or cultural enrichment. But in more sober settings, so it seems to me, the tacit model is unabashedly commercial. The business of a university is the production, marketing, and distribution of knowledge, the accumulation and cataloguing, in ever-expanding files, of fact, theory, and concept for extra- and intra-university consumption. Knowledge becomes a commodity desired by business, government, and the professions, and serves to certify graduates — they are prepared for a professional niche, fit for democratic duty as informed and critical citizens.

In this tenth chapter, I set out to undo the hegemony of these views. To be exposed to varied powerful moods and aspirations and their transforming powers should be a central aim of education worth its salt, especially in the humanities. Passion and imagination, for instance, are integral to ways of being and ways of being moved and transformed. We are shaken by images, aspirations, and terrors, and this stirring of the soul is part of what literature, music, and the arts display and enact. Surely such tilling in the soil of aspiration, hope, and fear is an educational adventure most worth praising. To get a better factual and theoretical grip on the world and to better wield a variety of critiques are tasks to embrace. But we also listen and speak in the business of reviving the sentences, books, music, and art of many worthy others. This is part of those ceremonies of transformation and illumination that in their endless permutations we call "teaching."

This preservative love flowing from imagination and the heart is at work in the classroom, and also in Thoreau's *Cape Cod*, as he brings Margaret Fuller to her proper stature. It's also at work in Rilke's rescue of a broken Apollo. In chapter eleven I encounter this poetic rescue (along with others) in my discussion of Glenn Gray and Hannah Arendt and the capacity of poetry to push back against the traumas of war. Glenn Gray was an early translator of Heidegger, and his friend Hannah Arendt, an intimate of Heidegger and a political thinker in her own right. The theme is poets (not only Rilke) in a time of war.

Gray gets through the worst of World War II with Auden's line in mind: "We must love one another or die." Arendt wanted to call her first group of essays from America, *For Love of the World.* Given her narrow escapes from the Gestapo first in Germany and then in Paris, and the necessity that she start life over again twice in new languages, in Paris and then in New York, with no wealth to tide her over—given all this, it's quite remarkable that from such adversity she could write "for love of the world." Yet not only Arendt but each American whose writing I engage in these pages faces extremity and models ways of writing that save the world from a darker fate.

My task in chapter twelve is to present Thoreau's impassioned defense of John Brown and his lyrical evocation of wilderness as two sides of a love of the world, conveyed not through theory or abstraction but intimately, imaginatively, poetically, and passionately. Thoreau is known both for seeking the serenity of Walden Pond and for his defense of John Brown, whose raid on Harper's Ferry in hindsight appears as the first battle of the Civil War, and in any case, an action for emancipation. Thoreau's rising in defense was as much against the local grain as his "retreat" to Walden.

* * *

Love of the world, abiding in wilderness, erecting a cairn against the ravages of early death—what all these may mean is the task and promise that I pursue in these pages. I hope these essays attain some measure of what Ortega meant by "salvations," even as the writers I attend write out salvations, delivering words that bring things and persons into light for praise or sometimes mourning, passing to us words of the world as love and grief for the world, speaking not in raw-boned argument but intimately in hope of striking sparks of life or empathy. Their redeeming interventions give us loves well worth reviving in times that skirt the dark.

Part II

_____

HENRY BUGBEE, THOREAU, CAVELL

Chapter 2

A PHILOSOPHY IN WILDERNESS

This theme of reality as a wilderness is the theme that unifies my life.
It enfolds and simplifies, comprehends and completes.
Whenever I awaken, I awaken to it. It carries with it the gift of life.
—*Henry Bugbee*, The Inward Morning

We sometimes think a dawn of meaning or discovery brings answers to a restless, questioning mind. But as often it opens new vistas, and sometimes boundless ones. Then life's streams and seas lift us bodily, offer glimpses of worlds too strange to know, and sounds of grief or celebration. This is the tangled and alluring place our lives are found, bound in wonders, urgent and captivating. Here we find the vital ebb and flow of world as it dawns, new and mobile, ageless and weathered. This is an inward morning, a home in wilderness. As Henry Bugbee has it, wilderness "carries with it the gift of life."[1]

* * *

The Inward Morning passes on a philosophy of personal address and place, played out in voice that curves in deliberate cadences, apt to the occasion. The setting may be a talk on Spinoza or a public hearing on securing wilderness preserves in Montana, a personal response to Heidegger in Paris or an invitation to a fellow artisan of reel and rod to brave the rush of current to gain just *that* enticing pool. In any case, the address of the writer, Henry Bugbee's address to us, will be issued from a heart immersed in vibrant life with others—things, persons, skies, earth, a streaming wilderness, a generous space of listening, of mutuality of address, and of presence.

---

[1] Bugbee, *Inward Morning*, 128.

Wonder greets us through the pages of *The Inward Morning,* greets us like great music might. It strikes home repeatedly: fresh, and irresistible. Without fanfare, Bugbee's journal provides a phenomenology or evocation of the human place that stills our will to master all we face. There we find our lives in question, yet not in ways that undermine. Whatever urgency or danger lies at hand, the writer's voice remains affirmative, sustaining a generosity, compassion, and respect. Here we live and move with other creatures amidst gifts of earth and stream and sky, a place we can inhabit dawning as creation in its manifold simplicity.

Bugbee's philosophical explorations are akin to Thoreau's expeditions. They also parallel the traditions of Wordsworth, Melville, and Emerson. Andrew Feenberg celebrates the *The Inward Morning* as "the only truly original American existentialism," and to catch its open trans-Pacific bent (and further break our easy pigeonholes), aptly calls it "Zen Existentialism."[2] Bugbee sees his philosophy simply as "a meditation of the place"—an animated, wondrous place.

A walking meditation evokes wonders encountered on the way, even as its words find their ground and stride: "my philosophy took shape mainly on foot. It was truly peripatetic, engendered not merely while walking, but through walking that was essentially a meditation of the place . . .[3] Walking tunes the body rhythmically and perceptively to take in an ever approaching and receding scene that when time and place are ripe, and if we but attend, can answer yearnings for meaning and the sacred. Walking can be pilgrimage.

Accounts of streams and snowfalls and perilous storms begin to shape a philosophy of wilderness. This is not a wildness apart, however, as if we were safe spectators to a tumult *over there.* Wilderness is a horizon surrounding us, but more importantly it permeates our existence as place, near at hand, wherever we are found. In some popular depictions wilderness is a distant forbidding Everest, meant to challenge reckless *provocateurs* or to prompt genuflection or fear among the faithful, or to lure city dwellers away from boredom and corruption. But Bugbee's wilderness is not a danger zone where heroes sharpen willful endurance in adversity, nor is it a wasteland where an ascetic negates temptations, nor is it a refuge for suburbanites. It's a place for

² *Wilderness and the Heart: Henry Bugbee's Philosophy of Place, Presence, and Memory,* ed. Edward F. Mooney, Foreword by Alasdair MacIntyre, Athens: University of Georgia Press, 1999), chapter 5.
³ Bugbee, *Inward Morning,* 128.

affirmation of wonders and terrors, the wildness of hawks and trout and storms, the flow of human fellowship at sea or in a city late at night.

* * *

As Bugbee has it, philosophy can approach the status of a poem.[4] He also writes that "Philosophy is not a making of a home for the mind out of reality. It is more like learning to leave things be: restoration in the wilderness, here and now."[5] This seems close to Heidegger's *Gelassenheit*. A "return to the things themselves" is a methodological imperative familiar to followers of Husserl. For Bugbee it has the urgency of a moral, even a religious imperative. It is in nearness to the things of creation, all living things and earth and sky, that we will find our way, our resolution, meaning, and conviction; in beholding we are held.

Humans are rendered alert among radiant particulars, infused by care and answerable to a call, underway and immersed in practices, placed so as to define a lively temporal existence. We might suppose the influence of Heidegger's "Forest Path," or *Being and Time*, yet the journal was complete before Bugbee encountered Heidegger; its themes come as much from Thoreau and Zen as from German phenomenology or existentialism.[6] Gabriel Marcel read parts of *The Inward Morning* in the early 1950s while Bugbee was his guest in Paris. Sensing a comity of interest, Marcel arraigned a gathering where Bugbee and Heidegger could meet. Perhaps curious to test a young Harvard professor's footing, Heidegger inquired how one *starts* to think profoundly, what *prompts* philosophical reflection? He got no flat American platitude, but caught his question socratically returned. Echoing a Basho haiku, Bugbee asked, Could the sound of a frog leaping to a fly at dawn suffice?

The counterquestion was Thoreauvian, but there was also an impish Zen-like ring to it. As junior faculty, it had been Henry Bugbee's task to shepherd D. T. Suzuki, the Japanese Zen Buddhist scholar, from talk to talk along the Northeast seaboard; later the two shared a summer on

---

[4] Ibid. 33.

[5] Ibid. 155.

[6] William E. Hocking was a distinguished Professor of Philosophy at Harvard from the late 20s through the 30s. He was acquainted with Bugbee in the late 40s and read the manuscript of *The Inward Morning* before its publication. Husserl's first American student, Hocking is author of *The Meaning of God in Human Experience*, New Haven: Yale University Press, 1911. Marcel dedicated his *Metaphysical Journal* to Hocking.

Long Island. Some years later still, Heidegger would fall in step with a Japanese scholar and acquaintance of Suzuki, and publish an account of their dialogue.[7] Without alluding to American wilderness in particular, Heidegger finds thought called out as one traverses paths toward forest clearings where things stand forth in luminosity. Whether or not Heidegger would remember the lean American's wilderness articulations, Suzuki knew the theme, especially the epiphany in *The Inward Morning* where a trembling line and leaping trout gather vivid definition blessed by stream and glistening pool.[8]

* * *

The moment of the leaping fish is a dawn of meaning that promises a place in and toward creation. How can this be? Well, the dawn we answer is surely always already underway, perhaps always already behind us, falling away just as we begin to grasp its shape. Could it be otherwise?

Let's note the mobile style of *The Inward Morning*. In contrast to an essay's argumentative drive toward closure, journal entries track and enact the *flow* of reflection, reenacting the motion attended to. Writing worth attending to delivers results of thought, but also, with luck, thoughts as they emerge, before they're wrenched from movement into finished static format. That's thinking at the edge. Gilbert Ryle could suggest that the origin of our thought is "systematically elusive," as elusive as our selves.[9] Catching thought-as-it-dawns is as tempting and impossible as jumping over our shadows. In *The Mystery of Being*, Marcel argues to the same effect.[10] Yet *The Inward Morning* seems to accomplish what argument would say is unattainable: it seems to give us thought at the moment of its forging or appearing, to give us dawning meaning outright through the sinews of its passages. Like Thoreau who sounds the cosmos and himself through sounding Walden pond or Mt Ktaadn or shipwreck on a sandy beach, we have writing that evokes a larger canvas through the particulars it displays.

---

[7] Heidegger, "A Dialogue on Language," in *On the Way To Language*, trans. Peter Hertz, New York: Harper and Row, 1971.

[8] Bugbee, *Inward Morning*, 86.

[9] Gilbert Ryle, *The Concept of Mind*, "The Systematic Elusiveness of the 'I,'" London: Hutchenson, 1949.

[10] Gabriel Marcel, *The Mystery of Being*, 2 vols. South Bend: St. Augustine's Press, 2001.

"I could wish for no more than to do justice to the instruction I have received from moving waters."[11] If we could countenance thought emerging from flowing waters, we'd have thought at the source and on the move.

The Inward Morning's unexpected success, in Alasdair MacIntyre's view, is found in its presenting reality outright-and-in-process, with an intimate directness. Its candid revelations are matched by its ease in taking up the creative spirit of founding texts in our tradition. Exemplary text and interpreting-thinker emerge alive together, outside the warehouse where an inventory of concepts, doctrines, or arguments accumulate on neatly labeled shelves. We glimpse a philosophical mind on the move through new terrain, finding its unique way. Melville or Plato or Eckhart appear newly framed, their meaning etched as subtle as the coming of a soaring hawk or new-laid snow. This matters when philosophy gets professionalized and dry and lets down those who seek a living thought.

* * *

The sensibility so evident in this journal challenges those who embrace a professionalized, tightly disciplinary conception of respectable intellectual endeavor. On this latter view, philosophy should be strait-laced, scientific, and impersonal. Remarking in the early 1960s on *The Inward Morning,* a writer in *The Journal of Philosophy* found the explorations quite unacceptable: "I fear that the philosophic point of such a venture escapes me utterly: I should think that it is a function of art, poetry, and literature—or mescaline—to yield up a heightened awareness of objects, of other people, and of reality in general, and that philosophy has quite different aims."[12] In the scholastic cloisters of the time (and, I suspect, in ours), to write philosophically of wilderness, or of a walking meditation, was unthinkable. Bugbee's zest for thought found greater scope along The Clark Fork in Missoula. He moved West to relative obscurity for a better blend of essentials: open space for an unfenced range of thought; space where an unrestricted breadth of books could be encountered in the classroom; wild country at one's doorstep in mountains, streams, and dramatic seasonal change; a tempered human pace and graciousness.

---

[11] Ibid., 83.
[12] George Pitcher, *The Journal of Philosophy,* 1964, 111f.

Today the presumption that philosophy takes only one, clearly demarcated path is in decline. One can now avow philosophy's common aims with art and literature. Stanley Cavell writes across the cultural map, on Thoreau and Emerson as well as on Shakespeare, Kant, and cinema. Henry Bugbee and he were together at Harvard in the 1950s. In interviews, Cavell attests to the need to root philosophy in one's own inner dialogues. That means disregarding any tacit or explicit bans on personal writing, or on writing that "yields up a heightened awareness" of things—bans on writing in the pattern of an Ortega salvation. Since Augustine and Plato, philosophy has been testament and confession and recuperative of the valuable—not just impersonal report. "In a sense," Cavell confides, "to write your own words, to write your own inner voice, is philosophy. But the discipline most opposed to writing, and to life, is analytic philosophy . . ." And he continues, "This is what my first essays are about—the suppression of the human voice in academic, analytic philosophy."[13] If *The Inward Morning* suffered academic neglect, it attained a sizable following underground. Its voice is refreshingly and unmistakably singular, frankly anchored in the vivid particularities of the writer's lived experience. Bugbee shows how "to write your own words, to write your own inner voice," and how to come to know in your bones that this is philosophy that you write. It saves writer and world.

These philosophical explorations lay out suggestive sketches of meditative, "experiential" philosophy, of the place of grief, compassion, and delight, of wonder, technology, and daily work; and of the difficult notions of finality and universality. Let me comment on responsibility and vocation, on perishing, and on the recuperative idea of reality as vivid presence.

* * *

Responsibility, in Bugbee's extra-legal sense, is apt response to claims on our comportment and being as persons with concern. Another's suffering calls on our compassion; your dignity claims my respect; a job can claim concerted effort; a sense of vocation can claim my long-term aspirations. Responsibility is as multifaceted as the claims it hears and answers.

The Inward Morning evokes moments of address and answer, solicitation and response. Bugbee recalls a swollen river carrying a camper

---

[13] See Giovanna Borradori, *The American Philosopher*, Chicago: University of Chicago Press, 1994, 126.

from a pool along the river's bank under a boom and then into the rush of downstream rapids. The man is swept under an overhanging willow branch, clutches at the trailing shoots and clings for life. He is swept in a wide arc toward the safety of a muddy bank. Henry arrives on the run, grasping the hands of the man in stunned relief: the nearness of death, the vulnerable strength of a will to live, a gratitude for the gift of willows—these suffuse the place. He finds himself released into a world reborn at the instant it passed the brink of perishing: "Not a word passed between us. As nearly as I can relive the matter, the compassion I felt with this man gave way into awe and respect for what I witnessed in him. He seemed absolutely clean. In that steady gaze of his I met reality point blank, filtered and distilled as the purity of a man."[14]

Here responsibility is grounded in perception and our native sympathy; it opens toward deep respect and awe. Perception aims at immediate features of a setting—say, the presence of danger—and also deepens in appreciation of "reality point blank," say, the profound presence of "the purity of a man." This appreciation of presence in its bearing on responsibility, sympathy, and respect is twofold. First, there is the particular man just rescued, his presence distilled to his unique singularity: just *this* man, at just *this* moment of encounter and desperate need. Second, there is his presence distilled to his essential universality: this man as reflecting persons in their vulnerability, "innocence" and "purity"—*standing for all.*

This bivalence of presence is rooted in particularities of person and place such that singularity and universality do not undercut but enhance each other. The singularity of the endangered man in his setting does not diminish his standing as embodiment of a broader simplicity, innocence, and vulnerability of humankind; nor does his standing as embodiment of universal worth calling on our respect, compassion, and commitment to aid and comfort in any way diminish his presence as a crystallized individual, here and now. An excess of meaning flows from and through the place sweeping these potentially opposing vectors in an arc of revelation.

Now if this rich expression of responsibility held fast in the grip of reality resonates convincingly, its authority will rest on the speaker's testimony, on the accumulated respect we have gathered for a voice trued to its experience in a world we can recognize as our own. This authority is thoroughly first-personal, avowed, and does not rest on

---

[14] Bugbee, *Inward Morning,* 172.

appeals to abstract reason or "the moral law." Of course interpretation can amplify the case, and our responses to this testimony can be closer or farther from the mark, better or worse. But the case to be interpreted lies before us as the givenness of reality, awaiting our reception. It is not to be mistaken for the production or projection of a detached, omniscient, or imperial self. Nor is it material for a disembodied reason to disassemble into lifeless components. The philosophical accounts of responsibility and compassion in *The Inward Morning* are not haunted by a wish to squeeze out a periodic table of their elements. They are lyrical revelations.

Henry Bugbee's work can be framed as a phenomenological project that renders the full reality of things. The appearances recorded are not "mere surfaces," deficient or illusory. Reality does not lurk behind them, nor is the very idea of reality a hoax. Bugbee's evocations pay tribute to a "surplus" of reality *gifted in* appearance, even as that reality declares itself ever mobile and awaiting our response. The real is confronted as value-laden (whether "positively" or "negatively") and head on. This makes his moral philosophy both contextualist (we are always positioned in a place and time, as *this* particular person, *here*) and also realist (we are not mainly in illusion, but confront real pain, and are capable of true responsive sympathy). His ethical reflections also hold out for a "somewhat absolute" in experience[15]: not some *thing*—a doctrine, say, or a piece of knowledge or an algorithm determining right action. What is absolute is an experientially delivered *relational* bond: I find myself gifted with, gripped by, a fulcrum on which action and understanding can be raised. This is necessity, the basis for a moral "must" as well as for those urgent, inescapable prompts that trace personal vocation.

Alasdair MacIntyre remarks on Bugbee's resuscitation of the notion of moral of necessity, of what we *must* do, as opposed to what we should or ought to do. He suggests that Bugbee's moral philosophy cuts a middle path between Hume and Kant.[16] Hume puts sympathy center stage but finds no deep ground for its necessity—it rests simply on our longing for social approval. Kant finds a deep ground for moral response but locates it, inappropriately, in reason's law-like necessity. Bugbee works to uncover an experiential ground of felt-compassion that carries the necessity not of law but of the heart—what in reality speaks to the person as a whole. Another's suffering is real and calls

---

[15] Ibid. 133.
[16] See MacIntyre's Foreword, *Wilderness and the Heart.*

not just to reason but to the very springs of wholehearted human responsiveness. An almost Buddhist sense of compassion is grounded in a necessity reminiscent of Spinoza.

If Bugbee can shore up human concern as responsiveness to others and the realities of our setting, then we have groundwork not just for ethics but for a deep environmental ethics.[17] Returning to things receptive to their meaning and cultivating a willingness to evoke those meanings in writing and speech makes good sense philosophically, as Edmund Husserl insisted. But returning to things themselves is also a homecoming in a moral and spiritual sense. Responsiveness, responsibility in and to our setting, means restoration to our place as wilderness, where nature and her creatures become far more than a decorative setting or exploitable resource. As orientation for our lives, such responsiveness opens a place for acknowledging vocation.

*   *   *

A capacity to be called arises in attending to exemplary lives. Philosophical reflection merges with biographical absorption—say in the detail of Thoreau's or Gandhi's life. In *The Inward Morning* the writer himself becomes exemplary. Quine's tribute, that in his friend he finds "the ultimate exemplar of the examined life," dawns on us as apt just as we find the writer grappling to true his life to his reflective vocation in the wild.[18]

> The aspens and larches took on a yellow so vivid, so pure and trembling in the air, as to fairly cry out that they were as they were, limitlessly. And it was there in attending to this wildness, with unremitting alertness and attentiveness, yes, even as I slept, that I knew myself to have been instructed for life, though I was at a loss to say what instruction I had received.[19]

---

[17] Bugbee's sense of experiential rapport with things, as it contrasts with a strictly empiricist position, is developed by Andrew Feenberg, "Zen Existentialism: Bugbee's Japanese Influence," *Wilderness and the Heart: Henry Bugbee's Philosophy of Place, Presence, and Memory*, ed. Edward F. Mooney, Athens, GA: University of Georgia Press, 1999, 81–91. See also Albert Borgmann's, "Finality and Universality: Bugbee, Heidegger, and Modernity," also in *Wilderness and the Heart*, and Charles Taylor, "Heidegger, Language and Ecology," in *Philosophical Arguments*, Cambridge, MA: Harvard University Press, 1995; also, Michael Zimmerman, "Heidegger, Buddhism, and Deep Ecology," in *The Cambridge Companion to Heidegger*, Charles Guignon, ed., Cambridge: Cambridge University Press, 1993.

[18] *Wilderness and the Heart*, vii.

[19] Bugbee, *Inward Morning*, 139 f.

Intimations of vocation can arise from sources at some remove from natural wildness. "It was music which first awakened me to the need for reflection."[20] Yet even musical awakening places one in wilderness: "wilderness is reality experienced as call and explained in responding to it absolutely."[21] There is a readiness to take one's life as in the question, to ask *Am I on track?* And there is a readiness to hear a summons to which one can authentically respond. Then we sense our lives as claimed, as called to a vocation, however difficult we may find the task of spelling out what such a claim might at last entail.

* * *

Listening responsiveness puts us at creation's dawn, full of life yet replete in the perishing of fluid streams and fading light, and in the perishing of our time: "It seems that every time I am born, the wilderness is born anew; and every time I am born it seems to me that then, if ever, I could be content to die. Surely it is here that I must research for the meaning of coming to be and passing away."[22] As we gather meanings in our setting, our place, it's clear that we are not minds apart confronting a machine in motion or a frozen heap of substance. The real is an ebb and flow that implicates us in its liveliness and perishing. We open to things rising into life and passing from it. Reverence then gains hold in gratitude for a reality "old and new and ageless."[23]

This readiness to see things in their passing vulnerability marks a vantage far from cool detachment or presumed control. It reveals the writer in a distinctive light: "Two dear friends and teachers of mine have said to me, independently of one another: 'You have written here as a man might write only near the end of his life.'"[24] This sense of death, he confides, has accompanied him since certain harrowing experiences in World War II, "Not in a way that saps life, but in a way that militates against putting off what one has to do."[25]

Death snaps us alert to the present, to the inevitability of our passing. Bugbee's journal finds roots in the crisis of war and the nearness

---

[20] Ibid.
[21] Ibid., 128.
[22] Ibid. 129.
[23] Ibid.
[24] Ibid., 11.
[25] Ibid.

of death. It is as if their inescapable impact readies the soul for praising recognition of things in their living and their dying. As he has it,
"the very perishing of what we love might be an essential moment in
the clarification of the worthiness of love of that which perishes." And
he continues: "There is weeping and gnashing of teeth; there is stony
impassivity; there is ribaldry, and vacuous staring. There is confusion.
But there is pure gentleness, and it is in this vein that perishing
speaks."[26]

If Quine, whose "official" philosophy hardly resembles Henry
Bugbee's, finds in his friend "the ultimate exemplar of the examined
life," it is in part because Bugbee is attuned to the wilderness of life-
and-death in which worthy philosophical revelation and testimony
must move. There we find whatever can give life density and direction.
Following such revelation is like traversing an expanse "as vast as the
Pacific and the music of Handel."[27] It finds us in wonder, a wilderness;
and however tested there, it can issue in compassion that leaves us
ineluctably alive.

* * *

The Inward Morning prompts us to amplify rather than strip down or
deconstruct. Bugbee's phenomenology of place as wilderness evokes
the "ongoingness" of the life of things that mark the place through
which we move. This walking in wilderness is participative, for the
place we *live* will continually be completed by our responsiveness: it is
not some static dot on an abstract map, but depends for its profile on
our steps in an openness to a life undertaken with others in a creation
that is emerging, underway.

Beyond cultural chatter and disciplinary conflict there are familiar
everyday experiences to be attended to: love and work, grief and
terror, wonder and celebration. In the work of Rilke and Emily
Dickinson, of Rousseau and Lao-Tzu, of Spinoza, Heidegger, and
Thoreau, we find these experiences consummately voiced, even
for the first time discovered. *The Inward Morning* amplifies and underwrites as a resource for survival the presence of the traditions these
names define. And as a philosophy of wilderness, of place, it cuts hubris
down, as meanings dawn toward the listening responsive self. Such an
"experiential philosophy" is post-empiricist yet fully realist. Like Rorty,

---

[26] Ibid., 138.
[27] Ibid.

MacIntyre, or Nussbaum, Bugbee shows philosophy emerge in concert with poetry, biography, and history as it unveils our worlds, configuring them narratively.

* * *

There were interludes in France and Pennsylvania before Bugbee found home along the Clark Fork and Blackfoot in Missoula. In Montana he found a solitude and inspiration where teaching and wilderness, swift water and reflection, could mingle and take root. Here is wilderness that bespeaks Spinoza's divinity-and-world, Suzuki's flashing Zen epiphanies, and Melville's dark sea and shipwreck. It is wilderness that embraces Marcel's availability to necessary others and Wordsworth's walking, recollective meditations of the place.

It is Christmas as I write these words. Sunlight sparkles through bare and feathery birch limbs, now drenched mysteriously by memories of New England snows. And I hear or see in all immediacy a passage from this journal. It is fellowship at dusk among a crew underway in the Pacific, caught up in war but for the moment caught up in song. "In the closing light of that day, riding to the endless swells, they sang the song of men in our position. And it was Christmas in the wilderness."[28] Like Odysseus, each was far from home, in danger, and full of longing. Yet amidst that awful incongruity time opened up for thankful memory and melody. I think of him today well over sixty years since that wartime sea-watch. I see him among family, friends, and the massive Bitter Roots where he taught and fished and climbed for years, where he was at home, looking out on falling snow, still against the mountains.

There is the book of tradition, of doctrine and argument, open for any to engage or rebuke; as inheritance it presents a raft of problems to take out, wrestle with, and make our own. But there is also the more private daybook of a philosopher's inspiration and advance, the record of philosophy's becoming a vocation for a writer here and now; as testimony it opens uncharted space—and simple sudden spots—where plentitude is found.

---

[28] Ibid., 71.

Chapter 3

A LYRIC PHILOSOPHY OF PLACE

A voice often comes to me,
and always says the same thing:
"Socrates, make music and compose."
—*Plato*, Phaedo

We all need some sort of homing device, an indicator that reminds us where we came from and how to return. When we no longer have the wonderfully reliable and mysterious sense of place that migrating geese or whales possess, then we make do otherwise, largely culturally, with equally mysterious and hopefully reliable maps to get us home. Sometimes an especially tuned text, like Henry Bugbee's classic journal of wilderness reflections, will point the way, mid-way in our journey.

The Inward Morning directs us toward a dawn that can show us home. In the footsteps of Thoreau, the writer proposes, as we've heard, that philosophy is a "meditation of the place" and that it "approximates the poem." A muse directs this odyssey. Perhaps searching memory lyrically, we'll find the faithful place from which we came, to which we return, to our loves and celebrations and sweet consolations, as well as to each grief and pain and anguish lying there.

A homing meditation of the place finds common ground, recovers common springs or sources. Still, this does not mean, for Henry Bugbee, that we forget the variety, the special detail, of the particulars along the way. Our most shared source is presence not to generalities but to single, radiant particulars. So he would have us stop at each bend in the river, at each pool, at each eddy—and there to watch for glitter, for color of leaves, and there to listen for the whisper of trees on the banks where feet have purchase and good standing.

Thirty years ago *The Inward Morning* came upon me as convincing as a sudden pelt of sleet. The mainstays of my philosophic background— Kierkegaard and Nietzsche, Hume and Kant—seemed barely relevant to my floundering. "I weighed everything by the measure of the silent presence of things, clarified by the cry of hawks, solidified in the presence of rocks, spelled syllable by syllable by waters of manifold voice, and consolidated in the act of taking steps."[1] This was *terra incognita*. And at that, a triple wonder: the wonder of the vast terrain, where landscapes, ships, and philosophic streams and sloughs seemed to intermingle wildly; the wonder of the smaller things presented then and there within this vastness: *this* bend of oar, *this* branch of willow, *this* line from Pindar; and last, the wonder of my eerie entanglement in this terrain and its particulars—up to my ears and flailing. But through it all, I could hear the reassurance that wilderness "carries with it the gift of life." "This theme of reality as a wilderness is the theme that unifies my life. It enfolds and simplifies, comprehends and completes. Whenever I awaken, I awaken to it. It carries with it the gift of life."[2] Since then, I've found my way more easily—though excitement does not abate—and find myself here again to recount these passages.

I raise a question that resonates throughout the book: *Can the circle of philosophy be widened to include lyric, religious philosophy, philosophy with a poetic, musical—even metaphysical—openness toward spirit or the sacred?* The text will answer YES, and I'll elaborate and endorse it, painting broad strokes on an oversized canvas.

Will this be doing philosophy as epistemology, or as environmental ethics or as some new brand of deconstruction or reconstructive metaphysics? Most likely not, and in any case, these boxes are not as fenced in as we suppose. Lyric should take us clean out of the corrals, clean out and into the open, where the niceties of compartmentalization can be set aside.[3] Henry Bugbee's thoughts are on the loose, immediate, in both their anguish and their joy—arching thoughts uttered in a moment of birth marking his own unique and fully recognizable voice. To stay close to the contours of lyric philosophy, I name three

---

[1] Bugbee, *The Inward Morning*, 139.

[2] Ibid., 128.

[3] Charles Taylor contrasts moral thought in the academic corrals, ethical thought in the open, and the spiritual forest beyond, in *Iris Murdoch and The Search for Human Goodness*, eds. Maria Antonaccio and William Schweiker, Chicago: University of Chicago Press, 1996.

temptations to shun, the vices of Dryness, Divide and Conquer, and Impatience.

(1) *Against Dryness:* Our ideals, or what matters, must be delivered in terms that evoke their presence. When we talk in moral or aesthetic or spiritual domains, it only harms intelligibility if we speak dryly without passion or involvement. We must evoke the domain of our concern. Failing that, sites of moral, aesthetic, or spiritual importance become dormant, or worse. We have the inverse of an Ortega essay in intellectual love. We have the opposite of salvations. Lyric brings the presence of what matters alive—vividly, musically.

(2) *Against Divide and Conquer:* Our ideals, or what matters, must be delivered whole, or in that direction, and not in terms of rivalries and battle lines—"binaries"—among the disciplines or less formal lines of comprehension. Divide and conquer can often make good analytical sense. But Balkanization is not always the best way to go. In retrospect, we can see the unintended damage that Kant exacts in erecting great administrative divides among a university's faculties—which then protect their fond preserves that serve as staging grounds for raids on weaker neighbors. Art, morality, science, religion, politics, and everyday life break apart from one another. Kant divides their territories and names their defensive ramparts so convincingly that we can now hardly see the world as less divided. But to parcel out the common tasks of understanding and reconciliation into a multiplicity of warring disciplines and corresponding institutions nips any moves toward wholeness or connection in the bud. Yet why should art and ethics, spirit and community, sky and earth be taken up in ways that increase their opposition to each other? The cure is lyric in philosophy. Lyric aspires to wholeness, linking streams of life within a single resonating verse.

(3) *Against Impatience:* Let the tumblers fall into place. Then the bolt can slide, the door can open. Don't push on doors that only open inward. We rush for answers before we're ready or know the true dimensions of what we face. Quietude, patience, a slow tenderness in thoughtful movement is too often taken as a vapid refusal to robustly join debate, participate, pull one's load, or be resolved. Yet the truth dawns as she will, not on schedules we impose and frantically pursue. We cannot force truth as suits our needs or timing.

> It was in the fall of '41, October and November, while late autumn
> prevailed throughout the northern Canadian Rockies, restoring
> everything in that vast region to a native wildness. Some part of each
> day or night, for forty days, flurries of snow were flying. The aspens
> and larches took on a yellow so vivid, so pure and trembling in the air,
> as to fairly cry out that they were as they were, limitlessly. And it was
> there in attending to this wildness, with unremitting alertness and
> attentiveness, yes, even as I slept, that I knew myself to have been
> instructed for life, though I was at a loss to say what instruction I had
> received.[4]

* * *

I pursue the themes of *The Inward Morning* in five sections, the first
called *Love and Strife,* the second, *Trust and Danger,* the third, *Affliction
and Release,* the fourth, *Death and Purity,* and the last, *Philosophy and
Inward Mornings.* Each becomes a meditation of a place: the place of
Diotima, the place of Melville's boatmen, the place of Job, a place on
the North Fork of the Trinity River, and a place for lyric philosophy.

I. LOVE AND STRIFE: THE PLACE OF DIOTIMA

Philosophy is not always indifferent to the lyric or religious. The
Presocratics had their gods and hymns, but perhaps that was extra
baggage. Some think the shift arrives as Socrates comes on stage. In
one disguise, he's there precisely to debunk the lyric and religious—
the poetic in all her forms. The figure of a skeptical antagonist stands
before us, the philosopher badgering his public with demands for
rational justification of any position whatsoever. But Socrates has
another side, one pertinent to our topic.[5]

   Think of the *Symposium.* We find him late for the party, delayed
by the grip of a trance. Later, when he's fully present, he rises to speak
on the evening's topic, which is love. Perhaps his earlier solitary
withdrawal into the quiet of a doorway was a kind of meditative prepa-
ration. In any case, as he begins to open up, the *persona* of the skeptic
has been put aside. For one thing, he instantly gives credit for his
insights to someone else, relying here on the authority of another
whose credentials he's had no time to check. The tale was told him by

---

[4] Bugbee, *Inward Morning,* 139f.
[5] On a religious, hymn composing Socrates, see *On Søren Kierkegaard,* Chapters 1–4.

a priestess—apparently without confirming witnesses, and as I imagine it, by a village well. More to our surprise, he claims for these fresh insights, not ignorance but knowledge.

Love, apparently, is the one thing Socrates knows about. His special knowledge—he knew that he knew nothing (of deep philosophical matters) is knowledge of ignorance, but this ignorance evidently does not wall out knowledge he picks up accidentally from a stranger. He learns of love from a woman who wears her authority on her sleeve, whose wisdom is then allowed to gently oversee and guide his rich and intimate excursus. His sense of love, conveyed in the tale of an ascent toward beauty, comes as a gift from Diotima. I imagine he meets her at a village well, a fount where earth and water mingle, where looking down one sees one's face, and also heaven's vault. Or perhaps the reflection of his face and heaven appears as he gazes at her liquid eyes. In any case, it's here that lyric words of love spring forth.

It is not like Plato, this master of theater, to let rapture last too long. If Socrates keeps his listeners spellbound with this story of a woman (who tells *him* a story), the spell is abruptly broken. The mood of gentle musing is broken as a drunken Alcibiades bursts in. Strife intrudes. Alcibiades has been jilted, his amorous pursuit rebuffed, by this old man. How dare a balding sage (no thing of beauty), reject *him*—a hunk, a king of homecoming parades? Thus Plato juxtaposes the view of love offered by the all-but-divine Diotima with the view of unrequited love offered by the pathetic all-too-human Alcibiades. We are left with rowdy pandemonium.

Is there a link between the somewhat frosty, unearthly Socratic love, and the riot of willful desire possessing Alcibiades? How can love embrace both the speech of Diotima and the disruptive rant that follows? What if the reality of love is not fixed for eternity but is completed by our answers to this tense standoff? Then the question depends on our responsiveness to love and its violence-tending underside. The question is not so much, *What is love?* as *How shall we answer?*—and in answering, vouch for love, and so complete reality.

Bugbee would tie love and lyric and the religious, looping them through discussions of celebration and rebirth, of idolatry and grace, and through narratives that move us to respond commemoratively, affirmatively. Love can open toward a wisdom that is immediate. "Might not the sound of a stream of running water call a man to his senses?"[6]

---

[6] Bugbee, *Inward Morning*, 226.

Or love's wisdom might emerge from the wild of immersion in a city's clamor. A single bell in Taxco can bring the writer through cacophony to a purity that lets him "come to love the place" in all its dissonant fluidity.[7] Or it might emerge along a track of fishing, where the writer "becomes the leaping fish" and so dissolves in Zen-like "emptiness."

> It is a glorious thing to know that the pool is alive with these glancing, diving, finning fish. But at such moments it is well to make an offering in one's heart to the still hour in the redwoods ascending to the sky: and to fish in one place, for one fish at a time. On such mornings, too, one may catch nothing at all.[8]

Lyric in Henry Bugbee's work sounds the wonder of a world—but not through dodging fractures. Creation is wilderness, an uncharted world that holds an abundant presence and passing eternity of finite things—things that stand forth, destinate and dense with meaning. But the violent disruptions of an Alcibiades, or worse, remain. There are moments we'd just as soon forget where *any* affirmation is cruelly tested:

> I think of the suicide planes which I *witnessed*; oh! they still call out to me, and what I make of them, of the lives perishing in flames, is still unfinished business which I feel I shall have to take upon myself until my dying day. What, what, indeed can I make of them?[9]

This question lingers tremulously. How can he hold within a single world-worth-being the savage terror of a kamikaze raid—and the saving testament of falling snow? We're stopped, transfixed. *How shall we answer?*—and thus round out reality.

II. TRUST AND DANGER: THE PLACE OF MELVILLE'S BOATMEN

Wilderness is not a solitude apart from communities of trust. Think of Bugbee's portraits of shiplife on the Pacific, where relentless danger, numbing fatigue, celebration, and mutual dependence are tightly interwoven.

> The ship is reeling through the night. Wrenched from oblivion, you sit upright, clutching the chain by which your bunk is hung, staring into darkness, swallowed

---

[7] Ibid., 230.

[8] Ibid., 86.

[9] Ibid., 225–226; emphasis in the original.

up in the crazed enormity you have been summoned to endure . . . By rushes and handholds you make your way to the pilot house. How is it the ship isn't pounded to pieces? You turn toward the man at the wheel and the ship tilts upward hanging in the air. She pitches forward, throwing you ahead: you grap the man before you and hold on against the shuddering shock at the bottom of the fall. "Don't grab me, take the wheel", he yells. "Course is two-three-five. Steering engine is out: it's on manual."[10]

See men in frail longboats, far at sea; a harpoon strikes, and all is burst alive and into risk. The hemp line, an instant earlier coiled neatly aft within its barrel, springs out, around the loggerhead, and forward, jogging by each boatman's oar and by his rowing wrist. The hooked whale runs and dives. Smoking rope races over oars and through its bow notch, pulling boat and crew at breakneck speed. It's called a "Nantucket Sleigh Ride," a place of boisterous, dangerous fun. But as Melville knows, that noosed whale is in dead earnest, and the line he pulls terribly ready to noose an oarsman's foot or wrist, flinging him and boat-mates fast into the deep.

That's an image of the place, as much as Diotima's place with Socrates. It's a place of danger that might open toward despair. There's the possibility of hanging. Melville's chapter ends:

> [T]he graceful repose of the line, as it silently serpentines about the oarsmen before being brought into actual play—this is a thing which carries more of true terror than any other aspect of this dangerous affair. But why say more? All men live enveloped in whale-lines. All are born with halters round their necks; but it is only when caught in the swift, sudden turn of death, that mortals realize the silent, subtle, ever-present perils of life. And if you be a philosopher, though seated in the whale-boat, you would not at heart feel one whit more of terror, than though seated before your evening fire with a poker, and not a harpoon, by your side.[11]

We're wrapped toward death. But the boatmen also give us strains of joy, common bonds, and the thrill of racing free beneath the sky. If there's doubleness here, the aspect of doubt or danger need not utterly prevail. A hymn to joy may yet survive.

If we succumb to images of distrust and violence, cynicism is not far behind, set to cleave us from our cares. Just as feedback loops of love breed love, loops of mistrust breed more distrust. Alcibiades and the

---

[10] Ibid., 83–84.

[11] Herman Melville, *Moby Dick*, New York: Penguin, 2001, Chapter 60, "The Line," 305f.

danger of that smoking rope remain, yet these have no *exclusive* claim
to truth. Frames of distrust or suspicion can be met with trust and
generosity, compassion or respect.[12] If pictures hold us captive, it is
only other pictures that can set us free.

The beauty we can see is often cracked and marred, yet we're not
just spectators. We work in ways we can against the triumph of the
worst, seeking beauty, if we can, beneath a scar. An Amish elder whose
granddaughter had been murdered recently spoke softly to his people:
"We must not think evil of the man." The elder sees under a frame
of forgiveness rather than retribution. This is a moral achievement.
Getting there can include imaginative, philosophical work. As Gillian
Rose puts it in *Love's Work*, "keep your mind in hell, and despair not!"[13]
Attend to evil, don't despair. Celebrating fellowship, grace—working
past a vengeful spot—can be good philosophy.

Wisdom is not just rational appraisal and prudent choice. In facing
fragility or cruelty, compassion and trust are more to the point. In this,
I follow Iris Murdoch, who holds that we cannot just hoard our trust,
awaiting propitious, guaranteed, investment—all rational warrants
secured before extending it. For one thing, there is no place of ultimate safety and knowledge, as Melville's boatmen know. For another,
a Hobbesian attitude of caution and mistrust, of fearing the worst and
sounding alarm, can *breed* the worst—which ensures that trust will
never flower.

Melville's persons are not on separate islands vying for protection,
but navigating common seas. In *The Inward Morning* there is work
with fellow seamen, work with rowers in an eight. In Melville there are
working whalers in their longboat. These are pictures of community,
of necessary mutual trust and risk in work. And there is an uncanny
sense that community even includes one's enemies. "I think of the
suicide planes which I *witnessed* . . . Is it not true that we were not
enemies? And who will believe this, how can it be believed?"[14] We
return to this unsettling but strangely consoling thought in the following chapters. Perhaps it's sufficient here to catch a deep, unstated,
even desperate hope, that care and trust and responsibility are inescapable, all the way down—even unto death. If this is to be believed,

---

[12] On trust and suspicion, see *On Søren Kierkegaard*, Chapter 5, "Love, this Lenient
Interpreter."

[13] Gillian Rose, *Love's Work: A Reckoning with Life*, New York: Schocken, 1995, the
quote is an epigraph, from Staretz Silouan, and reappears on p. 105.

[14] Bugbee, *Inward Morning*, 225–226.

the thought might clarify a soul, as that thought issues from the quiet, selfless, pondering of prayer.

This composite Melville–Bugbee image of persons joined in tasks and shared humanity counts against a contract theory of society. It reminds us that whether the setting is Hobbesian or Rawlsian, we must have trust already in place—trust, say, that others will heed contracts or bargain in good faith. Thus trust, and acknowledgment of the personhood and responsibility of the other, must precede any negotiation of contracts. We are always already somewhat faithfully in a boat, even as we ponder whether to jump ship or switch crafts. We are never utterly weightless, boatless; or if we are, no resolve can make the least bit of sense, whether for the good or for the worse.

To be resolved means that I take something to matter in what I do or don't do in the world and with others, and am ready to act on that. If mistrust leaves me untethered to any aspect of the world or to any relations with others, there will be no place where resolve can grip. It's worth noting too, against contract theory, that it has no place for the communal virtues of praise, generosity, and acclamation. These virtues establish and reaffirm the grip mistrust would dissolve. Is it not true that we acknowledge praiseworthy persons, actions, and aspects of the world *before* we devise rules to encourage the sustenance and legacy of such persons, acts, and worlds?

Communal values and working fellowship can resist zealous skepticism and adversarial distrust. Henry Bugbee's writing welcomes moments of celebration, joy, and commonality. These moments alone should win us over. There is danger, and also trust and generosity. If Bugbee understates betrayal, cruelty, or deceit, it's not because he doesn't see them, or feel their sting. Perhaps he anticipates the sting, not of a potential cruelty but of the potential loss of charity and trust, virtues that may themselves be weakened, understated, and in need of resuscitation. Philosophy should heed and speak for generosity of spirit. It is wisdom we can take to heart—and lyric holds the heart.

Philosophy is a meditation of the place—the place of Socrates, and of boatmen on a drunken sleigh ride. Next comes Job's ash heap. From there, he'll curse the very bowels of creation.

III. AFFLICTION AND RELEASE: THE PLACE OF JOB

Henry Bugbee finds a comity between the sacred and the everyday. Grace and gracefulness, renewal and redemption, release from bondage and accommodation to suffering play out this co-mingling. These themes cross back and forth over sacred–secular divides, and in crossing back and forth, underwrite a lyric-religious philosophy. Consider their place in *Job.*

Affliction and misery are never far away yet not so disabling or ubiquitous, we hope, as to numb compassion. Job's afflictions strike us terribly, as they strike Job himself in round on round of wounding disaster. In short order he loses fortune, family, health, and friends. We witness killing blows to body, mind, and spirit. His wife and erstwhile companions recoil in fear and self-righteous judgment. In his troubles, none remain to stand by him. His "friends" are empty shells. Worse, they peer with vacant curiosity or interfere with blame. If only they would abide with his fragility!

He's alone in tatters by his ash heap. Mind in hell, he despairs not. We watch his fierce counterattack. He demands reasons for his pain. Rage gives him strength. He shakes his fist at heaven in fearsome protest. Yet despite its righteousness, we come to witness a transformation of that protest and of the pain that feeds it. We witness a sudden quieting as he acknowledges the howling, lyrical Voice from the Whirlwind.

The voice from the storm is not bent on crushing Job, but on shifting him elsewhere, shifting the locus of his attention, delivering him to a world framed differently. The storm calls on his love for the world. He finds a sacred dimension of his world and hence the shadowed possibility of a sacred dimension to his cares.

His concern had been reason and justice. His friends accepted that framework too. All assumed there was reason for his affliction, and that Job's God must be just in ministering affliction. But the world delivered by the whirlwind sets matters of reason and justice aside. The storm responds to Job's questioning protest in terms that make reason and justice beside the point. The blizzard re-keys his attunement to his God, shifting that attunement from a register for lawyer-like argument and defense to a register fit for prayer—for what Bugbee will call "true prayer." His passions modulate toward humility and awe.

Earlier we heard Bugbee ask who could believe that in the midst of firing on a kamikaze, it was not an enemy that he faced. Similarly, we might ask, who could believe Job's outrage might be released to awe and quiet or believe that beyond his righteous protest he might be delivered to gentle silence, or believe that humility and emptying could be other than demeaning humiliation or servile acquiescence.

It's not that Job arrives at the "correct" or "proper" stance with regard to his suffering or to his God. Nor is it to say that his rebellion had been misplaced or in the wrong. It is not that Bugbee arrives at the "correct" or "proper" way to perceive an incoming pilot. If he had taken that pilot as an enemy, he would not have been in the wrong. In both cases the salient point is that the very framework of legalistic or everyday propriety or "right-and-wrong" seems suspended in the name of a stance we hardly know how to describe. Yet that stance seems to resist gestures of demotion, ridicule, or dismissal. A new insight is poetically garnered that cannot just be disowned as sophomoric. It grips in a wondrous acknowledgment.

The Voice with power to transfigure Job's suffering toward affirmation of the world and readiness for prayer had been preceded by the voice of Elihu. Elihu is a mysterious figure, a bit like Diotima, who reminds Job that wisdom and understanding will not come in a lawyer's brief; it will not come from forcing one's way by protest and argument into a hearing before the Lord. Law is not the final forum. Instead, Elihu foretells, wisdom comes in *dreams, visions,* and *songs in the night.*[15] Final words will be poetic.

Job lowers his fist and his voice and listens—not to an explanation but to something like songs and dreams. A whirlwind's voice arrives to roar and whisper in his ear. He hears no justification of his pain but an invitation to a grandeur that sweeps all around and through. His reality is completed then and there by the song of the particulars that speak. *He* does not complete reality; reality completes *him.* In poetry unsurpassed in power, fury, and sudden gentleness, the Voice commends to his sores and fissures soaring hawks, plummeting hail, and starry skies, creatures of the deep and of the meadows, one by one. As Job's listening awe expands, his affliction recedes. He's overwhelmed. But he's overwhelmed not as a stronger force subdues an enemy—reducing the other to servility. Job is subdued as great music subdues, sweeping over our will and power.

> Canst thou command the dawn?
> Like clay, the shape of things is changed by it;
> They stand forth as if clothed in ornament![16]

---

[15] Job 33:15; 35:10
[16] Ibid., 38:12–15, from Herder's trans., *Dimensions of Job*, ed. Nahum Glatzner, New York: Schocken, 1969, 149.

The dawn's transformative powers—its ability to dress the day—becomes an astonishing phenomenon. The point is not to insist on Job's ignorance or powerlessness *per se*, but rather to arrive at an appreciation of his subsequent astonishment and wonder whose arrival, perforce, leave his earlier knowledge and power as naught.

Job becomes open to radiant particulars that are intimate, yet also strange, uncanny. They can hold us at arm's length, even in their intimacy, intimating an excess beyond what we readily grasp. This frustrates lurking claims to master or control all that might approach us. Job's questions were in the space of reason and justice. They now disappear as a new space supervenes, the space of creation, delivered despite his protest—reality delivered point blank. In a vein more gentle than the whirlwind, Henry Bugbee reflects:

> It is well while looking at rocks
> to have the roar of a river in one's ears.
> Or to see still-standing trees
> through falling snow.[17]

The tale of Job's suffering, protest, and release toward a world transfigured can be heard in a roughly secular register. We stress *what* is named by the Lord—rather than what the *Lord* names. This allows *things* to speak, not just an imperial speaker. Speech and things are co-articulate as when we see the one we love and hear his name, all in an event that refuses to be divided between name and thing named. And things sing coordinate with a potential universe, assembled particular by particular, ready to sing what they might be—sing their emerging plenitudes. Rocks roar in rivers that hold rocks, both embraced by islands of earth; trees hold still to accommodate their mobile diaphanous kin, their still presence ready for a falling snow, itself in congress with a generous sky.

Viewing suffering in the scales of justice, the unfairness of Job's afflictions is evident. But the *Book of Job* does not conclude with a verdict on the justice of Job's afflictions. It questions the pertinence of Law's arena. Job hears no verdict but only creation's music. He "melts away" before its grandeur. (The Hebrew permits Job's final acknowledgment to be "I *melt* away," which surely bests standard renderings that would register humiliation or self-loathing—"I repent or

---

[17] Bugbee "The Philosophical Significance of the Sublime," *Philosophy Today*, Spring 1967.

abase myself in dust and ashes.") To melt away before creation is neither to admit impiety nor to abase oneself before bullying power.[18]

The gifts of this world are *gifts,* things with which we might fall in love, things to welcome graciously. And just as we might have words without an imperious speaker, so we might have gifts without an all-purpose imperious giver. Things speak and declare their giftedness—however silent they remain about their origins. We can see and hear the wonders of creation—with no assurance whatsoever about what we should say (if anything) about their source. We see the Lord's *gift*—not exactly the Lord. Or if, with Job, we now *see* the Lord (rather than having heard of him only), it is because we see the gifts of creation delivered in a voice from a storm. The storm itself, however transcendent, remains down-to-earth *wind*—swirling among things, one awesome thing among others. The whirlwind is in and of creation.

I can know Melville's lyric world—while the source of his lyrical powers recedes in mystery. I can know the lessons of moving waters—while the source of these lessons recedes. The mystery of how waters speak or teach is no deeper than the mystery of how mere lines of ink speak or teach in *Moby Dick.* I never catch the *source,* or the explicit process of *deliverance,* of a thought in the moment of my having it. This source is and forever will remain "systematically elusive."[19] Creation's source, the source and background of any present web of radiant particulars, is and forever will remain systematically, not just contingently, elusive—just as the provenance of a thought or of Melville's power will remain hidden, or just as the power behind a storm's creative force will remain hidden.

In forty days and nights of snow among the trees deep in the Canadian Rockies, Bugbee knows himself to have been instructed for life. We want a sense of the *source* of instruction. A capacity of rivers to teach or of falling snow to transform a soul, is perhaps no more mysterious and just as familiar as a capacity of blocks of printed letters and spaces to give us Melville's transforming words. Bugbee learned in the Rockies the passing of things, their fluid ephemerality and

---

[18] See Herbert Fingarette, "The Meaning of Law in The Book of Job," in *Revisions,* eds. MacIntyre and Hauerwas, Notre Dame: Notre Dame University Press, 1981; and Terrence Tilley, *The Evils of Theodicy,* Washington DC: Georgetown, 1992, 96, for a range of translations of Job's final "quieting," many far from the KJV's "abasement."

[19] Gilbert Ryle, "The Systematic Elusiveness of the 'I,'" *The Concept of Mind,* London: Hutchenson, 1949.

evanescence, their life, color, and momentary luminescence piercing the soul—their very being bespeaking spirit.

IV. Death and Purity: The Place on the North Fork

In *The Inward Morning* lyric testimony to the religious rises as a closing reflection on an arresting narrative. We've mentioned the incident in mountains of Northern California along a stretch of the Trinity River. The swollen waters carry an otherwise anonymous camper from a pool along the quiet bank under a boom and then into the down-stream rush of smothering rapids. He is swept under an overhanging willow. At the last moment he clutches at the trailing, tangled shoots and clings for life. The branch holds, and he's swept in an arc toward the safety of a muddy bank. Henry arrives at the spot on the run, grasping the young man with compassion and relief. Each registers the nearness of death, the vulnerable strength of a will to live, a gratitude for the gift of willows—a lyrically religious moment both wonderful and terrible.

In this event there is also for Bugbee a sweeping acknowledgment of release into a world reborn at the very instant it passed the brink of perishing. He gives us this instant of peril and release in words resonant with those unfolding realities. Danger comes as a call for response, and the wonder of release from certain death comes as a call to behold this man as newly born, as he gazes up from the muddy bank. Returned in memory some years later, those realities call for lyric rendering. Bugbee finds himself responding with an account of that danger, escape, and new life. The realities are rounded out and completed in words that are actions themselves, words that complete, preserve, and save.

If we limit our attention in music's domain to the rumpled fiber of a conductor's vellum score, or to the physical features of a wooden fiddle, or to the graphic behavior of acoustical rebounds, then we'd be refusing attention to what Ortega would call a realization of plenitudes in that particular domain—say, the domain of an evening's musical performance. Attending to plenitudes there for Ortega would be heeding the indications of overflowing significance that exceed and surpass and discard the fibrous printed score, the physicality of instruments, the evident small muscle alertness of performers. A nexus of emerging significance becomes the reality of music, completed as we respond to its full presence, refusing the temptation to strip it down to lesser elements. Its reality, Bugbee would say, arrives as we respond to its call.

Realities are at risk; they wax and wane. Completion can become interrupted or impossible: a doorbell rings, a siren wails, we fixate on a missed appointment. Our capacity to respond to an awaiting call is shattered, and so reality miscarries.

In Bugbee's renditions full plenitudes emerge as he responds to a call, say a call for help along a river bank, say a call from memory to bring events to their full significance. And Bugbee's attending to the singularity of a call from memory, or our own attending to the singularity of his lyric rendition of a singular event, does not, we should note, rule out universal appeals. The singular can deliver an invitation to hear relevance that (as we can hope) is infinitely wide ranging.

Philosophers have sought ways to carry contingent particularities, say of voice or locale or objects, beyond those contingent particularities toward the satisfactions of a general vision, carry over to a truth, let's say, that is universal and necessary. In answer to a call, we offer up a voice from where we stand, in hope of resonance felt to be necessary by an indefinitely extended audience, making that felt necessity of impact potentially universal. I draw on a faith or trust that my voice *does* answer to the necessary—the necessity, say that I respond to a call for help. And as a writer, or speaker, I draw on a faith or trust that my words will be heard in their urgency and necessity—not as only an idiosyncratic, contingent, or haphazard responsiveness of limited or negligible relevance. The rendering of particulars truthfully, responsively, can sound a universal and necessary note. To say this is to rephrase the insight that great poetry, great music, renders particulars as they must be. One won't alter a word or a note. And in the necessity of their being, they resonate outward. They will then be felt to be, for all in hearing distance, inevitable, necessary, and universal. Of course a pebble dropped in an attic bucket may resonate precisely nowhere of consequence. Yet a jar dropped by Wallace Stephens on a hill in Tennessee may rebound precisely everywhere.[20] That is the faith of philosophy and lyric.

Here is Bugbee's account of the moment after the young man's sweep from death to safety:

Not a word passed between us. As nearly as I can relive the matter, the compassion I felt with this man gave way into awe and respect for what I witnessed in

---

[20] The Stevens poem in question, "Anecdote of the Jar," begins: "I placed a jar in Tennessee, / And round it was, upon a hill. / It made the slovenly wilderness / Surround that hill.

him. He seemed absolutely clean. In that steady gaze of his I met reality point blank, filtered and distilled as the purity of a man.[21]

If these words persuade, their power must rest on the great cultural depth each word gathers and renews, on its ability to call on us, on our capacity to respond, on the living testimony of the speaker, whose words elsewhere we have come to know and trust.

Hume will grant us the compassion that emerges here as a moral pivot, and Kant will approve something like a dignity in human life that may underlie this telling of danger and rescue. But what are we to make of "the purity of a man" or of "meeting reality point blank"? The lesson of our times seems to be that it is only persons who filter and distill, and that reality can't be met, but only constructed. And reality is never distilled "on its own," as it were. We are jolted by the thought that a person might be encountered as "reality filtered and distilled" to its "purity."

There are plenitudes in Bugbee's prose or in Thoreau's discovery of shipwrecked bones or in Ortega's meditations on Quixote or in Job's capture by a whirlwind. These plenitudes point to and evoke domains of meaning, and particulars in those domains, that far exceed what we can know or master. We might sometimes distill reality, but then we might also, and more profoundly, *find* reality distilled, be *struck* by it so—in the purity or voice of things.

As teachers and shopkeepers, scientists and daughters, singers and priests, critics and builders, our lives are intercepted by exemplary persons. Their lives are direct testimony to non-manufactured value. Without access to their plenitude, I suspect we'd have no purchase on awe, respect, or compassion, no inkling what purity might mean. We'd have no access to what it might mean to be taught by moving waters, to praise creators and creation, to dispraise desolation, or to work for the better against the worst afflictions. Exemplars are given to our need, confusion, and affliction, not to a consumerist need for constructions. They are not ready-made devices or instruments of social fabrication but best seen as creation's gifts—or as the gifts of time, or of the place we inherit and presently inhabit.

That spot on the North Fork is a gift of purity and death, of pines and sun and still water—and danger. It is a place that bespeaks

---

[21] Bugbee, *Inward Morning*, 172.

exemplary action, perception, and the full setting of their reality, filtered and distilled.

> It was in the summertime, at a summer resort, along the North Fork of the Trinity River in California, on a day like so many summer days of bright sun streaming down through the tops of the pines. Most of the length and breath of that long smooth, flowing pool lay translucently exposed to the bouldered bottom. Children played on the sandy shores, or splashed along the fringes of the pool. The air was of ambient fragrance of pines, reassuring warmth and stillness, refreshing coolness of moving water, and frank with the murmur of conversation punctuated by shouts of the farthest remove from alarm. The roar of the rapids below the pool might have been but a ground-bass of contentment, filling us all.
>
> There came a cry for help, seconded with a cry of fright, and I turned toward the tail of the pool just in time to see a young man desperately, failingly, clinging to a great log which had been chained as a boom across the lower end (to raise the water level in the pool). No one could reach him in time. An enormous suction under the log had firm hold of the greater part of his body and drew him ineluctably under. He bobbed to the surface in the first great wave of the rapid below, but there was no swimming or gaining bottom to stay what seemed an impending execution on the rocks at the bend in this mill-race, some hundred yards on down. But it chanced that the river was abnormally high, and as it carried this helpless man doomward it swept him just for an instant under the extremity of a willow which was arched far out from the bank and erratically trailed its branch-tips on the heaving waters. With a wild clutch the young man seized a gathering of the supple branches and held. Everything held, that grim grip and that rooted willow, while the rush of the river brought him in an arc downstream and to the bank. He had barely the strength and the breath to claw himself up the muddy slope onto firmament.
>
> I had run across the log and arrived on the opposite side below the willow, where he now paused, panting and on all fours, unable to rise. Slowly he raised his head and we looked into each other's eyes. I lifted him out both hands and helped him to his feet. Not a word passed between us. As nearly as I can relive the matter, the compassion I felt with this man gave way into awe and respect for what I had witnessed in him. He seemed absolutely clean. In that steady gaze of his I met reality point blank, filtered and distilled as the purity of a man.[22]

Let me break the momentum of this passage for a moment to recall our discussion of Job, and hazard that the pure reality of the man is the reality of a Job. It is the reality of a Job cleansed by the storm, cleansed by the rapids of affliction and rescued into the wonder of a world

---

[22] Ibid., 171f.

reborn as a place of perishing, passing, and bountiful particulars.[23]
Bugbee continues: "I think of Meister Eckhart's 'becoming as we were
before we were born.' I think of what Conrad says of the storms visited
on sailors far at sea as chastening them."[24] These reflections likewise
resonate with Job—suffering, protesting, and resuscitated, cleansed
absolutely by the eye of the storm. Would that Job had had a human
hand reach out to him, in his tatters, on his bank of ashes—an eye that
saw with intimate compassion! Would that Job had had a witness who
could see his "becoming as he was before he was born"— see reality
filtered there and distilled to its purity.

V. Philosophy and Inward Mornings: The Place of Lyric

Henry Bugbee's view of the religious is rooted in his presence to the
splendid significance, even sacredness, of moments and things encountered day by day. He carries us toward the animating place where
sacred and commonplace commune. As he has it, the true mystery is a
religious one found in the countenance of the everyday. "The genuine
religious mystery is none other than that of the existence of things, of
ourselves, and of all finites."[25] It is neither the science nor the utility
nor the obdurate resistance of finite things or others that captures his
attention but rather their trembling mystery.

There's a rhythm to these reflective tales, encounters with trees
and wild seas: *adagio* or *allegro*. They're tales that open up as song,
emerging from an infinite expectant quiet before the exhalation of a
word. And they carry a stillness, a patience, forward into verse—a poise
of breath awaiting its successor sound.

Here is Henry Bugbee reflecting on Job's plight, giving us Job's
stillness, his quiet in affliction:

Tuesday, January 15, 1963
No wind stirs. At Zero Fahrenheit the flakes of snow are not at all large.
Incredibly light and unwaveringly they fall. A myriad of them fills our meadow
round the house. One sees them best looking at the trees beyond. Their falling
accentuates the still-standing trees, the dark trunks. And the still of the trees is

---

[23] See *On Søren Kierkegaard*, Chapter 9, on "repetition" that brings rebirth and world
as gift.

[24] Bugbee, *Inward Morning*, 172.

[25] Ibid., 160–161.

the nearness of falling snow. Occasionally, in the meadow, a weed nods and lifts again. The low fire on the hearth is even more discreet.

Tuesday, February 12, 1963
No great pressure of anything to say.
Doubt with respect to so much of past thought.
. . . a reticence almost to speak at all.[26]

Perhaps from silence, or perhaps from waste or welter, words skip like stones in rhythm, melody or color, or mourn the incandescence of a setting sun, or sound the stopping wonder of a harvest moon.[27] Lyric brings us there to them in sempiternal resonance. We're quieted, invited to take in a scene as if it were born again that instant: born through words at one with world, expertly joined, *both*—just then articulate.

Lyric testimony gives voice to the very things its songs enfold. The truth to which it aspires is truth not of statements or propositions but of the realities it conveys, delivered directly to us, point blank: true generosity—care—flux—perishing. And indeed it is realities that we seek, not just words to stand in for something else. So lyric philosophy lies toward the margin of a philosophy modeled on science or the law. Its testimony is far removed from the construction of a lawyer's brief or a physicist's proof—however elegant either may be in their own terms, and in their own right.

Here is testimony: "Two dear friends and teachers of mine have said to me, independently of one another: 'You have written here as a man might write only near the end of his life.'"[28] This sense of death, he confides, has accompanied him since certain harrowing experiences in World War II, "Not in a way that saps life, but in a way that militates against putting off what one has to do." As he has it:

> the very perishing of what we love might be an essential moment in the clarifi-
> cation of the worthiness of love of that which perishes.. . . There is weeping
> and gnashing of teeth; there is stony impassivity; there is ribaldry, and vacuous
> staring. There is confusion. But there is pure gentleness, and it is in this vein
> that perishing speaks.[29]

---

[26] "A Way of Reading *The Book of Job*," unpublished.

[27] God creates from "welter and waste" in Robert Alter, trans., *Genesis*, New York: Norton, 1996.

[28] Bugbee, *Inward Morning*, 11.

[29] Ibid., 138.

Like any other speech, testimony can fail, be false, drum helplessly on deaf ears. "We cannot rub each others noses in immanent reality by argument," as Henry Bugbee has it.[30] And neither can we be assured our witness will be heard. That is the risk when philosophy goes lyric. Yet its track record in presenting essential, existential truth is none the worse for that. We must know in our bones or not at all that at its height, testimony ascends to truthful song, verse that joins persons and their worlds.

Here is an encounter with Robert Oppenheimer.

> I can remember hearing Robert Oppenheimer on an occasion, when he was casting about for a way of communicating the "beauty" he found in the things he had investigated. Those with whom he was talking wanted to go on talking about quantum theory; how little they reckoned with the look in the man's eye as the meaning of his life's work suddenly overtook him anew, and he stammered with gratitude for the magnitude of the gift, in the appalling newness of essential truth. How shall we find a word to say it?[31]

The contexts for revelation of essential truth, then, are several and ever-surprising. The occasion might be fraught with drama of Job-like proportions—a matter of ultimate affliction, abandonment, and at last the restoration of a world. Or it might be a mid-size occasion, as in Robert Oppenheimer's sudden stammering attempt to assimilate the bearing of a life's work. Or it might be the size of a sudden danger of a man at sea gripping a rope-looped oar, or the size of a snowflake glimpsed in graceful fall upon a cabin stove.[32]

* * *

As in life, our endings should return to our beginnings. So I return to Socrates and the voice that whispered, "Socrates, make music and compose." Does this mean his life was off-course, that he should have turned to music, become less cerebral, more poetic? Or is he musing on a vision he has in fact partially fulfilled, that he finds himself answering in his action? If his life served to answer this haunting voice, to that extent it would already be not merely critique but musical, poetic.

Architecture has been called frozen music. We could alter this image to our advantage: when music freezes, it becomes architecture.

[30] Ibid., 99.
[31] Ibid., 169.
[32] Ibid., 121.

If Bugbee ever had to choose between thought as music frozen and thought as music fluid there's no doubt which he'd have. The music of our best builders aspires to erect a frame to outlast floods and fires and ravages of time, a frame aspiring to immortality. Yet the power and eternity of liquid streams is something else again. Music is the most passing of the arts, yet nonetheless eternal for all that. As music, lyric is not depleted by being transitory, caught only in passing. Its power lies in how it passes, how it grows and builds, winds down, and disappears into a silence not alien to itself but all its own—and lasting in its passing. It creates its own life, and its own wake and aftermath, which is its eternal glory or sadness—its lightness or heaviness—all spun out as flow.

If philosophy resurrects only Descartes' or Kant's architectural aims—to build a lasting edifice to span the ages—then we will sadly gravitate toward an impersonal, weightless language, and thus become weightless ourselves, good mainly for detached cogitations. There is an austere beauty in the static reflections of remote cables of logic and engineering that can attain the frozen eternity of geometry. But lyric philosophy will aspire to embrace the prospects of a contrasting and fluid eternity. It will be held in the fragile perishability of flowing streams and simple calling sounds.

* * *

Here are some relatively static ideas to pocket. For all the celebration of a world receptive to our love, fellowship, and walking, there will still be—and ever *will* be—an Alcibiades, a smoking rope, Jobs in affliction, men perishing in flames. The way to face this dispiriting, clanking mess is not to search for rationales but to care for the afflicted and broken despite the mess. Nothing will come of trying to rub out disorder through crafty explanations. We proceed in courage, perhaps in prayer, against the sharp grain of suffering. Lyric philosophy, while keeping a mind and ear in hell, helps us through the mess by praising what can be praised. And so it gathers a worthy yet marred and perishing world. If there is loss and devastation there is also a capacity to complete reality for the better (even slightly)—against the power of the worst. Lyric gives voice to raise up a world and raises us thereby. It becomes, as Henry Bugbee has it, a meditation of the place, and *in extremis,* true prayer that opens to the impossible. It opens to the unbelievable: the redemption of an ice-bent bough of birch. Relinquishing the world as a cognitive or practical possession, it allows thankful recipients to praise a world-well-worth-being, the only world we have.

It is a world of persons and things *given* to our care, and to our awe and wonder, to our gratitude and surprise. World attains a religious valence. Here again is that fitting and characteristic Henry Bugbee benediction—attesting to love of the world, to steadiness amidst the evanescent:

> It is well while looking at rocks
> to have the roar of a river in one's ears.
> Or to see still-standing trees through falling snow.

Chapter 4

DEATH AND THE SUBLIME:
Henry Bugbee's In Demonstration of the Spirit

What would that beauty be
if we did not mourn from the outset
the imminent destruction of such radiance?
— *David Farrell Krell,* The Tragic Absolute

Philosophy ought really to be written
only as a poetic composition
—*Wittgenstein,* On Certainty

How do religion, philosophy, and lyric prose or poetry intermingle and animate each other—the first especially in its commemoration of the dead and celebration of the living, the second especially in its exploration of reason and ethics at their limits, the third especially in bringing us to saving passions and epiphanies?

This is not a question I want to approach at the level of theory or culture or academic disciplinary charts. It's a question or conundrum—an uneasiness—that I explore by taking up the detail of one particular thinker's immersion in it. How does a particularly gifted individual, in this case, the American philosopher Henry Bugbee, play out in his arresting writing the inter-animations of a poetic, philosophical, and religious sensibility? We begin with a cue from the Spanish thinker, Ortega y Gassett. As we've heard earlier, Ortega takes his *Meditations on Quixote* as "essays in intellectual love." They are what "a humanist of the seventeenth century would have called 'salvations.'"[1] Henry Bugbee's meditations, from his 1936 thesis *In Demonstration of the Spirit* on through his mid-1950s *The Inward Morning,* seem to be

---

[1] See Ortega y Gasset, *Meditations on Quixote,* 31.

53

luminous instances of such "salvations." They take us through death folded *within* the sublime to a death rent and *overtaken* by the sublime. Writing "salvations" is writing redemptions. And hearing them can be. But that's to rush the story.

I. LIFE'S INTIMATE EXPANSE

Henry Bugbee graduated from Princeton in 1936 with a major in philosophy and a senior thesis to his credit. He titled it *In Demonstration of the Spirit*. His supervisor was Werner Fite, a well-known philosopher in his time whose name still appears as the translator of the Spanish philosopher Miguel de Unamuno's experimental (today we'd say "postmodern") *Mist, a Tragicomic Novel*.[2] In addition to pursuing philosophy and literature, while at Princeton Bugbee rowed varsity crew and pursued a lifelong love of music. He grew up in Manhattan, prowling all its neighborhoods, as Whitman had. He also held a seat at Carnegie Hall. If you check the last pages of *In Demonstration of the Spirit,* you will discover immediately following the last book entry a list of classical recordings that Bugbee testifies have made his philosophical ventures possible. He also cites, as inspiration, a cycle of Wagner performances he has attended during the Metropolitan Opera's most recent season. We sense this is no ordinary thesis, and no ordinary East Coast college senior.

The writer roots his thesis in then-current and still roiling debates about the aesthetic and the sacred, and how each relates to reason within a full life. He also enters debates about the tension between natural science and technical competence on the one hand, and art, social life, and religion on the other. No doubt "tension" is too weak an image. Bugbee fears that art, religion, and a vital sense of life itself are losing ground to a technocratic specter in league with a dogma, the debilitating view that only science asks the real questions. This dual threat haunts reflection and living alike.

Henry Bugbee wanted most of all to root his academic writing in the frankly nonacademic way he took up with music or works of Melville or Thoreau, the way he took up with city walking, mountain brooks, or lakes. Twenty years later, in *The Inward Morning,* we could

---

[2] *Mist: A Tragicomic Novel,* trans. Werner Fite, New York: Alfred A. Knopf, 1928; Chicago: University of Illinois, 2000.

read accounts that reflect the capacious range of worlds outside technical philosophy that he would claim as touchstones of reality—of that vibrant inescapable tactile reality that arrested, engulfed, and called him close to heart. Composed in 1952 and 1953 and first published in 1958, this philosophical journal shows the breadth, intensity, and lyricism of his thesis come to full maturity. Take this glimpse of school-day saunters in swamps. It is early spring, rotten ice still underfoot, and a strange wavering of mood befitting the change of season:

> Of course there were pines, darkly green here and there, or massed in bunches, but when they spoke it was in awesome chorus of a cold wind and grey sky. And when the pines said nothing, they just stood around inane, giving way to the visible aptness of the bare-limbed trees.[3]

Some years later there were mornings of concerted action, of college rowing, sometimes in an eight, sometimes in a single scull, the rigger and coach John Schultz an abiding and demanding presence:

> It was as if rowing had a kind of ground-bass meaning for him which underlay the constancy of his concern and seemed to him to demand relevance from the oarsman in each and every stroke. And so he momently expected each one of us to wake up on the end of an oar. This infinite expectation of dawn often made him seem unreasonable. What did he want of us, anyway?[4]

Mid-stream in the progress of *The Inward Morning*, we encounter Bugbee's sense that music was his entry into the realms of philosophical thinking: "but for the music which aroused and defined a sense of unconditional reality in me, I doubt if I would have found it relevant to reflect on our condition in a way that drew me to the works of philosophers as speaking to that condition."[5] And there are those moments he tells of life and death, beauty and destruction, searing accounts of suicide attacks approaching from the sky in the Pacific— not easy to read, nor to imagine having endured in anything like readiness or poise.

> And I saw the plane brought to focus in the sky by the converging cone of fire from ours and other ships. It kept on and on, and as it came on without deviation toward its target it seemed to be standing still in the sky, hanging,

---

[3] Bugbee, *Inward Morning*, 43.
[4] Ibid., 51.
[5] Ibid., 139.

hanging, hanging upon the air. In that hanging moment of the undeviating plane, in that moment when the Chief became continuous fire, gun and plane came to seem one, so that we might as well have had the pilot aboard and the Chief might have been at the controls of the plane.[6]

Still later in the journal, in that iconic passage we've encountered, he confides, "I think of the suicide planes which I *witnessed*; . . . what I make of them, of the lives perishing in flames, is still unfinished business . . ."[7] These apocalyptic, transformative moments came to pass eight years after *In Demonstration of the Spirit*, and eight years before he recounted them in *The Inward Morning*.

II. EVOCATIONS OF THE SPIRIT

Henry Bugbee was a serious student and also an adventurer. He walked Manhattan streets late at night, listened to jazz in Harlem, and hitched freights (it was the Great Depression) into the heartland plains to harvest wheat. He pursued music in concert halls and record shops. In *The Birth of Tragedy*, Nietzsche takes music to be the primal source of the vision, a tragic one, that alone is sufferable by a reflective person. As early as his Princeton thesis, Henry (as everyone was to call him) invites us to hear the power of music as speaking to—and from—the deepest levels of self and nature. He was impish enough to cast a musical lure across the path of the author of *A General Theory of Relativity*. Einstein would amble down the corridor each day to lunch, taking a short cut that led him by Bugbee's room. To hook the rumpled cogitator, Bugbee left the door ajar and raised the volume of a Mozart piece just enough to lure him into conversation. Of course the music of the *Psalms* and the insistence of Pauline letters also inhabit this writing. The surprise and shadow of lived experience—not excluding experience arriving through literature or scripture—play a commanding part for him.

As if to emphasize this breadth, he titles the thesis "*In Demonstration of the Spirit*." As we will come to know, "demonstration" is not accomplished by blackboard proofs or Hegelian dialectics. It will come by way of displays or evocations—evocations accomplished by music, by rivers, by sailors or flashing trout, by just *being* there

---

[6] Ibid., 188.

[7] Ibid., 225; emphasis in the original.

as witness to a man miraculously saved from certain death. Here is the setting and its drama, recounted earlier, and accordingly slightly abbreviated here:

> There came a cry for help, seconded with a cry of fright, and I turned toward the tail of the pool just in time to see a young man desperately, failingly, clinging to a great log . . . An enormous suction under the log . . . drew him ineluctably under . . . But it chanced that the river was abnormally high, and as it carried this helpless man doomward it swept him just for an instant under the extremity of a willow . . . With a wild clutch the young man seized a gathering of the supple branches and held . . . I had run across the log and arrived on the opposite side below the willow, where he now paused, panting and on all fours, unable to rise. Slowly he raised his head and we looked into each other's eyes . . . He seemed absolutely clean . . . I think of Meister Eckhart's "becoming as we were before we were born."[8]

These moments have their say as demonstration, display, evocation—instilled by and instilling spirit, bringing us to death and its undoing.

Bugbee's writing instills a listening absorption co-present with responsive articulation and sorting out. In *The Inward Morning*, we find this listening absorption as he brings us to the innocence of rivers or to routines at sea, to the serenity of trees or to terrifying fire from the sky or to the befalling grace of snow. His lyric passages—to tumult, wonder, or serenity—seamlessly give life to the remembered.

III. Spirit's Reach

The *Spirit* to which Bugbee alludes in his undergraduate thesis is meant to be as encompassing as possible within a broadly biblical tradition. It's unfolded as revelation or epiphany, a showing or "demonstration" that rings with St. Paul. *"I speak not in enticing words of man's wisdom but in demonstration of the Spirit."*[9] To Paul, it was primarily the Person, the Christ, who was called forth in demonstration of the Spirit. As Bugbee's writing matures, exemplary persons, rooted or walking in places that call on their depths, remain touchstones of what he'll call reality—an experiential, viscerally known reality. And increasingly he attends to the *things of creation*—in their bounteous unfolding.

---

[8] Ibid., 172; the full passage is given and discussed in chapter three, p. 47.

[9] I Cor 2:4; emphasis added.

Not unlike Heidegger, whom he had not yet read, they call forth, into a light of the place.

Each of the chapters of his thesis opens with a short biblical epigraph, unobtrusively entered, a framing device that we'd certainly find unacceptable in present-day academic prose. Inhabiting secular universities and colleges, we learn to deliver words appropriately distanced from intimations of a first-person religious sensibility. Between his undergraduate writing and his postwar publications, the style of academic thought had shifted decisively secular. But even for the 1930s, his writing is exceptionally personal. Of course in the intervening years, the hegemony of technical knowledge transmission and production has only consolidated its cultural and academic grip. Wisdom, insight, and illumination have become scraps in a stripped-down, rationalized academy, a mirror image of their meager interest in the wider culture, where they appear as shards, or abandoned sentimental objects, in an ever-expanding landfill.

In more ways than one, Henry Bugbee's thesis of 1936 seems dated. It evinces an intimate, passionate intensity that can, at least by present measures, seem well beyond the pale. It is unapologetic in its quite impassioned celebration of a European thinker, novelist, and public intellectual, Miguel de Unamuno, known for his existentialist meditations, especially *The Tragic Sense of Life*. Unamuno wrote from life's exigencies and exaltations as he underwent them, evoking the fragility of life, the wonder of love, the threat of violence spilling into the horrors of war and massacre. Without apology, the thesis cites an ineffable musical spirit as a source. Frankly biblical lines provide title and chapter epigraphs. And as an *undergraduate* thesis, there's something daring, extravagant, and surely imprudent in having chapters that in succession give his evaluative overviews not just of a writer like Unamuno, but of ethics and value theory, of philosophy of science and of a technological culture, of the nature of consciousness and of Kant's *Third Critique*. And in a final provocation, Bugbee ends his thesis with an unblushing "Amen"—as I hear it, a word that acknowledges a kind of blessing (as Cavell will put it in *A Pitch of Philosophy*) that has instilled voice and poise.[10]

---

[10] On his "Amen," see *On Søren Kierkegaard*, Chapter 12, and on blessing, see chapter six in this volume.

IV. A Kantian Sublime

In his thesis Henry lays out the collision between freedom and deadening constraint, between our sense that our lively, "existential" projects and self-conceptions have some real non-illusory significance, and the contrary conviction that nature takes our presence indifferently, even hostilely—paying no heed either to meanings that set free or to our powers of eloquence in the service of voicing them. The clash between freedom and an oblivious nature can frame a tragic fate. Bugbee finds tragedy confirmed in Unamuno, writing as Spain's glory spun toward death, and Bugbee even anticipates Deleuze, framing Kant as a tragic philosopher, defeated by the clash of freedom and nature.

The clash of brute force and freedom can be figured as "the sublime." In a single striking moment, we sense the convergence of external humbling power and of a strange uplift or cleansing, a quiet pleasure that one is witness to such power, partaking in a dangerous glory from a place where fate has been suspended or surpassed. Kant or Burke would have it that a raging storm humbles our will, yet energizes self-apprehension. It's a scene as old as the Whirlwind appearing to the *Old Testament* Job. Our aspirations to mastery and full cognitive grasp are depleted even as a freedom to be in dignified wonder or awe is instilled.

It seems likely that "the" sublime is not a single sort of phenomenal encounter but rather a family of such encounters in which one's expected wooden or routine apprehensions are radically shaken. Edmund Burke found "the" sublime in our fascination with terrible storms and mountain peaks (viewed from relative safety). Though they instill fear of death, we cannot avert our eyes.[11] Kant distinguishes "a dynamic sublime," found in power and turbulence, from "a mathematical sublime," where vastness stretches without limit, as in the case of starry heavens above.[12] George Pattison finds a sublime associated with the "spectacular city," a vortex of spectacles, where bustle, confusion, and dizzying kaleidoscopic sights threaten not death, but the anxiety

---

[11] Edmund Burke, *On the Sublime and the Beautiful*, *The Harvard Classics*, ed. Charles W. Eliot, New York: P.F. Collier & Son, 1909–14.

[12] Kant, Immanuel, *Critique of Judgment*, "analytic of the sublime," New York: Barnes & Noble, 2005.

and allure of radical disorientation.[13] Under the aegis of "the" sublime, a mountain is not just a mountain, a city, not just a city. Each site
so framed portents an uncanny, inexhaustible depth we're drawn to
comprehend but can't. Even persons might be sublime, a center inex-
haustibly coiling passions or unrest, as caught in The Mona Lisa's
smile, open to such endless troubling interpretation. Job's encounter
with the Storm is surely an epitome. It can be humbling and fearsome
and yet it portends life (as well as death). In a strange mix of anxiety
and fascination there is a momentary loss of will and cognitive grasp.

From Kant's point of view, that phase of depletion can't be sustained
for long, and shouldn't be. Yielding before vastness or power hints at
incipient servility or weakness (as the upright Kant hears it)—as if an
emptying of the self before wonders were necessarily humiliating.
Accordingly, he quickly posits a recovery of dignity in a subsequent
knowledge that only a rational being could witness such grandeur—
thus are the indignities of a near humiliation avoided. However great
the storm or mountain that I face, *it is I, a creature blessed with rational
consciousness,* who faces it.

Bugbee will amend this recovering phase of the Kantian account.
To gather poise after momentary deflation does not require an asser-
tion of rational dignity—as if the self needed to rear up to show its
most noble credentials. Without a sliver of humiliation, one might
bask in the sustained wonder that there are *things there* to speak!
To melt before powerful significance is to relinquish willfulness and
self-importance, and stay open to untold splendor. Self-emptying
might be salutary, a quasi-religious antidote to the pervasive liability
of overweening pride, a release from a drive to mastery. There is no
need to follow Kant (as Bugbee has it) in rushing to reinstall reason
and dignity.

In the current academic climate, the sublime has become an object
of dispraise or suspicion. An interest in the overpowering or vast, not
to mention a recovery in Kantian self-assertion and autonomy, is a
cover, so it's argued, for projects of domination and violence.[14] How
do we reach this unhappy pass? How does a bracing witness to an

---

[13] See *"Poor Paris!": Kierkegaard's Critique of the Spectacular City.* Berlin: Walter de
Gruyter, 1999.

[14] See "Toward an Ecological Sublime," Christopher Hitt, *New Literary History,* 30.3,
1999. Among leaders in a campaign against the sublime, writing from Marxist, deconstructive, and Freudian perspectives, are Terry Eagleton, Paul de Man, Frances
Ferguson, and Niel Hert.

awesome storm become reconfigured as a breeding ground for suspect cultural and political stratagems?

Perhaps it's assumed that praising the wild, spectacular, and threatening arouses the hyper-masculine fantasy of a counter-punch, as if the sight of a tiger triggered the scenario of the hunt: *if it's wild, shoot it!* But is the slaughter of buffalo or elephants really compatible with recognition of their sublimity? Edmund Burke took the tiger as a token of the sublime, but whether it counts as sublime depends on the disposition of the viewer. To the hunter, the hunted is not sublime but at best a noble adversary, and at worst a power to eradicate, a competitor to subdue. In any case, the problem is not that the sublime instigates killing but that a killing instinct cannot countenance a moment of sublimity when as a hunter (say) he might relinquish power, or sideline the desire to overpower any power he confronts. Aggression is hardly the only non-servile response to the momentous or powerful, it is opposite to a humility that the sublime instills.

Critics also link the sublime to mesmerizing and subduing political devices. The tyrant blares Beethoven over militaristic parades that dazzle the crowds. But why take these spectacles as instances of sublimity? The sublime (for Burke or Kant) has nothing to do with mastery of crowds through stagecraft. It's the final *refutation* of all such imperial dreams. In a pathetic miscue, just after the attacks of 9/11, the German composer Stockhausen remarked with cruel insensitivity that the event was "the greatest work of art in the world"—a spectacle that any artist would wish to have orchestrated! Thus can "the sublime" be co-opted and abused. Surely awe and wonder at creation, say, have their place. Wonder linked to human destructiveness is properly moral horror, not a melting before the sublime.

We might take some pride—reigned in well short of self-congratulation—in being present to the majesty of a mountain. Melville (and Bugbee) would even ask whether *a remnant of* pride is well-placed. A sublime impact—what Melville would call its mystic moment—can effect religious self-emptying. But this is not self-annihilation and coexists with satisfactions and ease that refuse grandiosity and self-inflation. It can refuse plans to tame or corner the unmanageable or wild. Mammoth waves can beckon the surfer, but they can also instill a reminder that our conquering has limits, and that to acknowledge them is not obsequious. In Kant's appreciation, death seems precisely *not* to foster the idea of rebellion or taking arms or steps toward mastery. "Starry heavens above" bring Kant to wonder, not to the imperial dream of getting to the moon.

When a Whirlwind accosts Job, his will-to-protest is silenced. Under stars or great whirlwinds we may realize we're only dust in the largest scale of things—and melt as before great music. In this, we learn the wisdom of letting be, of forgoing mastery, of a submission to the world that is a kind of love and acceptance of it.[15]

V. Death, Violence, and What Matters

Death is linked to the sublime, but not as the simple thought that you could die in an ocean storm. A storm can present imminent danger, and if I am about to drown, survival will preempt any impulse to bask wonderingly in its fury. To be swept or thrown off a jetty is traumatic or cruel, not sublime. Yet there can be something refreshing, restoring, in seeing high waves from the safety of a cliff. If I have room for awe, wonder, or fascination (as well as fear), death can be an occasion for transformative insight. The non-imminent but hauntingly possible presence of death reminds me that from the standpoint of the sea's vast power I could be alive or dead, perish or be spared, and it would *matter not a whit*—to the sea, to the sky, to creation.

Worse than my biological death is the thought that it doesn't matter if I live or die, suffer or rejoice, if others listen or turn a deaf ear. From the vast perspective of the sublime, we matter not at all. This dashes Promethean aspirations and belittles our wish for enveloping love and attention. But will can be flattened in an experience of the sublime, without portending annihilation of the *world*. *We* may matter not at all, but from that it does not follow that *nothing* matters. Things beyond our will can matter still—stars and storms, shafts of winter light, an infant's smile.

Artists can feel rebuked by the sublime, for it seems to undo their capacity to depict what is so massively *there!* It seems bent on eluding conceptual, linguistic, or imagistic grasp—as if genius were required to even start. There may be misguided *attempts* at capture, but mere mortals fail. Perhaps artists out to depict the sublime garner not success in *grasping* it, but success in grasping the truth that all we will ever have is *attempts that fall short*.

Think of how quickly the conceptual or psychological region we're testing eludes our grasp. Are we annihilated—or empowered—in the

---

[15] See chapters seven and eleven in this volume, on Cavell's theme of "Falling in love with the world."

presence of the sublime? Is facing it fearful—or fascinating? Does it exceed the power of poetry or music, or is it well suited to bring out the best in gifted artists? The impact of the sublime heralds both significance of surpassing *importance*—and a power to squelch all steps to convey it. As I see it, Bugbee finds that the sublime opens a necessary corrective to a number of standing, pernicious assumptions. In an age of ego, acquisitiveness, endless competition, and conquest, the sublime opens an unassuming, power-renouncing receptivity—at once moral, religious, and aesthetic.

By the time *The Inward Morning* begins to take shape, no vestige remains of Kant's view that the saving grace of the sublime is its affording an occasion for affirming reason and autonomy. That conceit rings of self-congratulation, and of denial of mortality and dependence. If the sublime exposes our mortal presence in an overarching creation, then it's fitting to halt ever-expanding autonomy, to embrace dependence on and with others, placed among the things of creation.[16] Bugbee tunes life-affirming flows of wonder, awe, and care, preserving and memorializing these in lyrical rendition and living speech.

Inward Morning is anything but morbid, but Bugbee does confess, in the journal's preface, to writing in a continuous awareness of death. Many of his exquisite narratives give us an uncanny *closeness* to death's dance with life—and life's, with death.[17] Witness the young man swept toward the rapids, the kamikaze descending, fish leaping high and hooked. This tensed interplay of life and death, power and impotence, clarity and mystery, displays the sublime in our presence to the wild (and within it, a presence to the serene). Although the sublime is not an explicit term of art for him in *Inward Morning*, the phenomenon bursts through, now indexed as "wilderness." One might even see in wilderness the transfiguration of what otherwise might be only terrible or traumatic.

Presence to wonders in music, art, and literature, and presence to wilderness becomes, he avers, the unifying theme of his life. The wild intimates a sacred place, a place of and for neighbors and companions where spirit speaks not just in human syllables but through fast water, distant peaks, and flurries of snow—through the cacophony and then music of night-bells in Taxco—through the plunging bow of a

---

[16] For a defense of dependence, see chapter nine.

[17] See the exploration of dancing with death in my "Transfigurations: The Intimate Agency of Death," *Kierkegaard and Death*, ed. Stokes and Buben, forthcoming. Indiana, 2010.

ship at sea—through attention to a campus bell that calls him to his next hour.

> It would seem to me that the bell spoke a final word in the soul, the meaning of coming to be and passing away, perennial, always and always, ever so, just as now . . . It seemed to key me to the vein of ultimacy in which philosophical reflection must move; many times, I know, it summoned me into the attitude of prayer, teaching me the namelessness of that which [we] must serve.[18]

VI. BEING AND BEINGS: THE DISSERTATION

As a graduate student at Berkeley before the war, Bugbee wavered between literature and philosophy. In his second semester he gathered his professors: which discipline should he follow? They demurred; in the event he chose philosophy. He would focus on aesthetics, working under the Hegel scholar Jacob Loewenberg. But he did not leave his literary, existential, and even religious sensibilities far behind. *The Inward Morning* would convey the arbitrariness of disciplinary and cultural divisions of labor. A journal is a thing of the day. Writing of the day, for this philosopher, will lay out a biblical site where we can live and move and have our being. It is a site for Eckhart and for Job's Whirlwind, for Shakespeare, Melville, and Thoreau. There are intervals on Spinoza's blessedness and necessity, on Stoic resignation, Kant's reflective judgments, and Tillich's ultimate concern. There is no discernible disciplinary grid. *The Inward Morning* invites us gently by the greeting of its title. The title of Bugbee's Berkeley dissertation is starkly forbidding: *The Sense and the Conception of Being.*

Completed in 1948, the dissertation develops a broad notion of the aesthetic as containing and revealing a sense of Being. For Bugbee, Being is not an onto-theological abstraction but fundamentally experiential, something *sensed* rather than only conceptualized or system driven. There were few signs from 1938 to 1941 of any such dissertation taking shape. Pearl Harbor put a quick stop to expectations. Bugbee became captain of a minesweeper that survived typhoons and kamikaze attacks. Before the war his sense of being and the sublime took heart from music, books, or mountain treks. Now in the time of the dissertation it is remembered under aspects more desolate, ferocious, and wounding. The sense of dangerous confluences of life

---

[18] Bugbee, *Inward Morning*, 229.

and death and the precariousness of survival must have enveloped absolutely everything. Yet there were also evenings at anchor, quiet, far from home. There was much to absorb of men teamed not just for battle, but for the everyday tasks of maintenance, moving through varied seas, lonely months on end.

There was time to think of these things in 1946 and 1947, yet as I read Bugbee's Berkeley dissertation, there's no discernible aftershock of war. Perhaps it was still all too close. Six years later, the war figures prominently in *The Inward Morning*, where it becomes thematically continuous with wilderness he had known since his youth, and to which he returned after the war. In Henry's dissertation "the sense of being" can be figured as a sense of the sublime. In a memorable evocation near its center, Henry in fact paints a majestic alpine scene that stands in as an experience of Being. It is Being experienced through attention to *beings*. Being is exposed in rising peaks, racing clouds, crumbling talus slopes, pines—it appears through attention to the soft coming of snow.

> [With the snow] each thing which had stood out, crying in resistance to the wind, now lapses and is lost in a pervasive still. Bird, bush, mountain, animal, stick, and stone—each is left to itself, alone, as in [a] timeless slumber. The wildness is sealed in silence . . . What blanches things visible, blotting mass and form, absorbing their very thinghood? What in this obscuring is hushedly revealing? What but the pure and secret presence that is snow?[19]

This is a precursor to Henry's later *Inward Morning* passage, that iconic passage where wilderness brings instruction in the Canadian Rockies.

> I weighed everything by the measure of the silent presence of things, clarified in the racing clouds, clarified by the cry of hawks, solidified in the presence of rocks, spelled syllable by syllable by waters of manifold voice, and consolidated in the act of taking steps, each step a meditation steeped in reality.[20]

An alpine storm, a vastness of the sea, a wilderness vista—these diminish, yet animate the self. Each conjures a spirit that supersedes, suspends, or transcends the vulnerability of the body to the ravages of nature or of war.

---

[19] Henry G. Bugbee, *The Sense and the Conception of Being*, PhD diss. 1947, University of California, Berkeley, 69.

[20] Bugbee, *Inward Morning*, 139.

Is Chief Johnson firing on a diving plane an instance of the sublime? It might be riveting to behold that plane against the endless sky. But in the event, it's primarily seen as impending death that must be met with counterforce. It might speak otherwise if I find myself in relative safety, but this safety is terribly unavailable to those on a ship under fire. The sort of poise in recollection that we find in Bugbee's journal, written eight years after the events, gathers from the years and distance now separating him from the actual attack. Perhaps the recollections in *The Inward Morning* are healing, a therapeutic retelling of terrifying and deeply wounding events that still call achingly for restorative interpretation. Even so, acknowledging the traumatic isn't by itself enough for a powerful sense of the sublime to emerge. That sense is muffled in battle and more available later. It saturates the image of the plane hanging in the sky, and then comes to link Chief and pilot.

Storms and a sea's vastness may intimate mortality, or scream its imminence. But perhaps in memory it can reverse the tide, can intimate mortality's undoing. Vastness and power overtake and rend the self, leaving *it*, in a sense, hanging timelessly—and thus, in that sense, in that moment, immune. The sense of Being is the sense of the evanescence of beings passing in and out of wondrous presence. So death is not the only word, nor necessarily the last word. It might always be next to last, as birth presages death, and from death springs birth in the ephemeral cycles of creation: mortality answered by natality, flowing always unfinished.

VII. Is There an Ethical Sublime?

The account of the firing and counter-firing in the Pacific depicts much more than exposure where individual survival is at stake. Skills, sure footedness, cooperation, and courage make life in such circumstances much more than a desperately thrashing fight to survive. There is also the moment of transposition. Bugbee imagines the Chief and pilot transposed in a moment that transcends this site of raw vulnerability. We are perishable bodies but not only that. Kant and Burke presented sublimity in wild storms or open skies, and it might also hover, as we've seen, over cities or a Mona Lisa smile. Now in a particularly wrenching moment of deadly fire in the Pacific, we might find ethics, too, infused by a dark sublimity.

Ethics might be a set of laws or rules or an array of Apollonian ideals. But it can also be a domain verging on the wildly Dionysian, a place of immediately impacting calls, solicitations, or demands.[21] The terribly wild terrain of this war-time event in the Pacific is a time that threatens to explode yet sustains an uncanny moral center. As such, it might instance an ethical sublime.

If the Chief might as well have been the pilot, and the pilot the Chief, then they are not *only* enemies, and perhaps not enemies at all. They share a moral status, a humanity, and in that become transposable. The perceived exchange of positions affects and seals this moment as an instance of the ethical sublime. Each now inhabits a status transcending their perishable bodies. Despite perishing as flesh and blood, they are and forever will be preserved as *persons*. This is to deny that in death each will be no more than a corpse, fodder for the sea, as if never having been born. Yet if each aims to *annihilate* the other, how do we fathom this status of equal imperishability, derived from their equal worthiness as persons?

When battle erupts for great Homeric warriors, neither hero preemptively casts his adversary as evil. Each is a worthy opponent to the other. Fate will bring them to battle, and sometimes a sense of justice will, but hardly ever, it seems, do they enter battle with the thought that the other is brutish or evil or subhuman. In this they are like Olympic wrestlers rather than flag-bearers for a cosmic good. (It's another story for Homer's warriors *after* a battle, when custom allowed the victor to desecrate the defeated.) Zen warriors might see each other as adversaries but not evil, and so might honor even he whom they set out to kill. The idea that behind each battle is the instigation of an enemy who is evil who must be destroyed with due heartlessness would be foreign to both Homeric and Zen warriors.

Bugbee says he cannot believe that the pilot and Chief are enemies to each other—or that he himself faced enemies, problematic as that sounds. "Is it not true that we were not enemies? And who will believe this, how can it be believed?"[22] If we grant this shared humanity we preserve in the midst of deadly confrontation the contrast between the unspeakable toll in death and suffering and the high moral standing of adversaries. Neither is subhuman to the other. But that is nearly impossible to believe. Controverting all "realist" instincts, it's as hard to believe as the belief (or faith) that in concrete hard-knuckle human

---

[21] See appendix to chapter twelve, "an ethical sublime," and *On Søren Kierkegaard*, pp. 197–199.

[22] Bugbee, *Inward Morning*, 226. See chapter five.

exchange, the ethical is always fully and inviolably present. I call this an instance of the ethical sublime because this moment to which Bugbee bears witness humbles yet exalts our sense of what ethics can and can't do.

Bugbee does not provide a detailed interpretation of that moment. No doubt he fears that switching to analysis would weaken its impact, for him and for us. It suffices for him, I suspect, that he leaves no trace that he or the gunner preserve the good against the assault of incoming pilot. But if this is not a collision of good and evil—what is it?

A tragic view—the sort of view that Bugbee embraces in his undergraduate thesis—would see these combatants as equally committed in the conflict that befalls them. The conflict is tragic because they are thrown into battle by fate, they have no escape, and they cannot but do grievous damage, however shattering their actions will seem to them in hindsight. This may be close to Bugbee's sense of things, but he doesn't say that it is. Why not? He tries in *The Inward Morning* to stay close to the particulars of his experience, which are—perhaps—too varied to be grouped under a single broad heading like "the tragic sense of life."[23] He is explicit in a refusal to generalize quasi-metaphysically about evil or tragedy or calamity.

Bugbee won't take some particular crisis or horror or delight as emblematic of some larger class of events and their general import. Looking for the generalization abandons the shifting specificity of what we do and undergo, in its telling detail. Necessarily more abstract summations, in his view, distract from the singular grain of experience in whose irreducible and often opaque complexities he and I must live (and die). And there are contrasting arrays of epiphanies that fall outside the heading of tragedy. Bugbee recounts moments of deep celebration and gratitude, of rebirth and dawn, moments of rejoicing and moving compassion, redolent of *New Testament* themes. What would it be to weigh disaster against dawn, as if we held a reliable balance, and the significance of one could be seen to shadow its other? Better stick to the grain of experience. Even in his student thesis, tragic and counter-tragic notes sound sequentially, like shifts from minor to major keys. He is haunted by death and by spirit strangely resurrected from the dead; by Unamuno's not solely tragic but tragi-comic vision; by mortality in phase with natality; by Eckhart's moment before

---

[23] Ibid., 225.

we are born—that we may be born from the dead into morning (and, let us admit, no small portion of mourning).

Perhaps no single narrative or lyric assembly of insight can gather all that calls to be gathered, allowing life under an unending sublime. In any case, both tragedy and comedy deeply discredit the illusion of one right, one wrong. Perhaps it's two rights, no wrong, or one good-enough right but no evil, or two wrongs. However you cut it, it's enough to make you weep, given such fateful suffering—even if a comic reconciliation were to supervene. Are we in Dante's dark wood, lost, yet yearning to emerge into creation's redeeming light?

Perhaps we should rest with that image, so reminiscent of Heidegger and of Thoreau, of a dark wood and clearing. But let me think, for a moment, of the relevance of Nietzsche's *Birth of Tragedy*. Nietzsche takes over from Schopenhauer the idea that music expresses the truths of our tragic condition. Now whether or not existence is wholly, or only, tragic, Bugbee could agree that music provides uncanny access to its mystery. His affirmation of a cycle's ephemeral evanescence resonates with Nietzsche's affirmation of eternal recurrence (all things go under and return—to go under again). But whereas Bugbee greets rebirth with unqualified affirmation—how could one *reject* morning light!—Nietzsche flirts with the possibility of a wholesale rejection of life, birth, or rebirth.

Nietzsche has a Silenus whisper unnervingly from an extreme edge of possibility that it's *"best never to have been born—and next best, to die early."*[24] This echoes Ecclesiastes (4.2–3): "And I thought the dead who have already died more fortunate than the living, who are still live; but better than both is the one who has not yet been, and has not seen the evil deeds that are done under the sun." Birth and life become a cause for *grief* (and death, cause for celebration). Yet Nietzsche also has Achilles: *"better to live as a day-laborer than to die, even if one were to become ruler of the dead."*[25]

In effect, Nietzsche valorizes the dark ambiguity created by this juxtaposition of Silenus and Achilles. A tension between tragedy and celebration permeates Bugbee's world, as well, but for him, tragedy is never as bleak as a Silenus extreme. On another front, still in *Birth of Tragedy* and in a sentiment Bugbee would recognize, Nietzsche

[24] Nietzsche, *The Birth of Tragedy*, § 3, Cambridge: Cambridge University Press, 1999, 22–24; emphasis added.

[25] Ibid; emphasis added.

laments the emergence of a theory-based Socratic-Platonic culture
that overtakes the dark vitality of tragic culture. Both join in praise of
a wilderness or wild that overwhelms any narrow Platonic aspirations
for abstract reason and rationalist clarity, secured only from a great
and distorting distance.

VIII. Not Death Alone: Ethics and Transcendence

The gunner fires in utter concentration at the oncoming plane, "making the prayer of his life." As Bugbee says, he's "burning out that gun
with the white fire of his soul."[26] Now the oncoming pilot, too, may be
making the prayer of his life. He emerges from behind the horizon,
out of sight at first. Bugbee can't read his full body. Yet the plane finally
comes close enough that he *can* glimpse his face, just before a glide
over the deck and into a surging wave. Why *not* attribute to each an
equal moral intensity? If pilot and Chief each make the prayer of their
lives, in that respect they bear witness to a shared dedication as well
as to a shared humanity.

This emphatic event carries a moral revelation in a powerful irrup-
tion whose scale and intensity resembles the sublime revelation Job
receives through the Whirlwind. The tie between Chief and pilot is
exemplary and includes transcendence. As Bugbee has it, in that
instant "I saw beyond the war." He adds, "Into this transcendence, the
Chief carried us all."[27] If war had become only heartless duty and
lifeless routine—that is now transcended. And if war was ever driven
moralistically, self-righteously, now that is transcended in the perception that the Chief and Pilot share common ground. If it were ever
a zealous or holy crusade, that too is now transcended. A radiant
sunrise can break through the stock perception that time transpires
at an even, uneventful pace. Morning light then throws us into the glory
and surprise of creation's dawn. Just so, the radiance of simple human
dedication can break through the dark of war's otherwise bitter
disasters.

In a passage further on in *The Inward Morning*, Bugbee takes up the
suicide attacks again. It's now many years later, far from the heat of
action, and a time we've visited, and to which we'll return in the following chapter. We hear an aching sense of responsibility for the deaths

---

[26] Bugbee, *Inward Morning*, 187.
[27] Ibid., 188.

of those he shot down. "I think of the suicide planes which I *witnessed;* oh! They still call out to me, and what I make of them, of the lives perishing in flames, is still unfinished business."[28] If he has glimpsed his adversary's humanity, how can he have been part of those fiery deaths? Some eight years later, he struggles to understand how he might answer for that—might *be* answer for *them.*

Their deaths cannot be undone, nor can his implication in them be erased or forgotten. This is a moment of tragic recognition. He will have "unfinished business" with those men through his dying day. He sees the horror of killing a man making "the prayer of his life"—yet how could it have been otherwise? Fate seems to rule over the encounter. And if he now cries out that he must *be* answer to those lives, then the cry is at least a prayer that he may have such strength to be answer in the *living out* of a gentle prayer. Bugbee doesn't respond to the approach of death with some version of the plea, *Why me!* —nor with the bromide that if evil is to be defeated, violence is (I'm so sorry) unfortunately necessary. The thought, "*I* don't deserve to die—*he* does!" counts as moralism. Bugbee sees only the soul that in the long run he alone must answer for.

There's a difference between giving an answer for one's deeds (where we imagine a short speech in something like a court of law), and *being* answer for one's deeds, where we imagine the pattern of one's actual living, its exemplariness, as the only "answer" that might in the circumstance even approach sufficiency. Bugbee calls his answer "articulating a true prayer," and doesn't amplify. But at the least this abjures the easier paths of patriotic self-righteousness, thoughts of revenge, plain indifference, forgetfulness, or outright denial.[29] More positively, it suggests a prayer for strength to be answer for those who have perished, for strength to understand (and perhaps forgive), strength for a lived-out compassion somehow commensurate, if only marginally, to the suffering in which he is implicated.

This complex event bears import for the spirit and even serves in demonstration of it. There's the primal level of a brute and devastating threat to life. Yet the occasion opens to other levels. The descent of kamikazes gives us a glimpse of the sublime: witness the plane hanging—as if it might hang motionless forever. There's a glimpse of an ethical sublime in the revelations of the transposition of pilot and gunner, in the concentration of action that takes on all

---

[28] Ibid., 225–226; emphasis in the original.
[29] See chapter five.

the force of nature, in the sense that the dominance of war's nihilism can be strangely transcended. And at yet another level these events occasion thinking through trauma. There are wounds, pure and simple, emotional and physical. And there are also *moral* traumas. If even for an instant Bugbee could take the pilot as no different from his shipmate, how could he bring him down? Only his working through that trauma in an unfolding life will tell if he can be answer to those fallen men: honoring them, remembering them in compassion, mourning them.[30]

IX. ETHICAL CALLS

Kant finds confirmation of a reflective being's dignity under "starry heavens" and under those skies Bugbee husbands wonder and astonishment. Things speak from their silent surround. An encounter in and with wilderness is aesthetic and religious and can intimate how a person might live. Bugbee's life at sea grounds communal solidarity and installs a vision of participating in creation that expands the moral or ethical domain. Ethics can answer more than questions of explicit duties or what a utilitarian calculus might dictate.

The sublime works in a moral or ethical vein against arrogance, self-importance, and egoism. A moral sublime (in a transposed Chief and pilot) makes a fight for survival simultaneously something more. A sublime creation overshadows the counterfeits of fame, riches, or power and occasions gratitude for the gifts of life and its many legacies—adventure, serenity, the voice of particulars that call us to an *openness to the world*. Without such openness—a broadly moral attunement—no moral or aesthetic or religious self could be alive and well.

Imagine a moral or spiritual self-unfolding, flowing stream-like through a venture in the wild, called by peaks or streams, seeking its next self around the next bend in the river. Bugbee hears the voice of *this* larch, *this* stretch of stream; he attends to *this* face by the bank of rushing waters, *this* face in an on-rushing fighter plane. Each voice and face has universal relevance but no link to universal law. Spirit is not lofted up above the clouds but embodied in the particulars of this ordinary–extraordinary world. It speaks in particular address: *this*

[30] See Robert Pogue Harrison, *The Dominion of the Dead*, Chicago: University of Chicago Press, 2003.

snow whispers, *this* pilot addresses him—as do the bells calling from the quad. Things of creation join, conjoin, voice in mutual address. They converge in acclamations, sound a world where persons can stand forth independent and together.

Bugbee's theme of life in the unknown of wilderness can verge toward what Stanley Cavell calls moral perfectionism. That perfectionism, developed from Thoreau and Emerson, does not posit a static ideal to attain.[31] It is to know that there's always something undone, more to be done, that one's evident imperfections are a reminder of steps yet to be taken in an unfolding wilderness. An ethics should not just give one the complacent satisfactions of a moral task completed, a rule obeyed, a result accomplished, a perfection in hand. When we know we have not got our relations or feelings quite right, when we know that we are, let us agree, less than perfect—this gives us the glimmer of a further perfection yet to be attained—and another after that, endlessly. Such is the spirit of this sort of perfectionism. This is a venture of discovery in a wilderness, as Bugbee has it. As Cavell has it, it is a discovery of my next and better self. Our status as perfectionist moral seekers is confirmed in knowing that we've fallen short, that there's more to be done; or in the idiom of wilderness, that there are always new vistas and dangers ahead.[32]

Here are three themes, severely condensed, of Cavell's moral perfectionism. As I see it, they provide a backdrop for Bugbee's vision of a moral life in wilderness. First, a crisis marks a threat to self, but also an opening for renewal: Henry might say, *we find ourselves at risk in wilderness; renewal comes through voice, calling us toward vocation.* Then the self finds itself beside itself in *ecstasis*, in enchantment and transfiguration: as Bugbee might say, *we're gripped in wonder and astonishment; we stand forth, to be born.* Third and last, the self transparently encounters that which it must answer, an exemplar, or the radiant things of an exemplary world: as Henry might say, *persons and particulars speak or call in invitation of an answering response, opening a dialogue for which we cannot but be grateful.* Perfectionism registers our sense of being drawn into unending, ever-open significant experiences, and into

---

[31] Stanley Cavell, *City of Words, Pedagogical Letters on a Register of the Moral Life*, Cambridge, MA: Harvard University Press, 2004. See also John Davenport, *Will as Commitment and Resolve: An Existential Account of Creativity, Love, Virtue, and Happiness*, New York: Fordham University Press, 2007, 291f.

[32] See chapters six and seven. On moral perfectionism, see *On Søren Kierkegaard*, Chapter 10.

acknowledgment of resuscitating perceptions of the new at every turn, perceptions that make *us* new.

Things of the place—moving waters, the song of an unseen bird— give vocational address. They call us to witness their presence and confirm that our calling is to listen, alert in the place of their habitation and becoming. There are shipmates to remember, and mentors like Gabriel Marcel, and the ghost of Bugbee's father as he learns at sea of his death. Eckhart, Melville, and Thoreau shimmer in texts that become *his* texts. Their words and worlds beckon. The path is his alone and also the general pattern of moral perfectionism. Creation holds exemplary persons and things of the place ready, one step ahead, calling to a dawning light.

A perfectionist moral stance doesn't aim at universal justification for a way of life. It aims to illuminate exemplary ways of living, inviting wider audiences to test the worthiness they instantiate. They invite universal resonance and appeal, and their staying power is tested through dialogue, meditation, and continuing exploration. Perfectionism of this sort foregoes the justifications that Kant or Mill or Aristotle might seek, and invokes instead the mysteries of receiving oneself, of losing oneself to find oneself, of encountering a call to stand forth, of relating transparently to others and to the luminous things of creation— things intimately at hand yet always somewhat out of reach.

X. Simple Transcendence

The sight of geese against the infinite sky, of the leap of a trout toward a morning fly—each is an *Augenblick*, a "twinkling of an eye," when "all shall be changed." Each marks an instant of awakening. Bugbee's smaller scenes can fall within the ambit of the sublime, even though they lack its characteristic vastness or power. Such small-scale wonders, in my view, expand the reach of the sublime by altering expectations of scale. There are small majesties. Creation holds even a snowflake in fluid wonder. Such majesties contest unmitigated suffering, and even death. Small wonders brush by in a wisp of breeze—or a wisp of a laugh.

The movie version of Ken Kesey's *Sometimes a Great Notion* has an unforgettably terrifying—yet strangely redeeming—moment of death. A logger is trapped beneath a great fallen redwood as the tide rises inexorably. We see nothing but tragedy. As the tide rises, a brother who stands free of the trap desperately breaths air into the lungs of this now submerged man. The camera views his doom from below, as if a curious fish were attending. Fatefully, in death's grip, a smile creeps over his face, then a bubble-expelling giggle—the silliness of a mouth-to-mouth dance between he-men. The exhale swivels into an intake of sea, and we watch him fail grimacing, a twinkle still playing on the eyes.[33]

It's impossible to watch and not to watch—*There's the laugh,* the grin, rising absurdly from the depth of the man's rejoicing life. Like a wink at his executioner, it makes his death other than unmitigated annihilation. Even in this most violent and helpless of circumstance, death's dominion is lessened, if by no more than a wisp of breath.

For Kant, an awareness of how easily we could be crushed by massive overhanging rocks prompts spirit to affirm that it is more than what can be so easily destroyed. For Henry Bugbee, awakening in the presence of death affirms the inviolate depths of a creation that is more than what can so easily be destroyed. It is an affirmation articulated in the particulars of creation—not least, among particular persons, close at hand. Transcending spirit is found in the intensity of Chief Johnson spiting fire, and in the pure gentleness of a young man's face, reborn from fast waters. And it's found in the voice of a stand of larches in late autumn splendor.

> Some part of each day or night, for forty days, flurries of snow were flying. The aspens and larches took on a yellow so vivid, so pure, so trembling in the air, as to fairly cry out that they were as they were, limitlessly. And it was there in attending to this wilderness, with unremitting alertness and attentiveness, yes even as I slept, that I knew myself to have been instructed for life . . .[34]

The transcendence at issue is not movement from a natural to a non-natural world, from death to afterlife, as it were. It is the transcendence Thoreau celebrates in "Walking" or *Walden,* the transcendence of night toward day, as from an *unawakened* self to one present at an inward morning. Transcendence brings us not *out* of the world, but back *into* it—alert, alive.

XI. Prayer

I find it striking that as early as Henry Bugbee's Princeton thesis we sense a deep earnestness, uncommon in any academic writing, but

---

[33] The 1971 film stars Paul Newman, Lee Remick, and Henry Fonda.
[34] Bugbee, *Inward Morning,* 139–140.

doubly uncommon in undergraduate writing, in the writing of one so young. It's a quality of commitment, intimacy, and urgency familiar in the pages of *The Inward Morning*. It is a quality that prompts two of his friends to say, "You write here as a man might write only near the end of his life."[35] In the opening preface to his undergraduate thesis he alerts his professors that they will not find just another philosophy major's culminating senior effort. He confides that the search undertaken in its pages is of more than academic interest to him. He senses a vocational stake—a life at risk—in the pages he delivers. This is an intimate revelation, and perhaps we'd rather not have intimacy in philosophy, or in academic writing generally. Knowledge is impersonal, isn't it?

But from a different quarter we might ask how we could ever know his writing, know it as *his*, if we failed to receive, and he failed to offer, that touch of intimate revelation? Later, in the *Inward Morning*, Bugbee gives us the point unblushingly: "[T]he merely *looked at* cannot be manifest reality. No intimacy: no revelation. No revelation: no true *givenness* of reality." He cites the Biblical sense of intimate knowledge: "[Without] the intimacy of touch, nothing is truly known."[36] We find the person in words that are touching, that touch us. A writer seeking and sharing insight won't wear a staringly vacant voice that announces anonymous truths from the distance of all time and eternity. We need an intimate place, an intimate voice, an intimate *now*.

As we've seen, that deep earnestness speaks also from his bibliography. There he lists classical recordings from Bach to Schubert to Rachmaninoff that on his account informed his writing as much as any book. The great works of Beethoven unleash and explore infinite emotion, and are paradigms of the sublime. Bugbee knew them by heart, well enough to hear silently on sea watch in the Pacific. He must sense that words do not always compete in expressive power with the music he so cherished. Writing was not easy for him; he wrote little in his life.

His final chapter on the then still-living Spanish existentialist Unamuno marks his homage to the thoughtful life of a man of tragic vision yet not devoid of hope. Henry thinks in the light of this exemplary figure, forced out of Spain and into exile at the height of his creative powers. Perhaps unsurprisingly, he characterizes the tragedy

---

[35] Ibid., 11.
[36] Ibid., 130.

of this silenced thinker in roughly Kantian terms as the clash of dignity and defeat. And this tragic clash in turn can be drawn out as resonant with the sublime and, at least partially, death's undoing.

* * *

I find the closing gestures of this mature yet youthful effort especially moving. That his effort had been religious throughout had been evident in the title, invoking St Paul, and symmetrically in its final lines, the lines that confess his stance and that give context for the title: "*I speak not in enticing words of man's wisdom but in demonstration of the Spirit.*" His writing of worlds and of the things of his worlds has been an evocation and demonstration of spirit, and a discipline of religious self-emptying. Then a final word discretely recalls the tenor of humility that saturates the course of his writing. Just above Henry's longhand sign-off is a simple closing word of solid and unmistakable intent: "*Amen.*"

This has been a "salvation," a poetic evocation of spirit, and a prayer.

Chapter 5

BECOMING WHAT WE PRAY:
Passion's Gentler Resolutions

Beyond the question of knowledge are
poetry, madness, love—
but if these are not and cannot be knowledge
they may yet be best of all
—George Pattison

Toward the end of *The Inward Morning*, Henry Bugbee recalls a searing moment in mid-Pacific during World War II where he served as captain of a minesweeper. He recalls bringing down Kamikaze pilots close enough that he and the crew of his small vessel could see the incoming pilots face to face. As that memory floods his present consciousness, he asks eight years later "is it not true that *we were not enemies*," though by all accounts they would have been. But if not enemies, how he could "be answer for those men, *living* men, perishing in flames"? He could be answer, as we've heard, "only as I could articulate a true prayer."[1] A prayer might temper that terrible moment, yielding life lived as unqualified compassion. That would be to follow in a place where passion and prayer co-mingle.

I. PRAYER AND THE HEART

Prayer belongs to the life of the heart, to the life of the passions, sufferings, and joys, of mood and emotion. It's perhaps close to the divine

---

Thanks to a member of Friends Meeting, Cambridge, for the words "we become what we pray."

[1] Bugbee, *Inward Morning*, 225f.

78

madness of love and poetic inspiration as Plato described these in the *Phaedrus,* where passion is linked to poetic imagination.[2] And prayer can clear the way for action or be a reflection on deeds past. Some pray for victory and others pray for forgiveness. But even here there may be imagination, madness, and love. Insofar as prayer is akin to contemplation or meditation, it can align itself with intellect. In any event, even as it reaches out to poetry, deeds, or intellect, prayer seems firmly centered in the heart, in those passions that infuse the center of the person, the center of the soul.

In the main at least since Plato, philosophers have been suspicious of passion, taking its clearest exemplars to be the irrational disruptions of violent fear, anger, or grief. The gentler passions—wonder, sympathy, or attachment—unfortunately get buried when attention gets fixed on the more violent passions that surely *can* subvert a worthy life. The disparagement of passion goes hand in hand with the elevation of knowledge and pure intellect, which are seen as models of *dispassion.* In a measured account, legitimacy would remain for a love of wisdom or attachments to friends or a quickness to be outraged at injustice. But the central story has passion signal a loss of composure, a wild abandon, a mindless zealotry. Bringing prayer to view requires bringing passion back from disrepute. Prayer is a refinement of passion, a tempering and realignment of the soul.[3]

In his moment of crisis, Henry Bugbee finds himself called to articulate—live out—a true prayer. This places prayer partly in inwardness. Yet the refinement of a personal identity, prepared by prayer, gets played out publicly, as well. Articulating "true prayer," in his case, will amount to meeting others with compassion. So however private prayer may seem, it often gets realized in community and can take its cue from there. When prayer is linked to vocation, its sense is negotiated in communities whose identities are themselves consolidated through ceremonial prayers and public pledges. Apart from prayers, personal callings, too, can be responsive to public attestations. Derrida's "I have lived in prayer" and his invocation of St Augustine is a call to Jack Caputo, who responds, inwardly but also publicly, with *The Prayers and*

---

[2] See David N. McNeil, "Human Discourse, Eros, and Madness in Plato's Republic," *The Review of Metaphysics,* vol. LV, no. 2, December, 2001, 142.

[3] W.E. Hocking takes the soul to be "the self taken in terms of its profoundest passion" (*Lectures on Religion,* unpublished, 1941). Hocking was Husserl's first American student, best known for *The Meaning of God in Human Experience,* New Haven: Yale, 1912.

Tears of Jacques Derrida.[4] And this then sets us all rethinking prayer, sometimes in solitude, sometimes in open forums. Public attestations can lay out a space for prayer.

The world or space of prayer that Derrida or Caputo circumscribe is quite other than the world of Teresa of Avila, say, whose prayerful tears watered the garden of her Lord. Kierkegaard, in still another vein, confides that prayer, like possibility, is the breath of spirit—and thus prayer makes space for life's necessary passions.[5] Another point of orientation for placing a prayer that could clarify the passion of our calling might be Wittgenstein's remark that "faith is a passion, while wisdom is cool gray ash."[6] Wittgenstein struggled with the view that sets wisdom and faith at odds. His attraction to Kierkegaard, I suspect, was based on a need to find a way to combine faithful passion with reason's critical wit—a combination Kierkegaard seems to have achieved. The perceived tension between faith and wisdom is a form of the tension already noted between the loves and faiths that set out and support our course or our calling, on the one hand, and on the other, the more dispassionate (yet still passionate) pull of cool reason or the subtle beckoning of wisdom.

II. THE HAPPY INEVITABILITY OF PASSION

Lacking time and resource for anything like a survey, let me offer an impressionistic sketch of the fate of the passions, starting back with the deathbed scene where Socrates sends the mourners packing. In keeping with distain for passion's excess, he makes an offering in his final words to Asclepius, a god of healing. It's as if he's thankful that death will bring relief from passion's tumults.[7] Tears and grief are false, misplaced, perhaps always, but certainly in the event of death.[8] It's the better part of wisdom to nip unruly passion in the bud. Yet surely

---

[4] For Derrida's "I have lived in prayer" and "I have never stopped [praying] all my life," from his *Circumfession*, see John D. Caputo, *The Prayers and Tears of Jacques Derrida*, Bloomington: Indiana University Press, 1997, 292.

[5] Søren Kierkegaard, *Sickness Unto Death*, trans. Alastair Hannay, New York: Penguin, 70.

[6] Ludwig Wittgenstein, *Culture and Value*, Chicago: University of Chicago, 1984, 56 C.

[7] On the other hand, we have Plato's non-Stoic Socrates of *Phaedrus*.

[8] On false passion, see Rick Anthony Furtak, *Wisdom in Love: Kierkegaard and the Ancient Quest for Emotional Integrity*, Notre Dame: University of Notre Dame, 2005.

there's a place not just for tears at the demise of those we love, but also for warm delight in welcome of the living. Furthermore, a strictly Stoic view can't credit Socrates with the passions to which he already accords great honor. I think of the Socratic passions of wonder, of love of knowledge, of hatred of pretense and fraud, and the passion to preserve one's civic hearth. Despite Wittgenstein's pronouncement, wisdom has its warmer side.

Plato's view is more nuanced than commonly assumed. He scorns lowly passions but prizes passion's outrage at indignity, a gut reaction essential to an effective military temperament.[9] And love of learning and of beauty and the good are undeniably essential. In Christian traditions, although lustful passions and many vices of the passions are appropriately demonic, an intense love of God can hardly be disparaged. Ascetic practices rein in passions, but only, so it seems, to make room for *proper* passion. David Hume, a pillar of Enlightenment, declares reason to be a slave of passion. Without a motivating passion, he saw no way for reason to gain traction. Kierkegaard links faith to passionate inwardness, and Sartre sees freedom as a passion—albeit a "useless" one. Tillich speaks of the primitivity of "ultimate concern," which sounds quite like a passion. Being gripped by a "passion for the impossible" is a familiar theme in Derrida, a thought that echoes Kierkegaard's passionate interest in "the paradox." In quite another vein, Bertrand Russell confides that "Three passions, simple but overwhelmingly strong, have governed my life: the longing for love, the search for knowledge, and unbearable pity for the suffering of mankind."[10] From these glancing allusions it's clear that passion can at times receive a positive philosophical review.

Let's look more closely at the *welcome inescapability* of passion in human affairs. Socrates prizes rational critique, but passion fuels its movements. Darwin notes our capacity for laughing and crying, which express the passions of grief, delight, and melancholy. Setting philosophical worries aside, it's hard *not* to take us as creatures of consuming joy and anguish, anger and fear, hope and despair, wonder, ambition, and envy. We're surely capable of great love and great hate. There's something deeply human about Achilles and Ahab *despite* the fact that they model rage. And it's clear that not all passion is dangerous or unruly. "Passion" covers a wide and varied field. We're subject to

---

[9] *Thumos* or "spiritedness" is the essential attribute of the soldier class in *Republic*.

[10] Bertrand Russell, *Autobiography*, London: Routledge, 2000, 9.

grand passions and lowly ones (envy, malice, and hoarding) and to a slew of unimposing ones. The *O.E.D.* takes passion as "an eager, out-reaching interest toward things," which allows love of reading, gathering stamps, or interest in the news to count as passion. Whether banal or grand or lowly, passion can be aptly characterized as primitive. Without it, no capacity definitive of our nature could get in gear.

Without passions there would be no urge to speak or know or do. We'd have no language, knowledge, or action. There would be no urge to care or to commit, to till land or measure stars, to make cities, art, or bridges. Yet the standard Anglophone approach to understanding human beings takes language, knowledge, and practical agency as the essential "primitives" from which to build.[11] The view that passion is a primitive controverts this standard view. Passion is what *animates* our language use, our pursuit of knowledge, our interest in free action, not to mention our concern for art or ethics, God or justice. Without that animating energy, we'd have neither cultural structures nor interest in them, neither recognizably human lives nor accounts of them, neither language, nor knowledge, nor action.

We might picture passion metaphorically as an energy that's wide and unsettled like the sea.[12] Bertrand Russell pictures the passions governing his life as "great winds, [that] have blown me hither and thither, over a deep ocean of anguish . . ."[13] This is preferable to some standard mechanistic views that figure passion as a set of "drives"; and it also improves on the common assimilation of passion to "Eros" or desire. Awe and grief are modes of passion but neither has the immediate look of a desire. Kierkegaard's Climacus speaks of grief's passion not as a sea, but as a river. He describes an old man bent in sorrow uttering a choked sigh. "Feeling," he observes, "is like the river Niger in Africa; no one knows its origin, no one knows its mouth, only its course is known."[14] The same might be said of passion: we know

---

[11] See, e.g., Donald Davidson, *Subjective, Intersubjective, Objective,* Oxford: Oxford University Press, 2001; and Arthur Cody, "Words, You, and Me," *Inquiry,* September 2002.

[12] Melville meditates on the sea-like variability of passion in *Moby Dick.* The sea delivers up Ishmael who ends his tale with these words: "Now small fowls flew screaming over the yet yawning gulf, . . . and the great shroud of the sea rolled on as it did five thousand years ago."

[13] Russell, *Autobiography,* 9.

[14] Søren Kierkegaard, *Concluding Unscientific Postscript,* trans. Walter Lowrie and David Swenson, Princeton: Princeton University Press, 1941, 237. See Pattison, "*Poor Paris!*" 97.

neither its source nor its terminus, but only its course at a particular time and place, even as its flow congeals as grief, or perhaps as awe or compassion. The several phases of the variable sea of passion can be mapped more systematically. States of emotion (say, rage) can be helpfully distinguished from pervasive moods (e.g., melancholy), which in turn contrast with irruptions of feelings (excitement), or long-term interests, concerns, or desires.[15] The capacious and informal view that I offer here takes moods, emotions, feelings, and concerns as so many forms that passion can assume.

III. Passion and Prayer

Say we become what we pray as we live out "true prayer." That will be true because our course and calling, what we become, is a matter of the incomings and outgoings of phases of passion. The detail of these eager outreachings and retreats makes up the story of our identity or character. The prayer-like plea "*Why has Thou forsaken me!*" might well up from fear, anger, or despair—in any case, a cry wells up as passion. Person, cry, and prayer are linked in passion's primitivity. Fear fuels flight, but also flows toward the anger of attack or toward beseeching, prayer-like cries for help. Tears fuel grief or mourning and their adjunct prayers. Passion phased as grief can migrate toward an aching need for consolation, and for such understanding as might lift the burden of this need. Such modulated grief can culminate in petitionary prayer: "*Help my affliction!*"—which is a cry of passion that sustains grief and pleads for recognition of a need. As a vector in the field of passion, prayer can gather grief and mourning to venture out beyond themselves: prayer can move the afflicted self from despair toward passionate reinvestment in the world. A similar fluid transformation can be traced from primitive elation to delight and celebration, culminating in prayers of gratitude or praise. Prayer then becomes an extension of delight-in-world.

The drama of a king in Shakespeare's *Winter's Tale* displays passion's fluid moves "from jealousy to rage, from rage to remorse, from remorse

---

[15] For a detailed analytic topography, see Robert Roberts, *Emotions*, Cambridge: Cambridge University Press, 2003. See also "Existence, Emotion, and Virtue: Classical Themes in Kierkegaard," *Cambridge Companion to Kierkegaard*, ed. Hannay and Marino, Cambridge: Cambridge University Press, 1998.

to mourning, from mourning to wonder, from wonder to serenity."[16]
A Christian drama might depict passion's moves from rage to fear to
stark despair, and then, perhaps to humility, joy, or a still serenity—an
ongoing tempering of passion ministered by prayer. Prayer can move
those passions that place us beside ourselves and out of sorts (in grief
or anger, say), toward less rending or disruptive ones. It can challenge
the arrogance of anger, remind a giddy joy that perishing, too, exists,
rescue grief from despair, and open doors on hope. We might imagine
Christian prayer as a fluid "energy-exchange" within a field of love,
with love's eager reaching out toward another love being met by a
returning loving reach. If love, through such mutual reinforcement,
has a capacity for increase within the ecology of passion, this might
explain its power to move more violent passions (anger, fear, or grief)
toward gentler, less self-assertive ones (compassion, wonder, or mercy).
Achilles directs his prayer toward a god who will intensify his wrath or
gird up his courage. A Christian prayer would call on love to palliate a
violent passion. Love flows reciprocally from above to below, and from
below, above. It's worth remembering that passions, as I take them, are
not agitations within a self-enclosed Cartesian consciousness. They are
channels or conduits of connection, of attachment, that carry animating two-way impulses and in fact *are* those impulses, both incoming
and outgoing.

Prayer is passion that is quiet but inwardly intense—a lively immobility. Physical immobility calms violent expressions making space for a
gentler passions' alert mobility. Prayer can start only as the vehemence
of an agitating passion subsides permitting change to quieter keys.
A devotee of gentle, petitionary prayer allows its ameliorating presence to work among the passions. In the event of grief or fear, it recognizes urgent need for rescue. It embodies humility in the recognition
that human artifice is unequal to the task of answering that need.
And it willingly, patiently awaits whatever deliverance may be offered
from a more than human source.

Reason might suppress wrath, taking on the role of a tribunal with
authoritative jurisdiction. But prayer would counter wrath differently,
through a caring, pleading empathy—passion to passion, mercy to
anger. From this angle, the question is not "Shall Reason prevail?" but
"Which Passion shall prevail?" Anger interrupted by prayer confirms
the ministrations of a quieter, tender passion that, however hidden or

---

[16] See Philip Fisher, *The Vehement Passions*, Princeton: Princeton University Press,
2002, 36.

unnoticed, is already presently engaged. Prayer takes up with fear or anger as like to like. It does not suppress a passion from the presumed superior vantage of reason, but instead cajoles and pleads and waits, one passion to another. Prayer awaits a gentler ecology of passion where love presides. Not only petitionary prayers, but prayers of praise or gratitude can work as passions that ameliorate passion. Say we're struck in astonishment at the grandeur of a scene, unsure if we're large or small before it, as in the onset of a wondrous sublime, itself a kind passion. Prayers of gratitude might ease the tension between this passion and its competitors—say, an inflated sense of self, or an abased humiliation. In clarifying gratitude, it might release one to a less anxious or intoxicated access to the world.

IV. CAN PASSION BE SELF-CORRECTING?

The *telos* of gentle, purifying prayer is openness to otherness, the otherness of all that elicits wonder or love, gratitude, or generosity. In the ecology of passion this *telos* encourages an equilibrium slanted toward the tender Christian virtues. (Of course, these virtues are not Christianity's alone.) When it's activated in prayer, this pull among passions toward the openness and receptivity of love is like the pull among opinions toward consistency and correctness. There's no guarantee we'll be correct in belief, or that we'll let a pull toward correctness have its way. Likewise, there's no guarantee that our dispositions will be correctly aligned, or that we'll let the pull toward love have its way. But a kind of regulative ideal may nevertheless be at work. Why not propose that cognitions and passions each incline toward propriety or truth? Of course truth is not single here, for if truth is a measure of worth, the worth of cognitions is assessed on a different scale than the worth of passions. We have true friends, true grief, and true prayer, as well as true opinion. In matters of truth, of whatever sort, we seek the rather abstract *desiderata* of coherence, appropriateness of fit, and proper causal and cultural antecedents. A person's grief should cohere with what we know of a wider narrative of her history; it should have fittingness to the situation of its expression; and it should not be induced by drugs or threats or brainwashing. Otherwise, we'd face false grief. The daunting problem is to fill in what concretely would satisfy these *desiderata* in contested instances where it is urgent to know of friends if they are true, or of grief or opinion, if it is true or false.

Our attachments—cognitive, relational, and passional—are constitutive of identity. To be cognitively truthful is to comport oneself
properly in the region of events, reasons, and causes. To be relationally
truthful is to comport oneself properly in the region of interpersonal
exchange. To be passionally truthful is to comport oneself properly in
the region of significance. These regions surely interpenetrate.

Hume held that sentiments can be self-correcting, a more worthy
sympathy reversing a less worthy indifference or aversion.[17] Just as
better cognitions keep worse ones in check, so better passions might
ride herd on unruly ones. Achilles prays to Apollo, mobilizing courage
to correct melancholy, complacency, or an anxious dispersal of interest. He pleads for the better passion to prevail. Similarly, a prayer
that one be enabled to forgive corrects a passion for vengeance, and
seeking a life of true prayer corrects a passion for violent confrontation. One shuns false passion.

We might picture the deep primitivity of passion fanning out as
mood, feeling, concern, or emotion, and developing a sort of open-
ended ecology of passion characteristic of identity or calling. Within
this loose ecology, the pressures of more "mature" or "reality-sensitive"
or "worthy" passions, through the alembic of their extension into
prayer, work to constrain those that are darker or lowly. They aim to
purify or refine the tainted heart in the way critique aims to purify or
refine a rough and tangled mind.

V. To Whom is Prayer Addressed?

Even if we take prayer to be a moderating phase of faithful passion,
to its devout practitioners it is more than gentle contemplation. The
faithful address their prayers to the divine, and then await an answer.
So far we've said nothing about the destination of a prayer. Perhaps
Henry Bugbee's plea for strength to live out true prayer puts the
stress where it belongs, on the living out rather than on whomever (or
whatever) might receive the plea. Nevertheless, there clearly is a plea
here, which raises the issue: *to whom is it addressed?* The uncertainty
of our response—the uncertainty of what we might name by "God"
or "the divine"—marks a feature of the playing field. It reminds us

---

[17] See Annette Baier, *A Progress of Sentiments: A Study of Hume's Treatise*, Cambridge,
MA: Harvard University Press, 1991.

that prayers are by their nature conducted in a surround of inexpugnable uncertainty. In detached, dispassionate objectivity, we know
next to nothing about how mortals and Gods communicate, if they do.
Nevertheless, those who pray have hunches and convictions that go
with a cultivated invested interest.

There's nothing unusual or irregular about this tension between
objective uncertainty and a living, engaged conviction, born of care
and cultivated sensibility. We "know" where the stress belongs in this
line of poetry, in this line of music, in this response to a child's effort.
Such instilled sensitivity is won through practice in the terrain. There
might be little of an objective nature that we could cash in in support
of our hunches here. By analogy, we might address our prayers to an
unknown and indeterminate recipient, and sense (or "know") in our
bones that we're on track with this. We've "been there," as we might
think, and know the feel of the place. Yet we'd quickly own up, if we
were asked for a less engaged, more detached appraisal of the matter,
to being beset by a troubling objective uncertainty.

Take a painter who sees her work as clarifying a passion and whose
activity is, in that respect, like prayer. As she paints, she may have an
audience or addressee in mind—but then again, she may not. If she
does, she nevertheless has no obligation to divulge the identity of her
addressee. One might say that the form of her activity presupposes an
intended audience. But she still might not know or reveal her "real-
life" audience, the person or persons to whom she presumably
addresses her work. She might feel her work was addressed toward
some vague and unnamed intended recipient whose reality is yet to
be established. "I paint for the eyes of another age," she says, when
asked. She insists that her primary attention as an artist, and our primary focus, as art lovers, should be on the painting itself, on what
it does or will do, on what it says or will say, on how it says it, on what
it shows and how. To inquire of the addressee is not only to ask (in this
case) a question without a helpful answer; it is also to distract from the
painting itself.

Or consider a love sonnet—an intimate expression of the heart that
is only haltingly made public. We might have no clue as to the real-life
identity" of the intended recipient. A Shakespeare sonnet might be
addressed to a man or woman, old or young, real or fancied. We
just don't know. But we're none the worse for this. Emily Dickinson
writes revealing love letters to someone who remains utterly unknown.
And perhaps our not knowing keeps our attention where it belongs:
on love and the work of love, not on relatively extraneous historical

concerns. The passion of the poetry shines through no less for all our ignorance. The passion of our prayers shines through no less for our ignorance.

Prayers of the form "*Grant us peace!*" or "*Forgive my impatience!*" imply an intended addressee, but to understand their thrust we needn't fill in the addressee's whereabouts, powers, name, or status. The epistemological challenge is defused as we grant an objective uncertainty while sustaining the certitude that accompanies trust in a venture, like composing a sonnet or a portrait intended for an indefinite or unidentified other, a trust that animates a sense of "knowing one's way about." A minimalist communicative frame specifies only an open place for an intended recipient, present or absent, attentive or distracted, namable or beyond names, all-powerful or less than all-powerful. Different prayers, different devotees, will articulate a trust in an intended recipient in ways implying different theologies. But these more theoretical elaborations rest on this narrower, minimalist assurance, that to ground the communicative thrust of prayer, it's enough to have the open-ended, incomplete idea of an intended recipient. This does nothing to unsettle but instead sustains the guiding insight that the fundamental context in which prayer comes alive is caught in a passion-based account.

Yet we can still ask why the intended recipient of prayer should be more-than-human. A brief answer would suggest that prayer sets out to temper over-weaning passion, and thus it makes sense that prayer calls on non-promethean powers to moderate or curb the urge toward total mastery. Calling on divinity is the other half of enacting humility.

Of course, critics can take petitionary prayer as craven supplication, and prayers of praise or gratitude, as flatteries, bribes, or payoffs. Prayer then becomes a gambit in a self-interested bargaining transaction. Yet prayer can also be read as non-selfish celebration of the open sky, deep gratitude for a musical talent bequeathed, and when a plea for possibility, even infinite possibility in deep distress, or for consolation in times of grief, then surely it is not selfish in the sense of putting one's own interest above that of others. In fact, in its appeal to a more-than-human source, when that appeal is not strategic or demanding but properly humble, prayer undoes selfishness, arrogance, and pride: it acknowledges a power sufficient to disarm a grasping, aggrandizing self, and presents itself disarmed.

Calling on "human-powers-only" in ultimate torment or distress *reaffirms* claims to human self-sufficiency, thus disowning finitude, disavowing deep limits to our effectuality. A more-than-human status for intended recipients of prayer keeps intact a humbling, tempering effect. This means that some thin content clings to prayer's intended recipients. But despite this thin content, skeptical worries about purported inhabitants of a transcendental realm will have little purchase if we concede sufficient ignorance to put *wavering* out of place. We pray or don't, and pray not in knowledge but in ignorance. Our deepest passions exceed objective warrant, for they provide the context within which warrants play their part. A passion for truth and the conviction that its pursuit is worthwhile necessarily predates the business of rounding up warrants for holding on to more local convictions. Conversely, to have full knowledge and warrant at our disposal would reduce the play of conviction and passion. Prayer abides this tension between passionate conviction and objective uncertainty.[18]

VI. Prayer in the Cadence of Life

We now take up a philosopher's evocation of prayer in the course of his reflections on an eventful life. Henry Bugbee wrote his philosophical journal at the end of his stay as a Harvard professor in the mid-1950s. Here is life with a full measure of delight and deep calling, of wonder and even terror. His reflections in *The Inward Morning* do not center on prayer, but this makes the few spots when it does rise to the surface all the more striking.[19] Such moments of prayer arrive unheralded, without fanfare. Prayer is linked to vocation, and Bugbee offers several angles on his calling, including *a meditation of the place*.[20] Perhaps the place that calls for meditation is the place of moving waters, or of teaching; it might be the place of still mountains, or of violent battles. We could say his passions are enacted as a mobile meditative prayer. And the prayers, the philosophical meditations, are worked out as William James put it, *ambulando*.[21] Their sense is worked out in walking them out, living them out, in what Bugbee calls a *walking* meditation of the place.

---

[18] This is, of course, an adaptation of Kierkegaard's (or Climacus') *Postscript* definition of faith as "an objective uncertainty held . . . with the most passionate inwardness," 203.

[19] See Bugbee, *Inward Morning*, 89, 229, and 225, and also 70, 143, and 214.

[20] Ibid., 139, and chapter three in this volume.

[21] See James Conant, "The James/Royce Dispute," *The Cambridge Companion to William James*, ed. Ruth Anna Putnam, Cambridge: Cambridge University Press, 1997, 205–206.

Midway through *The Inward Morning* Bugbee places us knee-deep in a rushing stream following a day of disciplined casting on the waters.[22] In that quiet moment beneath vaulting redwoods in the whisper of the river's flow, he offers prayerful thanks—*just for being there.* This thankful offering is continuous with the passionate attention, the reaching out, of the fisher's task. Thanksgiving is a phase of passion. The passions of work and gratitude become one as his identity gathers in a prayerful offering.

> It is a glorious thing to know the pool is alive with these glancing, diving, finning fish. But at such moments it is well to make an offering in one's heart to the still hour in the redwoods ascending into the sky . . . On such mornings, too, one may even catch nothing at all.[23]

Later still we join him as he meets a beckoning hour of teaching. A familiar bell declares the time across the campus green. It bespeaks, he says, *"the namelessness of that which we must serve."*[24] And he finds himself again in a prayerful mood, placed patiently, humbly, before demands he can hardly name. When teaching lifts above banal routine, we must all be struck by "the namelessness of that which we must serve." Mission statements hardly say it. "The good and true" are just other names for nameless mystery. And prayerfulness seems right as we absorb the yawning gaps between the gravity of what *must* be said, and our stumbling efforts. That which we must serve addresses us, even as we are at a loss to specify by whom or what we are addressed. And we pray for wit and strength to meet these demands, even as we are at a loss to specify the recipient of this prayer. Awaiting class, he waits on openness and energy to meet his calling gracefully, responsibly. He waits not in knowledge but in ignorance, and yet in trust upon a sea of faith that he may be equal to the hour. At that moment prayer might refine and clarify the passion of one's calling, the passion of one's being.

Prayer is also invoked dramatically on the occasion we have visited, an occasion more ominous than casting for trout, or casting for words to meet the hour. We remember that moment at sea in the Pacific when kamikazes descended on the ship in his command. Gunners open fire, ship and plane slide unwaveringly toward mutual doom.

---

[22] Bugbee, *Inward Morning*, 86.

[23] Ibid. The idea of fishing and catching *nothing* invokes the uncertain castings of prayer, as well as the "no-thingness" of the Divine.

[24] Ibid., 229.

On the bridge he waits, then returns fire, then finds the pilot so close they're face to face. *What is it to be known* by another in such circumstance? In a passage we know well, it is sometimes unspeakable.

> I think of the suicide planes that I *witnessed*. They still call out to me, lives perishing in flames. What, what indeed, can I make of them? Oh, I must be answer for these men. Men I never knew. Living men. How can I find answer except as I can articulate a true prayer? Is it not true that we were not enemies? And who will believe this, how can it be believed?[25]

There were no prayers at the time, only desperate action. Five years after, Bugbee can relive that crisis, working through the desperate horror. He's called to compassion, regard, even reverence, for all things of creation, under siege of war or no. He's called to honor his communal ties to others, expressed through his wartime service. Responding to this call necessarily rips the fragile remnants of would-be encompassing compassion. The heat of these colliding passions is by no means abstract. His guns bring down a man in flames—not a faceless "enemy," but a pilot he has known face to face.

In this impossible strait, he asks how his life can be answer for those lives, perishing in flames. He can address the "unfinished business" delivered on that fateful day, be answer for those lives, only as his life articulates true prayer. To articulate true prayer he first asks *"Is it not true that we were not enemies?"* True prayer does not continue violence by continuing to name enemies. Yet this refusal of violence is conjoined with another stark realization: *"And who will believe this, how can it be believed?"* The clash of these dark passions—that there are enemies, that there are no enemies—is answered, not intellectually, not dogmatically, not blindly, but by taking simple steps, steps that will enact the passional truth, "we were not enemies."

That this was not a confrontation of enemies bent on mutual destruction seems unbelievable. From the standpoint of ordinary possibilities, how could Bugbee hold the view, *"we were not enemies."* Yet in the grip of compassion and his deepest humanity, the writer holds to that impossibility, *"we were not enemies."* Prayer tips the passional balance toward compassion, and works out its resolution by taking steps. One is answer for those men, not as one speaks or thinks on this or that occasion, but as one *makes the truth of compassion true*— by walking through remaining life in compassion that's unstinting.

---

[25] Ibid., 225f.

As one *makes* something true, in the gentle composure of steps, one is answer for those men. "True prayer" tempers passional conflict through being true to gentler passions; its mercy and compassion consolidate identity in gentleness.

There are prayers of gratitude for world, and prayers that one may be equal to the day. Like these, prayers in dark times require maximal openness to otherness. The wholly other, in this instance, is the terrifying collision between Bugbee as captain of a minesweeper engaged in deadly combat and Bugbee as fellow creature embracing the preciousness of life. Prayer opens the soul to intractable passional collision, gathering those passions it must register truthfully. It opens the soul to the "impossible possibility" that a faithful passion can emerge from this cruel crucible. And it unfolds as a life in answer to those perishing in flames. It unfolds as steps taken to make the unbelievable now believable. This walk makes it true that writer and pilot known face to face are at last not enemies.

As gentle passions ease from violently conflicting ones, prayer becomes faithful encounter with the other, under whatever guise.

Chapter 6

TWO TESTIMONIES IN AMERICAN PHILOSOPHY:

Stanley Cavell, Henry Bugbee

in a sense, to write your own words,
to write your own inner voice, is philosophy.
But the discipline most opposed to writing,
and to life, is analytic philosophy.
—*Stanley Cavell*

our whole lives may have the character of finding that anthem
which would be native to our own tongue,
and which alone can be the true answer for each of us
to the questioning, the calling, the demand for ultimate reckoning
which devolves upon us.
—*Henry Bugbee*

For classic American philosophers, starting with Emerson and Thoreau, personal voice and evocation of a place are resoundingly essential. *Walden*'s philosophical instruction gets delivered through attention to the particularities of place and mood that *Thoreau* attends to—in just *this* voice, in just *this* phrase. At issue is self-articulation hinged on discovery of the proper placement or setting of the self he is and would be. Thoreau will address us intimately. We are informed of mood, insight, and place as their contours arrive in his articulations.

Yet on some construals of philosophy, voice and the particulars of its placement are impediments. The personal, on this view, is precisely what makes these early American writers not philosophers but preachers, poets, or sages. In its maturity, we learn, philosophy becomes professional and lean. It frames its questions with technical precision, and argues its case on the model of a scientific report or lawyer's brief.

Call this the positivist's construal. If it reigns, we lose something essential in Emerson and Thoreau, in Royce and James, not to mention, on the European front, in Sartre or Wittgenstein. If not for all philosophers, then certainly for these, the timbre, color, or rhythms of their philosophic voice is not just packaging. The intimation of the writer's fit-to-world is part and parcel of the philosophy conveyed.

Cavell writes of philosophy as the search for one's voice. Henry Bugbee, whose Harvard teaching years spanned Cavell's student years there, writes that he seeks in his philosophy the anthem that would be native to his tongue. Both Cavell and Bugbee find themselves in ambiguous relationship to academic philosophy precisely on this issue of the bearing of personal voice. Does it have a place in bringing philosophy into the open? Cavell's *A Pitch of Philosophy: Autobiographical Exercises* and Bugbee's *The Inward Morning: A Philosophical Exploration in Journal Form* bear witness to the struggle to find one's voice, and so to find one's stance, one's self, in philosophy as in life.

I

The American Philosopher, a collection of interviews with Quine, Davidson, Nozick, and others, repeatedly raises the question of what brings a person to take up philosophy.[1] The interviewer asks each respondent in turn to reflect on how his or her thought fits with the broader American tradition, with social and political events they might have been caught up in, and with personal attachments or crises. These questions seem somewhat awkward initially. A Paris intellectual might thrive with such questions, but we expect only a handful of American Philosophical Association celebrities to flourish in this setting. Happily we find arresting stories here—Danto, on his early wish to be a painter, Cavell, on how a class on Thoreau got started almost accidentally, Putnam, on left-wing causes and Jewish mysticism. Still, we might be bothered. Are these revelations, however interesting, at last only marginalia, anecdotes smoothing the way to something else, something closer to the true center of philosophy? In the larger frame of things, what are we to make of Cavell's "Autobiographical Exercises" or Bugbee's "Philosophical Exploration in Journal Form"?

---

[1] Giovanna Borradori, *The American Philosopher*, Chicago: University of Chicago Press, 1994, 126f.

Cavell wants us to hear what was compelling in his early attraction to language and music, something inescapably there that led him to his vocation. And he explores this notion of vocation, of calling, itself. The topics are best explored, he thinks, by taking up one's own case, by giving "autobiographical testimony." Yet this is also a philosophical exploration. We're reminded of Thoreau reflecting on what led him to take up residence at Walden. And reading Cavell, I'm brought to Henry Bugbee's account of what called *him* to take up a life of reflection and philosophy. At the risk of repetition, here, once again, is that lyrical account:

> During my years of graduate study before the war I studied philosophy in the classroom and at a desk, but my philosophy took shape mainly on foot. It was truly peripatetic, engendered not merely while walking, but through walking that was essentially a meditation of the place . . . I weighed everything by the measure of the silent presence of things, clarified by the cry of hawks, solidified in the presence of rocks, spelled syllable by syllable by waters of manifold voice, and consolidated in the act of taking steps.[2]

We pause, reflecting perhaps on the idea of a philosophy that "took place mainly on foot." And we might wonder how the "cry of hawks" or the "presence of rocks" could prompt thoughts on the way to their maturity as philosophy. Perhaps we have in these poetic recollections of youth a testimony to the struggles of "coming of age." But if we are to avoid self-indulgence and the loss of professional "objectivity," aren't we obliged to separate out a worthy philosophy and its defense from the struggles of the writer to come to an apt expression of that philosophy, reported confessionally, autobiographically? We might consider other philosophical exemplars. How prudent, or possible, would it be to divide confessional testimony from philosophy in Wittgenstein or Augustine? Or in Socrates' encounter with Diotima?

Richard Eldrige has pursued Cavell's early suggestion that Wittgenstein's *Philosophical Investigations* are confessionally first-personal, through and through.[3] As Eldridge has it, Wittgenstein opens a curtain on an intimate philosophical stage where several conflicting voices and characters, each with a distinguishable cast, try out their claim to our consideration. And this inward personal drama is

[2] Bugbee, *Inward Morning*, 139.
[3] See Cavell's "The Availability of the Philosophy of the Later Wittgenstein," Chapter two; *Must We Mean What We Say?* New York: Charles Scribner, 1969.

inextricably tied to our understanding of the growth, the restless on-goingness of Wittgenstein's explorations.[4] Moving further back in the canon, what would remain of Augustine's discussion of time or creation if we sifted out the "bare bones arguments" from his intimate report of how these perplexities came to possess him, call on him for response. These utterly "private" demands on his soul beg for completion in writing for an audience. And his philosophy is in large part the tracing out of this most personal struggle for insight. Then there are Socrates' utterly intimate encounters with Diotima, Alcibiades, Phaedrus, and others.[5]

If these exemplars persuade—and there are countless others one might appeal to—then it's a mistake to think that philosophy must maintain an impassable divide between professionalized discourse and intimate appraisal, between the personal persona and the public posture. Think, for example, of Martha Nussbaum's work on the voice of the novelist as essential to doing some kinds of ethics, and the easy identifiability of *her* passionate and discriminating voice underlying the power of her moral reflections.[6] The same could be said of any number of other contemporary writers, from Richard Rorty to Charles Taylor, from Ed Casey or Bruce Wilshire to Alphonso Lingis or Hélène Cixous. In each case, the philosophy written out is inextricably tied to a sensibility, to a personal voice that testifies, often autobiographically, and typically, quite intimately.

Bugbee invites us on his wilderness walks. Perhaps this is essential to his professional calling, and perhaps thus accompanying him is our way of access to the essential themes of his philosophy, to the path of his discovery of his voice, and of the anthem "native to his tongue." Cavell's book on Thoreau sets Thoreau finding *his* writing voice in learning to inhabit the geographical site, Walden. And in *A Pitch of Philosophy*, Cavell invites us to learn something of his journey through jazz and midnight journals and walks in the Berkeley hills. This journey is not a side show, a barker's "pitch" for philosophy. It's revelatory of the pitch, the musical line, or even the cant of the roof, that his thinking would assume in its maturity. I would think also,

---

[4] See Richard Eldridge, *Leading a Human Life: Wittgenstein, Intentionality, and Romanticism*, Chicago: University of Chicago Press, 1997.

[5] See *On Søren Kierkegaard*, Chapters 1–4.

[6] See Martha Nussbaum, *Love's Knowledge, Essays on Philosophy and Literature*, Oxford: Oxford University Press, 1990.

though Cavell leaves this unsaid, that the pitch of philosophy is the darkness, the "pitch black" of its moments of doubt and anguish.[7]

II

The title of Henry Bugbee's *The Inward Morning* comes from Thoreau, himself a prodigious walker who enacted, we might say, his own "meditation of the place."[8] He walked the environs of Walden Pond, but also along the Merrimack, the Charles, and the Concord Rivers, along the shores of Cape Cod, and nearly to the summit of Mt. Ktaadn in the Maine woods. Bugbee follows him in testifying to the steady, wondrous on-goingness of thought and experience as he ventures in the Canadian Rockies, along California rivers, and through long sea watches in the Pacific during World War II. The journal was written while he held a George Santayana Fellowship on leave in 1952 and 1953 from the department of Quine, C. I. Lewis, Morton White, and Henry David Aiken.

Just returned from harrowing wartime service, and on the verge of what promised to be a distinguished career, he felt compelled to give an account of himself that would mark the place of his philosophical explorations within the wider venture of his life. The journal did little to secure him favor as a serious candidate for tenure in the Harvard department. But he found it impossible to produce a standard issue philosophical commentary or critique of debates in the professional journals. Instead, he took stock of the several paths drawing him to his present place, as Cavell also would several decades later in *A Pitch of Philosophy*. This gave his work its meditative, autobiographical cast.

What could it mean, for a philosopher to reflect, Thoreau-like, on the meaning of hawks or streams or stones?

> What this all meant, I could not say, kept trying to say, kept trying to harmonize with the suggestions arising from the things I read. But I do remember that this walking in the presence of things came to a definitive stage. It was in the fall of '41, October and November, while late autumn prevailed throughout the

---

[7] I owe the thought of "pitch dark" in this context to my late colleague Mario Savio.

[8] See Dan Conway, "Walking with Bugbee and Thoreau," *Wilderness and the Heart*, Chapter 1.

northern Canadian Rockies, restoring everything in that vast region to a native wildness . . . And it was there in attending to this wildness . . . that I knew myself to have been instructed for life, though I was at a loss to say what instruction I had received.[9]

This passage startles in its candor, in its independence of what at the time (and still today) are the conventions of academic philosophy. The idea of Emerson or Thoreau as philosophers was not yet a glimmer in the academic eye. There were rumors that Rudolph Carnap, positivist *extraodinaire*, would come East to Cambridge to replace a retiring C. I. Lewis. On the prevalent "scientific" or "positivist" view, "instructions for life" had no place at philosophy's table, especially when such instructions were confessed to defy simple statement. If anything like such "advice" or "instruction" for life were discovered smuggled in, it was to be expelled from philosophy's domains forthwith. Any sentences that resisted explicit translation into verifiable protocols would be deemed meaningless, nonsense, failing to pass the threshold for serious philosophical consideration. To confess to have been "instructed for life, though I was at a loss to say what instructions I had received" was to place oneself far beyond the pale.

Bugbee reports that these hints of instruction were intimated through "flurries of snow," the cry of aspens and larches, "even as I slept." However alien to Harvard philosophy of the 1950s, these thoughts would resonate with the Harvard philosopher William Ernest Hocking, writing but a few decades earlier. As a student of James and Husserl, Hocking allowed the sensuous surround, flurries of snow in this case, to carry intimations of meaning, perhaps the lightness of ephemerality. He avers that Nature encases us sensorially, "even as we sleep"—say, in the damp air we breathe or the cushioning of leaves beneath our hips.[10] But a Hocking, James, or Husserl were only shadows in mid-century American philosophy, and the influence of a Cavell or Nussbaum or Rorty lay a decade or more ahead.[11] *The Inward Morning* fell by the way, largely unnoticed.

---

[9] Bugbee, *Inward Morning*, 139 f.

[10] See William Ernest Hocking, *The Self: Its Body and Freedom*, New Haven: Yale University Press, 1928, 120–121; and Bruce Wilshire on Hocking and Bugbee in *The Primal Roots of American Philosophy: Pragmatism, Phenomenology, and Native American Thought*, College Station: Penn State University Press, 2000.

[11] Wilshire weaves personal testimony and phenomenological description in the tradition of James, Emerson, Thoreau, and Black Elk, in *The Primal Roots of American Philosophy*, and *Wild Hunger: The Primal Roots of Modern Addiction*, Lanham, MD: Rowman and Littlefield, 1998 (see chapter eight in this volume).

Bugbee, no less that Socrates or Kierkegaard, Thoreau or Nietzsche, communicates how a philosophical vocation can crystallize by revealing how philosophy becomes a vocation for *him*, in the specific, non-exchangeable detail of *his* life, even if that calling or solicitation is hauntingly elusive and delivered through the "cry of hawks" or the "solidity of rocks" rather than through more familiar reports of how one glimpses what one must become.

III

If Henry Bugbee attended to wilderness amidst snow and streams, Cavell evokes a parallel moment of summons or promise delivered not in wilderness but in an undergraduate music composition class. Cavell remembers the instruction of Ernst Bloch as defining the possibility of vocation:

> All in all he bespoke a world of aspiration so vivid, a life of dedication so extensive and so constant—as if a wish were being granted me every moment—that I would at the end of a class sometimes find myself having trouble breathing, and I formed the habit of walking immediately after each of its sessions into the adjacent hills for an hour or so of solitude . . . It will take some years to discover another, but I knew from that time inescapably—not always hopefully—of the promise of some such existence.[12]

Vocation appears here as a haunting promise, at the moment more or less inarticulate, but nonetheless laden with conviction—the inescapable conviction that a calling was possible. Note that both Bugbee and Cavell find their deepest, most exhilarating thought, "consolidated in the act of taking steps."

These thoughts strike the thinker in solitude, and retain an aura of the uncanny, a mix of clarity and opacity to articulation. But they do not remain *only* a private talisman. The writer's poetic evocations afford public access, and with luck, another's thinking may be started responsively on its way. Perhaps these words consolidate our own belief in the possibility of true calling, something precious and available not just to the specially chosen, but to each reader, one by one. The hope and hint of such promise lies there in memory, if only we awaken to it, till it, bring it to light. The rhythms and timbre and anthem of

---

[12] *A Pitch of Philosophy: Autobiographical Exercises,* Cambridge, MA: Harvard University Press, 1994, 49.

another's eloquent voice reach a responsive ear. The listener, the reader, is thrown into a wilderness of half-remembered moments that may come to bear the marks of instruction addressed to oneself alone.

If these passages from Bugbee or Cavell find resonance, we have a happy reciprocity of mutual recognition. A writer undertakes to acknowledge the hidden springs of voice, of the place that feeds his work—her work—and however haltingly then proceeds to write them out for others. The issue is a proffered intimacy.[13] And if we take the words as such, as personal address, we can respond accordingly, intimately, in testimony of our own, just then brought out alive and true. This is the moment of mutual recognition: I acknowledge the voice; the voice acknowledges me. I walk with invitation of approaching paths, the dance of swaying boughs, the passing of light, the dusk in its singing.

IV

In Cavell's view, the responsive self lies deeper than our roles. The self that he pursues is encountered along the path of memory, through "a way of remembering who or what you are before you are known to the world." This phrase, "before you are known to the world," has an Emersonian ring. There are the familiar pressures to be as we are known to the world, to see and be seen in the throng, to be as the throng would see us. And these pressures, as Cavell has it, lead us away from discovery of the responsive self that we are, the root of our being.

We might contemplate an even more radical archaeological path of memory. We might seek, as Meister Eckhart has it, "becoming as we were before we were born."[14] To find that moment before birth would be to recover the self about to be born, about to be called into vocation. It is the moment when we find "that anthem which would be native to our tongue." And as Bugbee has it, persons present to things at their dawn, at the moment of their creation from darkness, see that

---

[13] As we've seen in chapter four, "No intimacy: no revelation. No revelation: no true *givenness* of reality. [T]he merely *looked at* cannot be manifest reality. [Without] the intimacy of touch, nothing is truly known." Bugbee, *Inward Morning*, 130.

[14] Ibid., 172.

"finite things themselves" are "born out anew."[15] Whether we hear Cavell's phrase as an improvisation of Emerson or of Eckhart, it clearly bears on our lives, and as philosophers, on our trust in what we might find as our unique and irreplaceable voice. Academic philosophy's constraints here are emblematic, for it can dictate an impersonal, technical style, stripped of voice—the personal voice subordinate to and perhaps buried by the dictates of impersonal reason, or by the obligation to review arguments and words other than our own, without the least eye to making them our own.

Bugbee confesses that he must reach to "who or what he is" before the world of technical philosophy impinges. As he tells us "It was music which first awakened me to the need for reflection; but for the music . . . I doubt if I would have found it relevant to reflect on our condition in a way that drew me to the works of philosophers speaking of that condition."[16] Cavell also remembers a musical moment of instruction that occurred before he was "known to the world." In miniature, it reveals the advent of vocation, the sense that calling and response are one. He recalls his mother, a pianist known for her ability effortlessly to sight-read absolutely anything, for her

> ability to bring to life whatever notes were put before her. It was precisely not to my mind a knack of interpretation, but something like the contrary, a capacity to put aside any interference, as of her own will, and to let the body be moved, unmechanically, by the mind of those racing notes . . . say that she was the music then and there; there was nothing beyond her to read into.[17]

No gap separates her playing and what she played. The self is "as it was before it was known to the world." This woman, in her playing, was receptive to the music, was present to herself in the notes, the pace, the run of her playing. She was present, as Cavell will put it elsewhere, through a "possessing that is not—is the reverse of—possessive . . . it is the exercise not of power but of reception."[18] That must be what it's like to be on track. The minds of racing notes bypass intervening will or detached knowledge to possess fingers that speak "music then and there." This account has its pair in Bugbee's peripatetic immersion in

---

[15] Ibid., 197.

[16] Ibid., 139.

[17] *Pitch*, 18.

[18] "Thinking of Emerson," *The Senses of Walden, an Expanded Edition*, San Francisco: North Point Press, 135.

wilderness, where sense is spelled "syllable by syllable by waters of manifold voice" delivered then and there, the encounter, as Bugbee has it, with "somewhat absolute" in experience.[19]

Perhaps we're at ease with the idea of a perfect fit-to-world found musically as notes rush for expression, as notes "speak" to, and possess our receptive fingers. The parallel in Bugbee is the voice of trees and stones already articulate to his receptive ear. If our ontology can handle the mind of racing notes, can it also handle roiling waters sounding out their very being, syllable by syllable? Hocking approaches this issue phenomenologically, noting that in encountering a familiar face, in the moment that we regard, we are (not untypically) *regarded*—such that "regard" somewhat floats between us.[20] In the hearing of whispering of trees, we are addressed in the moment that we address, in a mode attentive to the voice of the other. As music springs from the ink on the page, so syllables spring from the roar of a creek. Ears and hands that can hear are instructed, possessed, as is the heart, the very person in her entirety.

If the root of philosophical reflection is at times available only confessionally, through personal testimony, if the self is to be recovered at that horizon "before it is known to the world," then a philosophy attempting this confessional retrieval risks quick dismissal. For the context of philosophy and its culture is often adversarial public debate, and in that context, confessional retrieval appears to be little more than irrelevant, embarrassingly private revelation. So these moments become professionally repressed. Cavell writes adjacent to, rather than at the center of, analytic philosophy, and Bugbee removed to the wilderness of Montana, filling out his academic teaching life far from the mainstream.

Cavell confesses ruefully that "the discipline most opposed to writing, and to life, is analytic philosophy." Yet philosophy is, he says, "in a sense, to write your own words, to write your own inner voice." So the repression of professionalism is the repression of self. It becomes *outré* to suggest, as Bugbee does, that to find one's gait, one's self, one's voice, and to write it philosophically is to find that anthem "which alone can be the true answer for each of us to the questioning, the calling, the demand for ultimate reckoning which devolves upon us." A philosophical style or climate that rules out from the start imagining

---

[19] Bugbee, *Inward Morning*, 131, and 133f.

[20] For Hocking on "regard," see Wilshire, *Primal Roots of American*, 143. To be regarded (as we regard) is not unlike our earlier notice that we are held (as we behold).

moments of coming-to-insight, of coming to birth or vocation, risks losing voice to convey everything that matters. For without the seed, the syllable, the racing notes, there can be no answering self.

V

To stand on the verge of self-discovery, as Kierkegaard knew, can be a moment of anxious freedom. It can seem alien to stand with oneself, or with another, at the threshold of discovery. Here is Tolstoy sketching the necessity yet terror of assuming intimacy, of dropping a stance of formality toward another, or toward oneself:

> For the first time, he vividly pictured to himself her personal life, her thoughts, her desires . . . To transfer himself in thought and feeling into another human being was a mental activity alien to Karenin. He considered such mental activities as equivalent to indulging in harmful and dangerous fantasies.[21]

Is hearing—or telling—how one came to philosophy harmful or indulgent? Is it like becoming intimate, not just with one's wife (as Tolstoy has it), but with one's self? The fear may be the anxiety of self-knowledge, or knowledge of another. Yet there is also the companion fear, that in this uncanny region fantasy may take over truth— or worse, that we will be unable to distinguish the two. One treads dangerously the slippery circles of memory that encase what is of utmost moment to one's life.

It's not an accident, I think, that this tension between the security of formality and the terrors of intimacy is faced—when it is faced— autobiographically, or in journal form, and as a kind of last resort, after alternative attempts at conveying one's deepest concerns have run their course. We sense this in Cavell's reserve in assessing the full seasons of his teaching and writing and its seeds in his familial inheritance and its unorthodox bloom. And we hear this cautious reserve in Bugbee's concern that what he has to say resists easy expository shape, yet must be said—as witness to his world, his friends, his labors, his vocation. "Two dear friends and teachers of mine have said to me, independently of one another: 'You have written here as a man might write only near the end of his life.'"[22] The nearness of death has

[21] Leo Tolstoy, *Anna Karenina*, New York: Signet Books, 156.
[22] Bugbee, *Inward Morning*, 11.

accompanied him, as he has it, "Not in a way that saps life, but in a way that militates against putting off what one has to do."[23]

Some of the moments bringing him toward death appear in Bugbee's account of Kamikaze raids in the Pacific. Of course the thought of the nearness of death is familiarly existentialist and Heideggerian. Yet it also appears, perhaps surprisingly, in Thoreau's walk on Cape Cod weaving his way among corpses and those who have come to claim them, bodies washed up from an immigrant ship foundering in the surf.[24] And I'm sure Bugbee has in mind not just Kamikaze raids but Melville's reflection on boatmen risking their lives in whaling. In his chapter "The Line," Melville defines the philosopher as one who knows "the terror of the chase," "the nearness of death," no less intimately than the boatmen. The true philosopher, he says, will know the nearness of death "though he be seated by his fire, not with a harpoon, but with a poker in his hand."[25] Or, we might say, a pencil.

Perhaps philosophical reflection necessarily diverges from beaten paths, as the discovery of one's own voice becomes the discovery of one's intimate and unknown path, and of the risks, the terrors, that attend the journey.

VI

Cavell lays out conditions under which the public formality of philosophy and the intimate necessities of autobiography come to be "told in terms of each other" or meet each other's needs.[26] His account fills out and continues the themes of testimony, voice, possession, and place in a context of creation, on a stage at times blessed by the sacred.

First, one must sense that one has been addressed, by a text, a scene, a personal encounter—and one must take that address as a blessing, a promise, and confirmation deep and broad enough that it offers one

---

[23] Ibid.

[24] Thoreau, *Cape Cod*, Chapter 1, "The Shipwreck."

[25] *Moby Dick*, last sentence, Chapter 60, "The Line." A new member in the Harvard department in the fall of 1947, Bugbee introduced his interests for Quine, Lewis, and others by reading this Melville passage on "the true philosopher." See Quine's tribute to Bugbee as "the ultimate exemplar of the examined life," in *Wilderness and the Heart*, ix.

[26] *Pitch*, 38f.

permission to become who one is. This presupposes a radical openness to the address of another, whether delivered through falling snow
or rippling arpeggios or wizened eyes. Being called to become oneself
is, as Cavell has it, to be born, say, or reborn, in this case as a philosopher. And how can there be rebirth without creation? Being present at
creation, ready for blessing, one can embrace that promise or blessing
as one's own, and follow through. One knows in one's bones, or not
at all, that, as Bugbee heard it, one had been addressed among
mountains and flurries of snow and instructed for life.

Among other "conditions" that Cavell lists underlying the possibility
of philosophy and autobiography "answering each other's needs," one
must find a version of perfect pitch. As I would put it, one must have
a sense that one's ear is not dead, that in the anthem one finds native
to one's tongue, one's perceptual recognition is the recognition of
something unconditioned. As Bugbee would put it, one must have
faith that one can hear, or sense an Emersonian "somewhat absolute"
in experience. It is not a thing, but a "what" that is normative, absolutely normative, perhaps as aesthetic conscience—"somewhat absolute" in what one sees (or hears) and for what that seeing (or hearing)
demands. Life makes its ultimate demands. The extraordinary feature of absolute pitch, perfect pitch, is that one has immediate, non-
comparative, and infallible access to its rightness. The lesson for life is
that one seeks to have one's voice answer to a standard emergent in
experience that has all the clarity and call for response, for a pitching
up or down, on our part, to the inescapable demands, the measure,
of the oboe's exact 440 A. It is as if one has access to a measure of
perfection—unrealized, to varying degrees, though it will be. Answering to that measure will be testifying to the world one thinks. Philosophy will then emerge as testimony to one's sense of reality as it comes,
as blessing, and as containing a measure of our endeavors.

If these conditions are realized, that fact would find its ground in
a voice that witnesses—and we must accord that witness whatever
truthfulness it conveys. Bugbee writes "I could wish for no more than
to do justice to the instruction I have received from moving waters."[27]
And hearing this, I know that such a voice can appeal to little more
than my sense of its truthfulness. It is witness awaiting my response,
whether trusting or distrusting. Nothing deeper than the resonance of
his voice, and our sense of its accumulated power, could undergird this

---

[27] Bugbee, *Inward Morning*, 89.

sense of waters that speak syllable by syllable, of reality as it is reborn and completed in my attentive response, of its measure uncovered as a "somewhat absolute," and of one's calling as the demand to acknowledge these themes in the responsive action of a life.

This faith, in Cavell's case, in "perfect pitch," or in Bugbee's, in a "somewhat absolute" does not entail rigidity or judgmentalism. The stance is one of openness. There is ample room for revision or qualification in one's understanding of one's measure. As we have seen, it was the intensity of a music class from which Cavell fled for solitude. Yet he came in time to see that the lesson to draw would lead him on a course parallel to, but not vocationally within, music. "I would find that I was as interested in the understanding of what I heard [in a Bach choral], as thrilled by the drama of the teaching of it, as I was interested in the rightness and beauty of what I heard; they were not separate."[28] For whatever reason, the "drama of the teaching" and the "understanding of what [he] heard" led him vocationally toward philosophy, not deeper into music. But apart from the account of the life orientation that this moment contains, the moment's structure itself is revealing.

In attending to "the rightness and beauty" of a Bach choral, consciousness is dilated to include self-understanding in the listening, and awareness of the wider drama of the teaching. In such moments, any gaps between reflexive awareness of self and reflective understanding of a musical focus and the interpretative, instructional surround are diminished or closed, as are categorical gaps between reception, conception, and conviction. If this is a moment of philosophical insight, it is akin to musical insight or gestalt in its melding of feeling, perception, and submission of will. It is an experience to defy positivist construals of philosophy, yet one that falls full within the ambit of philosophy's concerns—so I'd think.

Granting the weight of these moments accumulated from Cavell and Bugbee, we open to exploration an expanded vista of concepts and relations. *The Inward Morning* takes them up one by one, and in their fugal relatedness, as does *A Pitch of Philosophy*. These are the themes of conviction, blessing, witness, dedication, and testimony, themes that move center stage. There they join more elusive notions, say Cavell's "perfect pitch," or Bugbee's "somewhat absolute in experience"—a rightness or perfection that confirms aspiration, a sense that we're on track, or that there is a track that's ours to be

---

[28] *Pitch*, 50.

on. And perhaps most important, there is the sense of the ongoing wonder of philosophy as a reflective way of life, half-way between sense and nonsense, a venture in wilderness, sometimes a high-wire act, sometimes an assured simplicity, always a creative and humbling pursuit.

VII

In Cavell's case, and for Henry Bugbee, too, there is more to philosophical voice and evocation of place than simple packaging. When such voice speaks in witness to the range of life from which a philosophical impulse springs, it can recast our philosophical agenda.

Over forty years ago a leading proponent of analytic philosophy had occasion to reflect on *The Inward Morning* in the pages of *The Journal of Philosophy*. He found the book, as we heard earlier, quite alien to his taste, and put the matter this way:

> [Bugbee's] . . . anecdotes are beautifully told and to me at least, strangely moving. But I fear that the philosophic point of such a venture escapes me utterly: I should think that it is a function of art, poetry, and literature—or mescaline—to yield up a heightened awareness of objects, of other people, and of reality in general, and that philosophy has quite different aims. But this is such a fundamental issue that it can hardly be discussed.[29]

The time has surely come, I would hope, when such a "fundamental issue" *can* be discussed. Revealing the world from which one's deepest vocational sensibility springs and to which it repeatedly returns for nourishment is not foreign to philosophy. This is to enact intimate, preservative care for our texts, thinking and teaching, the theme I develop throughout chapter ten. The autobiographical memories that we find in Bugbee or Cavell mark the springs of philosophical impulse that point toward completion in a sensibility attuned to a rich and varied sense of place and life unfolding in the inscrutable wonder of art and creation.[30] Here we dwell with readiness for voice and for anthem in the most sensitive of writers, writers who generously offer the turns of their paths for our appreciative response. Goods not to be refused.

---

[29] George Pitcher, *The Journal of Philosophy*, 1964, 111f.

[30] Cavell writes out autobiography as philosophy, or philosophy as autobiography, again in "Excerpts from Memory," *Critical Inquiry* (36), 2006.

Part III

SIX PRAISING EXPLORATIONS

Stanley Cavell

Bruce Wilshire

Henry James

Preservative Care

J. Glenn Gray

Henry David Thoreau

Chapter 7

STANLEY CAVELL—ACKNOWLEDGMENT,
SUFFERING, AND PRAISE:
A Religious Continental Thinker

Can we make—or find—a bridge between Stanley Cavell's work and
continental philosophy? And what about the burgeoning field of
continental theology? Does Cavell's work in any way shed light on the
unanticipated thaw in conversations, and even mutual support,
between continental philosophy and theology?[1] Looking at the span of
books I might reread in responding to these questions presents a
daunting prospect. I suspect that sketching a genealogy of Cavell's
writing would be as impossible as sketching a genealogy of continental
philosophy or theology itself.[2] So I'll set myself a less intimidating
task. I'll give an informal account of how I hear continental themes

---

[1] Note the interest of Agamben, Derrida, Millbank, Marion, Caputo, Zizek,
Pickstock, and others in St Paul and Augustine, and in themes of "The Gift," boundless
responsibility, and so on.

[2] Some of Cavell's titles: *Must We Mean What We Say? A Book of Essays* (1969); *The
World Viewed: Reflections on the Ontology of Film* (1971); *The Senses of Walden* (1972);
Pursuits of Happiness: The Hollywood Comedy of Remarriage (1976); *The Claim to Reason:
Wittgenstein, Skepticism, Morality, and Tragedy* (1979); *Themes Out of School: Effects and
Causes* (1986); *Disowning Knowledge: in Six Shakespeare Plays* (1987); *This New but Unap-
proachable America* (1988); *In Quest of the Ordinary: Lines of Skepticism and Romanticism*
(1988); *Conditions Handsome and Unhandsome: The Constitution of Emersonian Perfectionism*
(1990); *Philosophical Passages: Wittgenstein, Emerson, Austin, Derrida* (1995); *A Pitch of
Philosophy: Autobiographical Exercises* (1995); *Contesting Tears: The Hollywood Melodrama
of the Unknown Woman* (1996); *Emerson's Transcendental Etudes* (2003); *Cities of Words:
Pedagogical Letters on a Register of Moral Life* (2004); *Philosophy Day after Tomorrow* (2005).

weave in and out of his work against the background of my own encountering them.

I. The Necessity of Voice

The voice is unmistakably and inimitably *his*—as recognizable as our favorite tenor or contralto, as recognizable as early Nietzsche or late Beethoven. He seeks a musical voice. In *A Pitch of Philosophy, Autobiographical Exercises*, he claims his mother's sight-reading at the piano as his earliest and, we'd guess, most lasting model for expressive attunement to the world.[3] Her voice in playing, her perfect musical intimacy with her text as her fingers delivered Brahms or Schubert, immersed her so fully that there was no gap, as it were, for interpretation. Text and voice were seamlessly connected. This was her love of the world and her suspension of doubts. Is this grace, or an accomplishment?

A singer's inflection, pacing, and coloring of lyrics are of a piece with the words conveyed. The manner, the métier, of delivery is inextricably mixed with what arrives as delivered. Cavell's *mode* of interpretative uptake of a text and simultaneous delivery of it merge soundlessly with the significance of the passage that he takes up. The idea that a mood of intimacy, say, and non-assertiveness, might be essential to unraveling concepts and themes that interest Cavell—the idea that the mood of a military tactical analysis of love will miss love—is anticipated by Kierkegaard:

> The fact that science, fully as much as poetry and art, assumes a mood both on the part of the producer and on the part of the recipient, that an error in modulation is just as disturbing as an error in exposition of thought, has been entirely forgotten in our age, when people have altogether forgotten the nature of inwardness and appropriation in their joy over all the glory they believed they possessed, or through cupidity have lost it, like the dog which preferred the shadow. However, every error begets its own enemy. An error of thought has outside of it as its enemy, dialectics; the absence of mood or its falsification has outside of it its enemy, the comical.[4]

As one commentator puts it, "The mood proper to ethical discourse [on love] is . . . a mood of personal address, expressing that a proper

---

[3] Cavell, *Pitch*, 17–19.

[4] Søren Kierkegaard, *Concept of Dread*, trans. Walter Lowrie, Princeton: Princeton University Press, 1957, 13.

response to hearing the concepts expounded is self-examination, passionate appropriation, and action."[5]

Cavell's "prose arias," as one insightful commentator calls them, invite a reader not only to thrill or shudder slightly at the music heard, its rendering, or even rebirth in performance.[6] They prepare one to walk away with a mood and melody still vibrant, singing still in commemoration, and in one's own voice. What rubs off from his performances is permission to hear the texts in one's own voice, in a register of emotion, uncertainty, and conviction somehow attuned to his own. Raising an evocation that *moves* a reader or listener seems entirely appropriate, however infrequently we come across contemporary writers or philosophers willing to write that way. But if one speaks of love, of love of the world, for instance, one can't forever postpone bespeaking it, evoking it. Cavell's voicings complete themselves as they evoke *my own* capacities (or lack of them) for revoicing a strain of the heart, of the world.

II. Passion's Placement and Denial

It was less love I suppose, than infatuation, or even prurience, that fed my first serious "book affair." In the *Brothers Karamazov*, I found words to carry me toward what in retrospect is philosophy and equally literature or even, I've come to see, theology. The lyric excess, the mad swings from spiritual ecstasy to the stink of murder, from the cool edge of argument to back-alley debauchery, was melodrama pitched just right for adolescence. It put me in line for further literature or philosophy. I couldn't know it at the time, but I was reading existentialism. And I couldn't know that existentialism would be a style of thinking that in the last quarter of the twentieth century would be supplanted by structuralism, deconstruction, postmodernism—and then lumped unceremoniously under the label "continental philosophy and theology."

At the time, what I did come to learn was that the sort of philosophy I found in Dostoevsky was not the real thing. In college, my best philosophy instructors dismissed Dostoevsky and those writers such as

---

[5] Robert C. Roberts, "Kierkegaard and Ethical Theory," *Ethics, Love, and Faith in Kierkegaard*, ed. Edward F. Mooney, Bloomington: University of Indiana Press, 2008, 91.

[6] Garrett Stewart, "The Avoidance of Stanley Cavell," in *Contending with Stanley Cavell*, ed. Russell B. Goodman, Oxford: Oxford University Press, 2005, 140–157.

Sartre or Camus perceived to be vaguely in his camp. Novels, especially those as reason-averse as this Russian's, were well beneath serious *philosophical* consideration. Even "The Grand Inquisitor" was, for them, too murky, wild, and threatening.

I was being fed the growing split between continental and Anglophone philosophy, yet also fed, unintentionally, a way to disown that split—and from an unexpected quarter. Wittgenstein was the single star of that decade (the 1960s), and *Philosophical Investigations* was valued in my small world far above the *Tractatus*. But Wittgenstein's later writing—I mean especially its style, what it evoked, what it insinuated about its author—was clearly neither Descartes, Hume, nor Kant. It lacked the philosophical grace and drama of a Platonic dialogue, and the expository orderliness of Aristotle. It seemed to be a jungle of aphorisms and instructions and reminders *against* Descartes or Hume or Kant—against the false clarity of their presumptions and arguments. It was a jungle that Oxbridge was trying desperately to domesticate. It was too minimalist, unornamented, to be Romantic (so I thought). Even so, brave souls bypassed the usual analytical domestications in order to link Wittgenstein to Schopenhauer and Kierkegaard. One might suspect a connection to Dostoevsky, as well. Yet how exactly could one join the enigmatic one-liners of this Austrian now-British genius to the wild theological bent of a Russian existentialist?

By graduate school I had rumor of a Wittgenstein read (as we'd say today) *continentally*. Cavell's Berkeley lectures were packed. By 1964 he had published an article in *Daedalus* that found Wittgenstein and Kierkegaard were, if not kindred spirits, then non-combatants: there needn't be a *battle* there. You could hear a pin drop as he put those two together in a prestigious cultural journal. If Cavell were to be believed, the file labels "Existentialism" and "Analytical Philosophy" should no longer seem so absolute and absolutely opposed. Yet professionally, the oppositions were only hardening into a cold war of mutual disbelief and not-so-muffled indignation at the temerity of the other.

Dostoevsky was my earliest entry into philosophy, which placed me roughly continental. Yet my attraction to Cavell—based on his dramatic "existentialist" reading of Wittgenstein—gave me an "analytic" base, as well. Cavell opened up affinities between Wittgenstein and Kierkegaard. More generally, in his earliest works he displayed his own affinity for a personal, as he called it, "confessional" style of philosophy, the sort of writing we might find in Pascal or Nietzsche. And that dedication to a personal voice, along with a willingness to roam imaginatively with no regard for disciplinary fences, has characterized Cavell's career over the succeeding decades.

All this suggests a device for tracing out some of the major themes of his career, and for developing a sense of what he might bring to continental philosophy and theology. The device will be to imagine Cavell providing a reading of some themes from *The Brothers Karamazov*. To my knowledge, he never treats this novel directly, but imagining an encounter gives me a way to bring out what's central to his way of reading texts, and a way to consider the merit, if any, in placing him among the continentals. Four themes will help place Cavell's work: perfectionism, romanticism, skepticism, and acknowledgment; each involves what Nietzsche calls affirmation.

III. Modes of Affirmation

Early on in *The Birth of Tragedy* Nietzsche averred, against theodicy, that life could be sufferable only as an aesthetic phenomenon. Later he came to see that even the redeeming gestures of art relied on a more basic sense that something was worth affirming—perhaps the materials and skills an artist wields, perhaps aspects of the world or self calling for aesthetic response. We might see Cavell's grounding themes as modes of affirmation. Affirmation is inescapable in the call to become who one is (the central strand of "moral perfectionism"), in the call to give passions and "this world" their rightful place (a central strand of "romanticism"), and in a move past doubt (the central strand of skepticism). I'll give a thumbnail sketch of each, starting with Cavell's idea of "*moral perfectionism*." This is his name for something like ongoing yet never realized self-realization.

"Moral perfectionism" captures the thought that persons are always on the trembling edge of the unexpected, on the verge of becoming themselves through shedding what is less than perfect, emerging from a kind of spiritual tumult or unrest while unfolding toward their next and potentially better self—all this an *unending* process of becoming, a forever *unfinished* striving. These forever unfolding reconfigurations of a self articulate the drama and enigma key to the productions of those inaugurating figures we label "existentialist" or "continentalist," Kierkegaard, Nietzsche, and Dostoevsky. Each of the better Karamazov brothers desperately pursues his next and better self, through crisis after crisis. With the theme of moral perfectionism, Cavell shifts his question from *"Must we mean what we say?"* to the continental question, *"Must we become who we are?"*

A second connecting theme is Cavell's *recovery of the romantic.*[7] The subtitle of *City of Words,* his most recent book, is *"Pedagogical Letters on a Register of the Moral Life."* This is a tribute to Schiller's *Letters on the Aesthetic Education of Man.* Film is our most evident contemporary vehicle for aesthetic education, and Cavell has his pedagogic chapters alternate between texts from the canon of moral philosophy and particular films that illuminate or continue their themes. Dimitri Karamazov quotes Schiller profusely. Of course Dostoevsky's romanticism is not Schiller's, and Cavell's is not a Karamazov mix of desire, impulse, and poetic effusions of love for "the sticky leaf-buds of spring, the blue sky."[8] But we're in the varied land of Romanticism, and it seems likely that major swaths of continental philosophy—if it's something anywhere near single—are best characterized as a continuation of German Romanticism.

A third theme crossing Cavell and continentals is *skepticism.* This might take a classical Cartesian form, or it might be allied with unmasking social certainties, the sort of skepticism that Marx, Nietzsche, and Freud ply, earning them the title "masters of suspicion." Yet again, purveyors of objective uncertainties, *aporias,* deferrals of closure, undecidability, or irony might advance skepticism. As Cavell sees it, skepticism Cartesian style, when carried through, amounts to a "refusal of the world." It's of a piece with tragedy and pride.

In Ivan Karamazov's case, skepticism is a refusal of others that's linked to cruelty and finally murder. The cruelty may not be immediately evident: "I'm returning the ticket," Ivan confesses to his brother. He's returning his ticket to life, to creation. But it's clear he speaks this way to lure his brother *away* from creation, away from his love for others and most especially, from his attachment to the revered Father Zossima. No argument can possibly bring Ivan into affirmations that would quell his skepticism, so he's left denying the world and others in a kind of nihilism. Cavell would frame the impasse between

[7] Parallel are "recoveries" by Richard Eldridge, *The Persistence of Romanticism,* Cambridge: Cambridge University Press, 2001; Charles Lamore, *The Romantic Legacy,* New York: Columbia University Press, 1996; Frederick Beiser, *The Romantic Imperative,* Cambridge: Harvard University Press, 2003; and Anthony Rudd, *Expressing the World: Skepticism, Wittgenstein, and Heidegger,* Chicago: Open Court, 2003.

[8] Ivan's line, but on this the two brothers agree. Feodor Dostoevsky, *The Brothers Karamazov,* New York: Penguin, 301.

Ivan and Alyosha as a failure not of knowledge or argument or reason but of affirmation, or better, of acknowledgment. To succeed in acknowledging the world and others would be, as Cavell says, a love of the world, and there's no surefire access—certainly not an exclusively intellectual one—to that requisite love.

Here is a passage that frames the only way that Ivan's doubt and world-denial might be answered. Cavell spells it out as his response to skepticism, but it's also Dostoevsky's way of response to Ivan, and has a familiar ring for those who read Kierkegaard, as well.

> To live in the face of doubt, eyes happily shut, would be to fall in love with the world. For if there is a correct blindness, only love has it. And if you find that you have fallen in love with the world, then you would be ill-advised to offer an argument of its worth.[9]

Cavell is prompted by Wittgenstein's gnomic question and answer: "Do I doubt?—My eyes are shut." Cavell's elaboration is that skeptical doubts can go unrefuted and yet lose their grip, as when we close our eyes before a kiss. Our fearful mutual vulnerability is for a moment shelved. This is the blindness of love, the only blindness that can be "correct." It's living *happily* in the face of doubt, which isn't possible all the time nor for everyone—nor can it always be justified. Yet the world would be far less without such blindness, aptly present and as needed.

I have slightly truncated Cavell's words. The last sentence, in full, and its immediate successors, read:

> And if you find that you have fallen in love with the world, then you would be ill-advised to offer an argument of its worth by praising its Design. Because you are bound to fall out of love with your argument, and you may thereupon forget that the world is wonder enough, as it stands. Or not.

Note that there is no guarantee that you will find the world "wonder enough." Perhaps since the Holocaust we have lost what Arendt calls the capacity to write or act "for love of the world." Cavell interrupted his Berkeley lectures on *Moby Dick* in 1963 when Arendt's *The Banality of Evil* appeared. Eichmann has nothing in common with Ahab, yet if there is evil, they are each instances.

In the last pages of his *Postscript*, Kierkegaard's Johannes Climacus revokes *arguments* against distortions of faith in favor of "falling in

---

[9] Stanley Cavell, *The Claim of Reason: Wittgenstein, Skepticism, Morality, and Tragedy,* Oxford: Oxford University Press, 1979, 431.

love," with a certain way of life, Socratic and Christian. Arguments have limits. Take the haunting story from Eli Wiesel. A small group of rabbis find themselves putting God on trail from the midst of a concentration camp. How could a just God mete such affliction on his people? They find God unforgivably guilty, and then pray.

To block a too-piercing, vivid sight allows us, as Cavell puts it, "to fall in love with the world." It is the opposite of Oedipus' self-loathing blinding, even though this brings him into new contact with the world. This startling thought—that we need blinding—seems exactly right for evoking a risky yet apparently inevitable link of skepticism and affirmation, even as the Whirlwind averts Job's eyes from suffering to allow affirmation of the world. Skepticism about the source sorrow is set aside—not refuted—as he melts before the wonders of creation. Such a paradoxical link of blindness and sight allows life latitude and incidentally provides a clue to the moving center of continental philosophy and theology, where attestations of *aporias* and undecidabilities vie for prominence with affirmations of friendship, love of God, or justice. This co-presence of doubt and affirmation is no more fragile—and just as fragile—as love itself.

For Cavell, skepticism about others—about other minds—should be framed not just as a failure of arguments to get us to the reality of another, but as a *denial of persons,* even violence toward them. One thinks here of Levinas, who builds the acceptance of the other into the very basis of any responsible philosophy, long before any epistemological compunctions are allowed to surface.

Cruelty drives Ivan Karamazov's skepticism. He returns to his family from Enlightened Paris because he smells his father's blood and wants to look in on the murder he will slyly instigate. He enjoys unleashing his Paris-trained intelligence against his younger brother's love and faith. His cool Euclidian "understanding," brought to bear on things human and divine, amounts to a refusal of others that culminates in killing. He is, as his brothers say, a tomb; he must, they say, resurrect his dead. Alyosha is a fount of affirmation flourishing in the company of Zossima and the young boys for whom he's a saint. His imperfections prod him to further compassion. Ivan has no such sense of a next or better self, and is ready to watch his father killed, and to puncture the spirit of Zossima. Thus he's set on killing Alyosha's spirit. The story of the Grand Inquisitor, relayed to his little brother when Alyosha is especially vulnerable, is meant to crush him. Ivan delivers it in an offhand manner on the very evening Alyosha heads to the monastery to comfort the dying Patriarch.

Ivan's famous "poem" or legend introduces an aged Cardinal who oversees the Spanish Inquisition and its immolation of suspected heretics. He turns to suddenly discover Christ returned among the throngs. The Cardinal jails Him. Just as Ivan demeans Alyosha's love, so the Cardinal demeans Christ's. Visiting Him late one evening, the prelate accuses Christ of heartlessly placing an impossible burden of responsibility on his people, delivering an impossible freedom whose terror kills their spirit. Out of a greater compassion than Christ can know, the Church, so the Cardinal avers, relieves the people of their burden. Christ had his moment in history, failed, and has no right to upset the Church's restorative project of compassion, which succeeds where Christ's failed. The Cardinal makes his case in Christ's cell as the inquisitorial fires are readied to claim Him once again.

Ivan's skeptical invention is brilliant and strangely resistant to philosophical refutation. Just as important, Ivan deploys it for sadistic ends, which reveals its skeptical sophistication to also be a cruel refusal of others—not to mention a hatred of the world. It's Ivan's way to imprison Alyosha and mock his love of Zossima, a love that spills over as a love of God and of the world. Ivan is a demonic anti-perfectionist here, ambushing his brother's next and better self.

IV. ACKNOWLEDGMENT, SUFFERING

In addition to moral perfectionism, romanticism, and skepticism, there's a fourth theme that weaves Cavell and continentals. It's *acknowledgment,* an idea we've already touched on, and that resonates with the ground-bass theme of affirmation.

From his two late 1960s essays "Knowledge and Acknowledging" and "An Avoidance of Love," on through his later collection of Shakespeare essays called *Disowning Knowledge,* Cavell leads us away from hope that a knowledgeable refutation will put an end to skepticism. Redemption from its despairingly endless coils requires not knowledge but an ability to acknowledge the world and others. If we could avoid an exclusive focus on doubt, if we could avert our eyes and love or at least acknowledge others and the world, then skepticism would not disappear but at least it would be inconclusive, leaving room for its other, not dogmatic certainty but confident affirmation. It would lose its grip.

To acknowledge others is to turn refusal and disowning upside down. Alyosha is willing to fall in love with the saintly Zossima "eyes happily shut" to the world that Ivan would make salient. In his death-bed sermons, Zossima reminds his listeners that hell is being unable to love, and that heaven is wherever two are joined. And Ivan's justly celebrated "poem" of the Grand Inquisitor gives a marvelous instance of the quiet power of acknowledgment in facing down a mind like Ivan's, or the Cardinal's. Ivan has the Christ of his mysterious tale sidestep the Inquisitor's arguments. Christ's response is a gesture of personal engagement, of love, of acknowledgment of the person who suffers there before him.

Having seized Christ earlier, the old prelate now visits the prison cell at night to give opening and closing arguments in defense of seizure. The striking fact of this encounter is that the old man's arguments go unanswered. They are not met philosophically by counterargument, or by knowledge that would undermine their force. Yet if not his arguments, the man himself is answered. A silent gesture puts a seal on his loquacious disquisition. Christ "draws near and quietly kisses him on his bloodless lips." This affirms, acknowledges, the person before him whose fate is human, that is, whose fate it is to suffer, to undergo affliction—and to deny that fact. In the Cardinal's case, denial takes the shape of cloaking power under a sham benevolence. He asserts a wider fellow-feeling than Christ's. Yet Christ's gesture intimates that the Cardinal's tyranny springs from his unacknowledged suffering, which is recognized by a kiss. This gentle recognition of the icy suffering of his soul shakes the Cardinal to the core; he blanches, turns, and then lets Christ go unharmed.

Have we found Cavell a home among the continentals? Hearing his motifs resonate so powerfully through this founding continental text makes a case for his cultural location in that tradition, in both its philosophical and theological guise. But there may be less than we hoped for in finding this convenient label for his work. We've come nowhere close to locating the full range of Cavell's concerns, and so-called continental philosophy itself is not a unified phenomena. But from both sides, the continental connection can be illuminating. From the European side, it shows definitively that the themes central to the tradition marketed as continental flourish this side of the Atlantic, not only in Cavell, but in his mentors, Emerson and Thoreau. And from Cavell's side, the continental connection brings out the centrality in his work of interlocking philosophical and literary modes of expression, the interplay of skepticism and romanticism, the awareness of our readiness to refuse others and the world, and the idea of a striving to shed one's imperfections, of a restless, relentless search of the soul as definitive of a person.

V. THOREAU: A CONTINENTAL

The tumultuous worlds of the Karamazovs are distinctively Russian. Squabbles like that, heroism, sainthood, and devilry like that, couldn't happen just anywhere. Cavell doesn't write about the Russians but he does present his own local exemplars of affirmation, of romanticism, moral perfectionism, averted skepticism, and acknowledgment. They're precisely placed, in Cambridge or in Concord, at Walden or in Boston. We might want to call them American continentals, or perhaps hope for the day when such tags were unnecessary. In any case, Cavell's work takes him through Kierkegaard and Wittgenstein and Austin on toward a surprising and daring widening of the circle of texts he makes his own. I can't pursue the themes of moral perfection and acknowledgment in the works of these Americans, Emerson and Thoreau, but I can allude to one feature of their writing that makes them unmistakably American—not European. And that is simply landscape.

The upstream Charles I knew flowed at a simple walking pace among abandoned ponds and swamps. Explored by canoe, it spoke of Emerson's self-reliance and Thoreau's escape from quiet desperations. In quite a different mood from Dostoevsky, these writers, too, ministered, their voices beckoning through the leaves in the way childhood words mysteriously can. How, then, could I *not* find my heart miss a beat discovering *The Senses of Walden*, newly minted from the author of "Existential and Analytical Philosophy" and "Must We Mean What We Say"?

Under pressure from our moral and philosophical exemplars, the mind extends. There is the stretch from Kierkegaard to Wittgenstein; then the stretch from Wittgenstein to *King Lear*; and yet again, from any one of these to Concord, Emerson, and Thoreau. I've come to sense this array of texts as wildly different districts of a single city, but as I first encountered Cavell's readings of such apparently divergent worlds, only desperate leaps of faith could join one to the next.[10] For a budding philosopher, this sometimes somber, sometimes

---

[10] Cavell's *Must We Mean What We Say?*, New York: Charles Scribners, 1969, included essays on Beckett, Kierkegaard, Shakespeare, Austin, Wittgenstein, contemporary music, and a polemic with Benson Mates—what could unify this book but the voice of its author?

effervescently diverse city seemed just right—and then, impossibly surreal. Still later, the city included film, a woman's voice in opera, the fact of television, autobiography, Derrida, Plato and Levinas. Do we have another mind so capacious?

VI. WORDS AND PASSIONS

It helps to reread Cavell's early '62 essay "The Availability of Wittgenstein's later Philosophy," in a continental, even theological, vein. Imagine the shock of an article in the numbingly impersonal *Philosophical Review* that opens with a literary epigraph—any at all, let alone this one in particular, and at this length—and almost operatic. It's from Giraudoux:

> Epochs are in accord with themselves only if the crowd comes into these radiant confessionals which are the theaters or the arenas, and as much as possible, . . . to listen to its own confessions of cowardice and sacrifice, of hate and passion . . . For there is no theatre which is not prophecy. Not this false divination which gives names and dates, but true prophecy, that which reveals to men these surprising truths: that the living must live, that the living must die, that autumn must follow summer, spring follow winter, that there are four elements, that there is happiness, that there are innumerable miseries, that life is a reality, that it is a dream, that man lives in peace, that man lives on blood; in short, those things they will never know.[11]

At the time it must have read as an affront to philosophical sensibilities, but we can now hear this epigraph as an existential invitation to read *Philosophical Investigations* as if it mattered, as a confession, as theater or prophecy; as responsive to the crowd; as showing what we can't help but know (yet will never know)—that we are mortal; that we can have or lose a voice; that there can be a passion for God; that God can be passionately denied; that there can be no passion; that one can fall in love with the world or out of love with it. These are fragments scattered in a broken revelation of the epoch's alienation from itself. Two years later Kierkegaard and Wittgenstein are given equal and equally respectful time in Cavell's "Existentialism and Analytical Philosophy."

---

[11] Ibid., Chapter 2.

VII. PERFECTIONISM

Confession and theater are linked to dialogue, which for Cavell can also be musical. He engages his present responsive listeners with his readings as a singer might engage her audience. When all works well, his voice brings present listeners to sense the possibility of a successor self, even as he listens for his own. As a moral, transformative discipline, his writing allows words to span our common work. Writing becomes a spiritual discipline. As interpretation, it has an uncanny resemblance to Midrash: taking up a text with great care, turning it this way and that, opening it toward new readers and their present as if our very souls depended on hearing each word faithfully.

This progress is perfectionist in the sense of sharp awareness of the endless withdrawal before us of what we would be, perfectionist in being unsatisfied with the imperfection of merely "good enough" moral aspirations, requirements, or accomplishments. Especially in intimate relations, including with oneself, we want more of ourselves and others than just compliance with civil law, or adherence to a utilitarian or Kantian counsel, or interest in a Platonic or an Aristotelian virtue. (As we will see, this is the lesson of Henry James, as well.) Cavell comments sideways on why Rawls or Kant must be silent on such issues as how high you or I might set the bar for our own sense of decency or accomplishment on any given day; or even whether we set a bar at all for what might be required of us beyond the commonplace. The moral struggles Cavell brings to light are invisible to what's most explicit in the theories of Mill or Kant or Aristotle. They hold out at least the hope in principle of achieving rest, of satisfying a moral principle or standard, of hitting the mark once and for all. The perfectionist refuses the presumption that moral work might ever end, that life is moving toward a satisfaction or completion at least in principle attainable. The wheel of work for them is never stilled. That, in their view, would be a sign of complacency or self-satisfaction or a denial of the ever beckoning allure of worth or felt-necessity.

A moral perfectionist is sensitive to the endlessness of the struggle to find one's voice, a moral voice, say, a voice one can believe in; to find a social framework one can believe in (apart from its meeting certain abstract requirements of justice, or being "passably" good); to find one's way through betrayal or grief to forgiveness or mourning; to find praise or gratitude or to welcome prayer or benediction. The struggle for intelligible expression of what we can own, of what we might believe in, of what we can be, is a wonder, terror, and blessing, and here our stripped down theories from Mill or Kant or Rawls don't help. Yet if Cavell succeeds, his articulations display and instigate transformations. Listening is moral formation. As figures in a text find voice, and as we become interlocutors in his dialogues, the impact of what it's like to find a voice can uncannily rub off, suggesting where our next step might lie. His interpretative spiritual discipline becomes our own.

VIII. MIDRASH, PRAYER

Hilary Putnam defends the view that the highest form of ethical life for the Jewish tradition is approaching, honoring, and acknowledging God through study of sacred texts.[12] Reading is both critical and pious, and one courts change in oneself through reading and then retelling, recreating what one has read, with new and questioning elaborations. In an Aristotelian sense, this life of reading the text and one's soul being read by the text would be the good life. It's a kind of disciplined textual critique, affirmation, and praise that Tyler Roberts calls "critical piety."[13] Does Cavell's writing then become a kind of Midrash, critical and praising elaborations not just of scripture, but of Shakespeare, Emerson, Wittgenstein, or film? Is he rabbinic, serious, and playful with his text, all along working for the glory of the word, the glory of the world? Or in quite a different mood, he might be off on an inspired late-night riff, Midrash heard as a jazz improvisation on a theme just then inherited from a horn. There is a musical as well as a conceptual side to all interpretation in Schleiermacher's view.[14] As we've seen, Cavell seeks out the music in the texts he hears and plays it back to us, transfigured. He writes as if his life depended on it—as if ours did, too. There's no explicit call, "*You must change your life!*" But it's lurking in his meditations.

Even in reading the early polemics, "Must we mean what we say?" and "The Availability of Wittgenstein's Later Philosophy" we sense

---

[12] Hilary Putnam, "Jewish Ethics," in *The Blackwell Companion to Religious Ethics,* ed. William Schweiker, Melrose, MA: Blackwell 2005, 160–165.

[13] See Tyler Roberts, "Criticism as a Conduct of Gratitude: Stanley Cavell and Radical Theology". *Post-Secular Encounters: Religious Studies, Humanities and the Politics of the Academy,* New York: Columbia University Press, 2011.

[14] The on-line *Stanford Encyclopedia of Philosophy* entry on Schleiemacher gives a good account of his view that any powerfully effective reading of a text relies on a melodic and rhythmic rendition. I take up the pedagogical necessity to read poetry (and some prose) aloud in chapter ten.

that the authors and views he scrutinizes are under *moral* scrutiny. More obviously, his alluding to Augustine or Freud reminds us how our lives can be brought under broad and painful indictment—they demand our lives be changed. Reading Cavell can make us feel under them, too. We're asked to change.

Cavell wouldn't be disturbed if his words were indicting, I think, provided only we had heard him in the right way, in the right register, with well-tuned ears. I said that this tone was unique, and I should qualify: it's unique in the writing that easily comes to mind as typical of professional academic philosophy in the last fifty years in English-speaking countries. Others know better than I whether this tone of moral urgency—that an interpretation of a text will matter to the contours, say, of your spiritual life—is to be found among professional philosophers in Paris, Rome, or Berlin. That urgency was surely present in the 1930s there. I'm placing Cavell's voice of mild but insistent urgency against a backdrop of Anglophone philosophy since the 1950s. There's still some distain or at least resistance toward writing that carries emotions, or "the personal" among philosophers allied with cognitive science, or standard epistemology, which means that Cavell's study of love and affection, or of shame and violence, or of being deprived of one's voice will be ignored: it is intimate, and forebodes change in the makeup of our passions.[15]

Writing can address us in many ways, inviting different kinds of response. The meditations of Marcus Aurelius, Midrash, or the prayers of Kierkegaard invite us to participate in a spiritual exercise, to entertain a moment when writing might purify or heal or transform the self. But Cavell occupies an endowed and distinguished chair in philosophy within a modern secular university. Can he deliver from that site a kind of prayer, Midrash, or meditation without thereby forfeiting the academic status of that writing? Perhaps that threat of forfeit shouldn't matter. Perhaps he writes person-to-person rather than professor-to-professor, or professor-to-student. But if Cavell's writing transgresses the boundaries of a strictly professorial approach to texts, academics may feel justified in refusing to take his efforts as straight-forward contributions to academic discourse or theoretical inquiry. Accordingly, they may feel quite unwilling or unable to respond to words that seem to invite or even demand a kind of spiritual discipline.

---

[15] Cavell "invites improvisation in the disorders of desire." He beckons toward moral alternation. See his discussion of "passionate utterance" in *Philosophy the Day After Tomorrow*, Cambridge, MA: Harvard University Press, 2005, 185.

We have it on the good authority of Garrett Stewart, chair of a prestigious Mid-West English department, that scholars from within the
discipline of English literature don't respond to what Stewart affirms to
be an extraordinary literary achievement. He suspects that Shakespeare
and Thoreau scholars fail even to read Cavell, let alone, disagree with
him.[16] That resistance to Cavell might derive, as I've suggested, from
an unwillingness or incapacity to respond to writing that addresses and
so makes demands on a reader's moral–spiritual convictions, that
invites participation in a spiritual discipline, that asks for a kind of
self-transformation or movement toward a better moral self.

Garrett Stewart refines our sense of where the resistance to Cavell is
focused. "In Cavell's writing," he says, "argument and articulation grow
indissoluble at the level of affect—and hence of conviction."[17] Cavell's
words engage passions and seem to call on our commitments. The
appeal of his sentences goes well beyond an appeal to our capacities
for theoretical assessment. Stewart finds mainstream scholars unable
or unwilling to respond at this particular level of appeal. He puts this
fact quite dramatically and disturbingly. Literary scholars, he says, have
lost the "skills and taste and aspiration" for literature.

What is it to lose the "skills and taste and aspiration" for literature?
I suspect it means to become unresponsive to the literary expression of
affect and conviction, to fail to hear writing as witness and testimony to
the life of passion, affect, and emotion. As it now stands, Stewart
implies, there is no room within the academic study of literature
for responsiveness to praise or shame or grief "at the level of affect—
and hence of conviction." But if literary scholars have no ear for this
dimension of literary articulation, they will have no ear for Cavell.
The very idea of prose in the service of moral perfection is not just
objectionable, but ideologically an object of derision. Reading is not
"reading for life" but a matter of unmasking or decoding an ideological product.[18] Critique of society in the nineteenth century

---

[16] A June 1999 *New York Review of Books* account of Thoreau reception failed to
mention *The Senses of Walden. The Vehement Emotions*, Princeton: Princeton University
Press, 2002, by Harvard English professor Philip Fisher, sneers at what he takes to be
academic philosophy's neglect of emotions. Quite astoundingly, even as he writes on
The Winter's Tale, he fails to mention Cavell's essay on it, or Cavell's "The Avoidance of
Love," on *King Lear.*

[17] Stewart, "The Avoidance of Stanley Cavell," 153.

[18] See Margaret R. Miles, *Reading for Life: Beauty, Pluralism, and Responsibility,* New
York: Continuum, 1997.

was framed as a critique of religion. Today it's framed as a critique of literature and the humanities, which are confronted as false consciousness, as ideology, as opportunities for target-seeking strategies of "cultural studies, discourse analysis, and the semiotics of social energy." What's lost, as Stewart puts it, is a capacity "to *encounter* writing *along the very contours of its expression.*"[19]

We might think of Cavell's writing as exemplary in allowing us to encounter words delivered "along the very contours of [their] expression." Here's a line Stewart takes up from Cavell's first book on film. Cavell evokes the soaring birds and sunlight from the final scene of Dreyer's film *Jeanne d'Arc*. Dreyer's birds are locked in Jean's gaze at her final moment at the stake. They're given by Cavell as "wheel[ing] over her, with the sun in their wings," words that relay the film's epiphany, and words that allow Stewart the space of that epiphany, letting his words relay the life of Cavell's words on Dreyer on *Jeanne d'Arc*. He hears Cavell draw out "the tacit stream of immolation and immortality" as wheeling birds, light in their wings, deliver *a love of the world*. To love in the face of doubt, eyes happily shut, would be to fall in love with the world. The brush of sun in their wings is a flicker of immortality, anointed in Cavell's final words: "*They, there, are free*"— words returned in Stewart's reprise.

Cavell's tone, the "contour of his expression," is something like acknowledgment or affirmation against the background of terrible death. These feathered flyers are heralds of immortality—an *immanent* immortality (as Stewart hears it). There is something more than somber, hushed affirmation in these words—no doubt a frightful shiver, and more one fears to utter. Jean's death tests those eyes, happily shut . . . or open. Those sunlit wings link uncannily to her demise. His words, "*They, there, are free*," must then approach a register of prayer. Stewart exclaims and pleads "What is this but philosophy as criticism as poetry!" I'd just add "philosophy as criticism as poetry— and *yes, as prayer—as benediction!*" In tracking Cavell's "contours of expression," Stewart flies free of calls for professional decoding. For the moment, then, he's there, free, caught in what he calls Cavell's "tacit four word ontology of all projected screen presence"— *They, there, are free.*

---

[19] Stewart, "The Avoidance of Stanley Cavell," 153; emphasis added.

IX. Affliction, Benediction

Cavell lays out words and silences and gestures that draw us in with lyric urgency to change a life. His dialogical spirit does not transfer information but transforms spirit. Such liberating effect, such epiphany, brings listeners one more step beyond their imprisoning inhibitions. Philosophy, poetry, religion are conversion. This should not be alien to a continental theology.

We might hear Garrett Stewart lifted toward a better self, and we with him, toward a more uplifted sort of reading self, through those words he passes on, voicing in his elaboration of them his own animation, his freedom found in finding words: "*They, there, are free.*" As Stewart further confides,

> In the . . . swift gust of the verb across the cadenced swoop of
> 　　[Th]　　ey　　/　　[th]　　ere　　/　　are　　/
> we audit, on the underside of writing, a pervasive "air," the subliminal breath of
> airiness itself, all but spelled out as the medium of uplift.[20]

Thus we're swept by a gust of breath, a love of words and the world, and some of the best immortality we'll get.

---

[20] Ibid.

Chapter 8

BRUCE WILSHIRE:
The Breathtaking Intimacy of the Material World

At its best, the study of the human can evoke wonder at its topic, have
ameliorative effect, and shake our understanding not only of familiar
phenomena but also of disciplinary methods and domains. Weaving
gracefully through anthropology, gender studies, philosophy, medi-
cine, and literature—nomadically at home with each—Bruce Wilshire's
Wild Hunger: The Primal Roots of Modern Addiction artfully defies our
disciplinary assumptions.[1] He shakes our understanding of addictions—his stated topic—by showing how these destructive habits
are coded pleas for a world we've lost—and hardly know we've lost. His
startling diagnosis is that we're still wounded by the loss of the primal
awe-filled world of hunter–gatherers—a loss that in the vast sweep of
human history is relatively recent.

Imagine stripping a hunter–gatherer culture of its expressive rituals
and ways of linking to the earth, to each other, and to simple things
such as eating, walking, and smoking; imagine stripping them of their
ways of passing on wisdom, generation to generation, their ways
of marking time and timelessness, of finding ecstatic experience. As
we surely know, to strip them of this would be the spiritual—and
physical—death of the people. The death might be sudden, or it might
be gradual, as disease, alcoholism, despair, and violence replaced
the vanishing old ways of being. If we were once these primal people,
perhaps this death, gradual or sudden, in fact is our own. We suffer
ancient wounds. Elaborating this troubling suggestion is not easy.
But if we are receptive to Wilshire's many leads, we can move beyond

---

[1] Bruce Wilshire, *Wild Hunger: The Primal Roots of Modern Addiction*, Lanham, MD:
Rowman and Littlefield Publishers, 1998.

resignation or despair at our fractured world to marvel at the human
and at the human place in the widest, wildest scheme of things. As he
puts it in an essay on William James, we've lost a sustaining sense of
"the breathtaking intimacy of the material world."[2]

Wilshire's task is to bring a primal world alive to us by dissolving
walls of incredulity, conceptual and experiential barriers that locate it
well beyond the pale for denizens of an industrial, bureaucratic state,
for inhabitants, as Max Weber would have it, of a distinctly "disen-
chanted" world. This means changing our focus on familiar phenomena, from eating to walking to taking in mountain vistas. Restoring the
sense of an awe-filled primal world places addiction in perspective.

Perhaps we begin to grasp the roots of addiction in little things.
I note my breathing stops cold as I begin to problem-solve—something
dies within me and makes me crave revival; I reach for a comforting,
and deadly, cigarette. Or we note the roots in big things. I glimpse,
despairingly, that my "normal" interest in my career has become a
compulsion to "get ahead," geared at a dead run: work has become
dangerously addictive, destructively out of control.[3] Grasping what
would make our lives less meaning-depleted can mean, as a start,
refiguring the pace and rhythm of work and breathing.

Patterns of ordinary life, so familiar that we cease to "know" them,
take on new and unexpected meaning under Wilshire's attentively
articulate pen. We come to wonder at our world and at our wondrous
placement in it. "In archaic modes of truth, self realizes itself ecstati-
cally—realizes itself by communing with itself in the very act of communing with the rest of the world."[4] When meaning slips away,
what will replenish us? "[W]e are body-selves creating meaning in
improvisory concert with the world around us; ourselves-augmented-
by-the-world replenishes us."[5] The question remains: How do we make
contact with ourselves or the worlds that augment them?

I

An Inuit fisherman graces the cover of Wilshire's *Wild Hunger*. Attending his line, the Arctic hunter becomes a metaphor for meditation,

[2] "The Breathtaking Intimacy of the Material World: William James's last thoughts,"
The Cambridge Companion to William James, ed. Ruth Anna Putnam, Cambridge:
Cambridge University Press, 1997, Chapter 6.
[3] Wilshire, *Wild Hunger*, 207.
[4] Ibid., 179.
[5] Ibid., 173.

for focused readiness to respond to the unknown—all senses alive and vibrantly alert. Just as much, he is a metaphor for nourishment—bodily, social, spiritual. And as much again, this is a metaphor for adventure, replete with risk. To imagine this Inuit is to know the fullness, danger, and simplicity of an art of living connected to a span of human needs and satisfactions as these interweave in Nature's depths.

Poised on the ice, the hunter feeds his line through a crack to snare the dancing fish below. Thus he meets a need for protein and oil. But he also meets a hunger for the wild, for exhilaration on thin ice in lively contact with a vastness just beneath. And remembering the Inuit artist who first brushed in a fisherman like this on bark or stone or sealskin, we are reminded of the primal need to celebrate in paint or dance or song the rituals of hunting and nourishment. We remember the need for creative art that both embodies and commemorates ecstatic ties to nature, to the ever-present Whole. Following the trajectory of this expressive hunter, Wilshire subtlety unfolds a primal philosophy, where myth, art, and religion coalesce. The root meaning of "religion" is to "re-tie," to restore lost links. The art of living that Wilshire celebrates is reconnective and regenerative, a healing reabsorbtion in what Emerson called the "always circular power returning into itself."[6] When stymied or shut down, the hunger for experience, for a sense of live connection, leads to self-destructive, addictive substitutes. When we cut ties to alert and animated bodies, or to our need for adventure, for sensing the trembling line at our fingertips, when we neglect body-spirit nourishment, in desperation we grab the nearest fix. We violently ingest or "shoot up" anything that promises to break the stagnant pall of lifeless routines. We cannot wait with the Inuit hunter for a strike from the deep unknown. Deprived of real adventure, real nourishment, we despair of real exaltation at contact with a fathomless surround. The Inuit hunter artfully tied to his totem, to his meal, and to the family that will share it, reminds us of a loss. We have forgotten how to feed out lines for real fish, for real souls, for real contact with an animated Whole.

Wilshire's chapters tell the story of the tenuous but still present hold this primal world has upon our lives. We are invited to acknowledge our need for ecstatic connectedness, for wilderness, and for links to nature's regenerative cycles.[7] Through careful phenomenological

---

[6] Ibid., 22, 47.

[7] Ibid., Prologue, and Chapter 1.

description, we are offered a new framework for understanding the lure of smoking and the loss of ritual settings that might make it other than addictive.[8] We come to sense the hopeless insufficiency of medical models of addiction and of a narrowly "scientistic" approach to human meaning and fulfillment generally.[9] We see how, despite its ubiquity, art in our age has become marginalized as a source of lasting regeneration—and not least because art has lost its primal connection with truth, with truth as the *way* of recuperation. "Whatever keeps meanings alive in memory is true. Art can do this."[10] There are chapters on the forgotten importance of smell and gut feelings to our sense of place and identity and on the phenomenological complexity of spatial and temporal dimensions of our identity.[11] Wilshire writes on the role of trance and possession: he speaks of the "angelic possession of walking with my dog."[12] He details the perils of technology and the potential of shamanic healing.[13]

In invoking what we have all but lost, a saving reality becomes present to the receptive imagination, if only for a moment. "Meaning as truth is a benevolent spell—a call to return home to the awesome world that formed us."[14] "Things allowed to emerge in experience and be what they are compose for us a kind of sacrament. This is the deepest freedom for it washes out the deepest blockage to development: dread of disclosure."[15] In Wilshire's evocations of primal hungers and primal satisfactions, we feel our own deep selves awakened as the world about us dawns.

II

The contemporary addiction array includes eating disorders (bolemia, anorexia), compulsive shopping (and shoplifting), obsessive sexual fetishes or rituals, heavy drinking and drug dependency, excessive gambling, workaholism, and nicotine, caffeine, and sugar dependencies.

---

[8] Ibid., Chapter 8.
[9] Ibid., Chapters 6 and 7.
[10] Ibid., Chapter 10, 178.
[11] Ibid., Chapters 2 and 9.
[12] Ibid., Chapter 7, 131.
[13] Ibid., Chapter 12, and Conclusion.
[14] Ibid., 183.
[15] Ibid., 178.

We reach for a second piece of pie as if possessed, as if a ghost extended our arm. We fleetingly consider returning an extravagantly priced book but quickly give in to the somewhat alien force that would have us buy. We remember someone close to us in the grip of shoplifting; another is a jogging junkie. These moments of partial, strange compulsion rob life of meaning and pleasure. Only half-desired, the extra slice tastes slightly rotten. Purchased against prudence, the book seems fugitive, not fully ours. There's no end to what our shoplifter grasps, his or her desire never satisfied. The symptoms of addiction are familiar: a repetitive, recurrent need or hunger that seems insatiable, out of control, and destructive of what, in better moments, we realize is best for us.[16] Wilshire conceives of addictions as abortive, false starts mimicking a legitimate quest for ecstatic experience. It's as if the world of the addict gets flattened, drained of the several, alternative rich sources of ecstasy, say in music, fulfilling work, or wilderness experience. In such a flattened world, all that remains is a cheap, momentary, and ultimately destructive fix.

As opposed to a pleasure-fix, rich ecstasy impacts sensation, emotion, and mood, each of these modulated by imagination, intellect, and action. A sunset will rivet the eyes, frame the fiery heavens, and force one into awe; or it will whisper gently, sing of all things infinite, and cradle the willing soul; or it will move one to reach for a camera, a pad and pen, a friend's hand. Its poor substitute, the addictive, *ersatz* version of ecstasy, of "getting outside oneself," jolts one's senses momentarily but offers no prod to elaboration in wider worlds of emotion and mood. There is no potential in the sensate impact for ritual or artistic re-creation. One's thought, affect, and action remain largely disengaged and hence isolated from a world that can sustain meaning or satisfy the complex structure of human needs.

Beyond those of "mere" physical survival, the rich complex of human needs that gets thwarted in the flattened world of addiction is summarized by Wilshire. There is

> the need for exploratory movement and for a wide variety of stimuli to incite and reward it; for sharing in the group's placing of itself in the World-whole,

---

[16] Wilshire links addiction to the sense of "compulsion" and lack of control and to patterns destructive of life. He avers, "If the ingestion of these [drugs] is a necessary condition for actions that are in fact constructive and meaningful in the long run for selves and the world of which they are members, they are not addictive, I believe." 105.

its origin stories. And then despite deep cultural and cosmical identification, a need to develop what each of us is in addition, an individual being.[17]

And he continues:

> Sensuous and graphic—frequently playful—satisfaction of these needs is intrinsically valuable and ecstatic, and imparts to us a conviction of our significance and vitality as persons. Taken as a whole our primal need as bodily selves is to *be*, fully through time, in cycles of exertion and restoration, probing exploration and recollection: to progressively discover our being in the wide world, not just to have it, as if it were a possession.[18]

These are the needs that are increasingly denied in a fast-paced, technological, bureaucratic, and careerist culture.

III

Wilshire invites us to change our philosophical worldview. To that end, he provides data from psychology, sociology, and anthropology. He provides moving autobiographical passages, and a sustained critique of pervasive philosophical presumptions, academic and cultural. He promotes the promise—and necessity—of a broadly phenomenological standpoint as a way of understanding human existence in all its dimensions and depths. The underpinnings of this broad critique are already visible in the struggle of the American philosopher William James to come to terms with the depth of experience, especially in its ecstatic dimensions. Appreciating Wilshire's long-standing absorption in James allows us to see not only the genesis of central themes in *Wild Hunger* but also to see the sense in which the vision Wilshire invites us to embrace is a distinctively philosophical and American vision.

It is as if Wilshire has excavated ever-deeper strata of philosophical experience, beginning with turn-of-the-century European phenomenology, digging back to its links to James, then finding still deeper connections between James and early-nineteenth-century German Romantic philosophy (especially Schelling), and at last establishing the link between themes crisscrossing in these traditions and themes in the wisdom of hunter–gatherer, Paleolithic, or "primal" societies.[19]

---

[17] Ibid., xii.
[18] Ibid.
[19] Ibid., 93.

This itinerary suggests that Wilshire s account of primal philosophy is meant to be read not only as a plea to reconsider the depth of Native American thought and practice but also as another and crucial step in a dialogue between American and continental philosophy that begins with Emerson's influence on Nietzsche and James's influence on Husserl. This dialogue continues through Husserl's influence on the neglected Harvard philosopher W. E. Hocking and then Hocking's influence on the French philosopher Gabriel Marcel. It proceeds with the indebtedness of Marcel to the Harvard/Montana philosopher of wilderness, Henry Bugbee, and the indebtedness of Bugbee to Marcel.

At this point, we have another step in this trans-Atlantic dialogue that stretches out over more than a century. We have Wilshire's own marshaling of the work of James and Husserl, Emerson and Merleau-Ponty, in the interest of an appreciative exposure of the lineaments of a Primal philosophy—a philosophy that can be fully articulated only after these earlier phases of an American/Existential-Phenomenological dialogue have been absorbed and understood. It is as if only a much later age is fully ready to understand a much earlier one. I should note that Wilshire provides one of the most thorough and helpful bibliographies that I've seen on the theme of wilderness— in general, as it relates to American thought, then as it relates to psychology and primal thought, and (of course) as it relates to addiction, anomie, and human fulfillment.

Relying on Wilshire's most recent essay on William James, we can lay out key themes linking primal thought, the vision of James, and the view proposed in *Wild Hunger*. His plea, first, is to reject Cartesian dualism. It is just unintelligible to suppose that we can assess and inventory our "inner thoughts" without acknowledging that we are embodied creatures already fully placed in a world. James comes to see that to study human experience in an open way inevitably leads one beyond the classic philosophical-scientific presuppositions that mind and matter must be kept distinctly apart (mind–body dualism) and that in reflecting on experience, the person reflecting must be kept out of the story. James develops a third way between mentalism and materialism, between detached objectivism and fuzzy subjectivism. Thunder is as much in a real world of things apart from me that then suddenly suffuses my consciousness as it is an "impact in my mind." There is no absolute contrast here between "inner and outer," or "mind and matter." More generally, there is no final opposition of persons and their setting: we belong to the world as much as the world belongs to us.

A second theme is the need to set atomism aside. Experience doesn't come in isolated, discrete "bits" but far more holistically, and in ways that blend the focal-point of attention with the spatial and temporal surround. Temporally considered, I don't experience an isolated clap of thunder, but rather a clap emerging out of prior silence and feathered forward into quiet. Spatially, the sound arises not just from the sky above the peak straight ahead, but from an aural canopy that first defines the region behind me as vacant of sound, that rushes toward me and in fact overshoots my position, finally filling all the sky.

Then there is the plea to affirm the aesthetic and visceral aspects of experience. These are in no way "less real" or important than those aspects of experience of interest to a physicist, chemist, or mathematician. The inherent awesomeness of a giant thunderclap is as real as its decibel level or distance from my observation point. Consider the universe as it feels to a diver along a tropical reef, or to a climber from a just-ascended twelve-thousand-feet peak. Consider the world revealed through the music of Handel or the art of Cezanne or the pen of Homer. These alternative worlds illustrate James's pluralism, his conviction that each of these contrasting stretches of human experience is fully as important, fully as revelatory of reality, as anything delivered from the precincts of natural science.

This is related to a fourth strand in his case, the invitation to acknowledge the super-abundance of reality and its "mythic" suggestiveness.[20] There is more to reality than we can know; its "voluminousness" continually overflows our momentary sense of having it in our grasp. "The numinous altogetherness of things animates us lovingly. Our song and theirs are one. We allow ourselves to be addressed and drawn out."[21] Wilshire finds undertones in James's work of "very ancient notions of cyclical, ever-generating life, the dark depths of Earth, interdependence of light and darkness, clarity and vagueness, birth-death-rebirth."[22] And this invitation leads to his last theme, his sense that we have lost, and must reclaim, a taste for "the mysterious" as an encompassing aspect of experience. Wilshire finds James, in his last thoughts, speculating on the possibility of an "Earth-Soul," representing the profound (and fundamentally mysterious) identity of earth-and-spirit.[23] And James speculates on the possibility of moments when

---

[20] Ibid., 199.

[21] Ibid., 183.

[22] *Cambridge Companion*, 107.

[23] Ibid., 120.

the deep past, the fullness of the present, foretastes of the future, and the "otherness" of that which we encounter are caught up simultaneously in a consummatory intimacy that is not just an aberration of experience but revelatory of the truth of our personhood-and-worlds. At last, if we take it so, ours may be a "sacred place" where, embraced in the sacrament of life, we acknowledge our kinship with all living things, with Earth, with our deep past, and with a cyclical, regenerative eternity.[24] One can't avoid resonances, here, with the work of Henry Bugbee—yet Wilshire was to encounter *The Inward Morning* only in 1997, after the essay on James as well *Wild Hunger* were completed.[25]

IV

Healing an addiction-prone world requires a change in vision and a change in practices. The creative, healing link we lack is a **spiritual tie to others, to self, to sustaining Earth, and to an encompassing Whole. "Spiritual" is marked by a double asterisk—Wilshire's innovation—to signal his insistence that "the spiritual" is not non-bodily and "ghostly" (the Cartesian misconception) but part of the expressive, communicative capacities of embodied humans. "The body is **spiritual in its powers of communication, in its abilities to express, recognize, be recognized, and to incorporate others' recognizings. The body is **spiritual in its dangerous interfusions and cycling transactions in the world."[26] As sensate, sensual creatures we are connected to "inner selves," others, and the place we inhabit through a felt-sense of body, place, and meaning. Lacking that connection, or aspects of it, we descend to addictive practices. A quick fix, from whatever source, fills the void we feel when work becomes lifeless, eating becomes a bother or an outright enemy, when conversation becomes chatter, exercise is a chore and our own and other's suffering becomes an unwanted imposition. Lacking the essential **spiritual connections, life is stagnant, dull, routine, a matter alternately of boredom and frightful desperation. The Earth is unsteady beneath our feet, would-be friends flee, the consolations of philosophy or any public achievement

---

[24] Wilshire, *Wild Hunger*, 125, 163, 178, 211.

[25] Wilshire was taken with Bugbee's work, once it came his way, and included a striking essay on *The Inward Morning* in *The Primal Roots of American Philosophy: Pragmatism, Phenomenology, and Native American Thought*, College Park: Penn State University Press, 2000, Chapter 9.

[26] Wilshire, *Wild Hunger*, 141.

are empty. Addiction must be understood, not just medically, or as a sinful moral failing, but against a general background of cultural and individual stagnation and anomie. **Spiritual regeneration is the saving response to our dolorous state of ecstatic deprivation.

The tasks Wilshire thus sets himself are formidable. At the philosophical level, several "paradigm shifts" are required. A Platonic bifurcation of bodily experience from fulfilling experience of the good must be erased in favor of a holism of value-saturated experience. A Christian bifurcation of "the true self" from its physical embodiment must be erased in favor of a body-self open to the **spiritual. A bifurcation splitting the human from an Earth that is conceived only as material for production or exploitation must be healed by something like Emerson's idea of a World-Whole of energy cycles in which we humans can be co-participants. And privileging the patriarchal over the maternal must cease. This is no small order to fill. The default assumptions are not easily dislodged. Even as they are brought into question on a number of contemporary intellectual fronts, they grip the culture in its literary, religious, civic, familial, and economic strata at a depth that makes it almost impossible to shake them loose. They are mutually reinforcing. There is no beholding or pilgrimage or being held. The Cartesian picture of a disembodied self is linked to the view that we surveyors of all things human are detached and shielded from the object of our study, and both pictures are implicit in the view that nature is alien, to be understood only in a reductionistic way as machine-like, devoid of value fit for fully human response. So we must fight the conceptual battles, and the related battles over practice, on several fronts at once. As Wilshire has it, until we relearn our participative place in Nature's cycles of birth and death, of effort and relief, of growth and decline, of sunlight and night skies, we will continue to lead half-lives, stagnant spans of empty, desperate business.

V

We tend to think of addiction, and meaning-deprivation generally, as an individual affair. But Wilshire is aware of the economic, social, and political structures that encourage or discourage propensities for addiction. He leaves ample space to outline the social construction of addiction, and to envision the social edifice that would satisfy ecstatic needs sufficiently to make addiction an anomaly.

Now we might agree that addictions are rooted in the dysfunctions of modern industrial-bureaucratic society and "cured" through renewed access to wild experience, in art or wilderness, in ambulatory or gastronomic experience, in imitation of the lives of primal peoples. But it's also highly probable that ecstatic deprivation has roots in the loss of fulfilling intimate or familial relationships, the absence of rich work experience, or in the harsh realities of grinding poverty. Nothing Wilshire writes excludes the parallel, complementary debilitating effect of such factors in the lives of ever-so-many inhabitants of "advanced societies."

The vision Wilshire evokes is of the embodied self at home and vibrantly alive amidst the wonders of earth and sky and each day—the lineaments of a primal world. But suggesting, as a practical proposal, the retrieval of a hunter–gatherer's awe-filled world as a way to stem a pandemic of addictions seems all too close to fantasy, a philosopher's pipe dream. Perhaps it's a Thoreauvian fantasy, or the dream of a modern shaman.[27] But in any case, it's hardly likely to veer the massive course of politics or culture. So we might think.

Consider a paradox of Wilshire's account. Say we concede that our daily lives become deadened in a technologically driven, consumerist and dangerously exploitative economic juggernaut. And say we concede that its regimen shatters vast regions of experience otherwise available for life, insuring alienation from restorative, ecstatic connection to nature's cycles and our own rich needs and hungers for the wild. Precisely to the extent that we concede this picture, the possibility of reversing the momentum of these trends seems correspondingly a hopeless cause. If we face a juggernaut of these proportions, then our confidence that we can reconnect to primal roots on any scale large enough to stem the wash of meaning-deprivation and addiction is seriously undermined. But I think Wilshire can respond to this apparent conundrum. And his response here also bears on the fear that his suggestion of a return to primal roots is fantasy.

He can ask us to consider—consider carefully—the alternative. It seems to be some form of despair, capitulation, or cynical detachment. But *must* we abdicate what freedom we retain in resigned accommodation to this shattering of the human?

Given the bleakness of the alternative, we should at least give this vision an honest chance. In fact, at times the closeness of this

---

[27] Wilshire, *Wild Hunger*, 49, 93.

liberating vision is palpable. In reflective moments we may come to believe that our present malaise can be transcended. It is this sliver of hope that fuels Wilshire's vision, and our own hope in reading him. This is not at last a pessimistic book. It finds heart in Black Elk, in Emerson, Thoreau, James, and Dewey; it finds heart in the simple pleasures of walking, eating, embracing; it finds heart in recuperative memories of childhood and yesterday, in the primal stories of origins and in the ancient counsel of elders; it finds heart in great art and in attunement to the restorative cycles of an undomesticated wild.

Throughout, Wilshire reverts to short, autobiographical interludes that bring home hope through the intimacy of first-person testimony. He confides his own epiphanies, encounters with a saving wild, struggles with mastering compulsions, moments of ecstatic tenderness and healing, encounters with life-depleting academic walls, restorative ambles with his dog, shamanic image-journeys. Through these confiding revelations, what might otherwise be framed as an abstract general problem (not mine, but largely one for others) is converted to something I can see as *my* problem, and hence amenable to healing through my initiative, however meager that effort might seem in world-historical terms. A general, abstract wisp of hope for restoration can lodge as a deep hope I can feel in my bones. And if one wants more, then one can follow Thoreau in knowing that if enough readers feel hope in their bones, a tide will rise to float an Empire.[28]

---

[28] "[a] tide rises and falls behind every man which can float the British Empire like a chip", *Walden*, chapter 18.

Chapter 9

HENRY JAMES—AN ETHICS OF INTIMATE CONVERSATION:
Is the Unacknowledged Life Worth Living?

Robert Pippin joins a distinguished line of recent Anglophone philosophers who find "the ancient quarrel" between philosophy and
literature (or poetry) somewhat *passé*. In his remarkable book on
Henry James, we find literature and philosophy engage with equal
passion the questions of moral skepticism, of the reigning ideals of an
age, of the sources of unfreedom, the formation of a meaningful life,
and the centrality of reciprocal acknowledgments and affections in the
establishment of an identity one can call one's own. Over the years,
Pippin has provided fresh and meticulous readings of Kant, Hegel,
Nietzsche, and Heidegger, and of the wide-screen phenomena of
modernity. Now, as a further inquiry into modernity, and as an expression of his love of the literature in its own right, he plunges into the
exquisitely contoured inner landscapes that Henry James both travels
and dissects. Pippin composes a seamless rapprochement between
genres, between the novels written to entertain (and morally inform
and explore) and a philosophical sensibility attuned to a tension
between ethics conceived as imposition or acceptance of rules or
guides or of exemplary virtues, and ethics as a subtle quality of
conscience revealed in intimate conversational exchange.

I. Achieving Moral Weight

Personal acknowledgments and mutual recognitions are central
themes in Pippin's account of the moral tone and accomplishments of
James' more admirable characters. In the articulation of these themes,

we hear echoes of a neo-Humean emphasis on care and sympathy, and of Hegelian master–servant scenarios, or of Sartrean scenarios of would-be lovers struggling for recognition in a zero-sum game—the gain of one immediately offset by a loss to the other, making the hope of mutuality a dismal futility. Interest in the interpersonal, in the development of an "inner" life through personal exchange, accounts, I think, for American fascination with British "upstairs–downstairs" films (*Howard's End*, or *Remains of the Day*, or even the adaptation of James' *Wings of the Dove*), a fascination that seems to mourn and sentimentalize a class-tradition and a tradition of leisurely conversation alien to a busy America.

Major claims in *Henry James and Modern Moral Life* are that moral freedom relies on my capacity to answer the question what my life might mean to me—an answer I can believe in; that I will arrive at such an answer through a subtle expansion of consciousness; and that this expansion is part and parcel of my acknowledgment and enactment of dependence on others.[1] Quite early on, Pippin suggests that contrary to Kantians, Aristotelians, and Utilitarians, "the key issue in morality might not be the rational justifiability with which I treat others but the proper acknowledgment of and enactment of a dependence on others without which the process of any justification (any invocation of common normative criteria at all) could not begin."[2] And toward the end of his investigations, he follows through with the thought that morality might be

> the cultivation of a kind of understanding, imagination, taste, awareness, felt life, that amounts to the fullest achievement of freedom . . . the freedom at issue does not involve the exercise of will, the absence of constraints, or the satisfactions of interests or desires . . . it involves an expanse of understanding, and so finally in one's life, a greater capacity both to take account of others better, and just thereby to be oneself. This is an expanse so subtle, so delicate, that it has no real content, no real new thing one learns, no straightforward moral truth.[3]

Following James' lead, Pippin holds that achieving moral weight and meaning in one's life rests not on a simple assumption of rational autonomy or fundamental self-interest matured by formal enlightened

---

[1] Robert B. Pippin, *Henry James and Modern Moral Life*, Cambridge: Cambridge University Press, 2000.

[2] Ibid., 10.

[3] Ibid., 175.

discourse, but on attaining and exercising a rich subjectivity consisting in a heartfelt acknowledgment of multiple and mutual dependencies enacted in intimate contexts of exchange far from public forums of legalistic or philosophical debate.

II. MODERN MORAL LIFE

Pippin returns repeatedly to "issues of modernity" of concern to James, issues that motivate his sketch of morals based on mutual acknowledgments, and that in many ways make his "moral voice" unique, or at least, of special interest. Among these issues, listed here in increasing order of intricacy, are (1) the importance of freedom as an inescapable value presupposed in any action we could call our own; (2) the diminished valorization of will, mistakenly seen as an intervention in the otherwise "natural" (and "hence" unfree) formation of a moral life; (3) the correspondingly increased importance of a willingness to acknowledge our "necessary others"; (4) the pervasiveness of an anxiety, sometimes verging on skepticism, about the force of moral claims on us; (5) the pervasive and philosophically under-appreciated difficulty of knowing one's own wishes, desires, and actions "as really mine"—and not merely pale imprints of another's desires, or fragments of a whirl of desires, responses, or beliefs circulating like media images and sound bites in an anonymous social milieu; (6) the haunting confrontation with finitude, facing two unnerving thoughts in particular, first, that irresolvable moral conflict tracks a moral life inevitably, both deeply animating and deeply scaring it; and, second, that insight, wisdom, or reconciliation come always partially and too late, in the mode of my living what "will have been" my life in shared memory's retrospect, rather than living it in an "immediate" pastless or fully present time or in an inviting future prospect.

III. DEVELOPMENTAL NARRATIVES

In Pippin's view, these facets of Jamesian "modern moral life" are not merely threads in those novels so fascinating to James aficionados. They are as close as one can come to a faithful description of that mobile, uprooted, electric, and dangerously alienating (yet not hopeless) condition we now call "modernity." Characterizing "modernity" is not offering a "moral theory" but offering a sketch of the broad issues

and conditions any theory meant to engage "modernity" must confront. This sketch underlies the Jamesian picture of morality as a
crucial expansion of imaginative vision, as a way of seeing or understanding in a better, more truthful way, a dilation of moral vision that
is established cooperatively in close relationships of mutuality. And
there are interesting parallels between James' characterizations of
"modernity" and the attaining of a moral life within its context, and a
familiar story of "modern moral theory" in German idealism.

In his essays on history, politics, and anthropology, Kant sets aside
his architectonic, demonstrative expositions to adopt a *developmental*
style of tracing philosophical ideas. Hegel takes up this methodologi-
cally historical, "biographical" unfolding of moral concepts as the *only*
proper way to gain insight into the meaning of moral concepts and
moral life more generally.[4] Such moral phenomena are themselves
constitutive of, and realized in, the context that "carries" them. So it's
not the case that we can initially develop a non-moral context and then
place moral "elements" "in" it. Moral phenomena cannot be "stripped
off" an historical/biographical context, any more than context can be
"stripped off" the phenomena contextualized.

For Hegel, ideas of freedom, slavery, inequality, resignation,
"unhappy consciousness," family life, or civil society are not static,
"eternal essences" or abstract principles but possibilities, ideals, and
assumptions that gain substance as they become actualized in concrete
practices of specific times and places. This means that philosophy,
in Hegel and subsequently in Nietzsche and Heidegger, unfolds as a
narrative meant to capture the "struggle" of its ideas and assumptions
for historical "recognition" and practical embeddedness. Analogues
to Hegel's stress on the historical unfolding of life-meanings are found
in Kierkegaard's stress on temporality and repetition, Nietzsche's
favoring a "genealogical" style, Heidegger's stress on "historicity," and
even Wittgenstein's advice to unravel confusion by tracing its elements
back to a Heraclitean "flow of (human) life" that is itself rooted in
"natural history."[5]

---

[4] See, e.g., Kant's "Idea for a Universal History from a Cosmopolitan Point of View,"
in *Kant's Political Writings*, ed. Hans Reiss, Cambridge: Cambridge University Press,
1970.

[5] David G. Stern notes Wittgenstein's early use of "flow of life" for the phenomena
that in *Philosophical Investigations* became "forms of life." See his *Wittgenstein on Mind
and Language*, Oxford: Oxford University Press, 1995. "Natural history" is an explicit
term of art in *Investigations*.

Henry James has no avowed systematic philosophical intentions. He places the desire to entertain first on his list of narrative objectives. He invites us to enjoy an arresting drama of issues of "recognition" and "identity" unfolding among the restricted upper-class, wealthy, sophisticated cast of characters whose doings, sufferings, and reflections James describes in painstaking detail. Yet Pippin shows the unfailing currents of philosophical exploration flowing crisscross through the multiple surfaces of these narratives. Someone skeptical of a novel's capacity to deliver a philosophic point of view will be skeptical about the claim that it can carry a theory of moral development that is more than shallow and impressionistic. But in Pippin's hands, what is at first of primarily aesthetic, psychological, or superficial social consequence emerges as a philosophical stream of moral insight that becomes increasingly translucent and convincing.

IV. RECIPROCITY OF RECOGNITION AND RESPONSE

Morality, as Pippin has it, concerns what we owe each other. In the Jamesean context, this amounts to "owing each other a mutuality and reciprocity of recognition" that makes a life, a moral life, something we can acknowledge and hold as our own.[6] This conception of mutual recognition at the heart of moral sensibility revises or replaces familiar alternatives. It is not a claim that our mutual benefit requires rules of cooperation and coordination of effort. Nor is it a claim that each of us is of equal worth "in the eyes of God," nor a promotion of excellence of character. Perhaps in a quasi-Kantian sense, we recognize each other as beings capable of forming our own ends deserving of respect. But this would be only a small part of the story for James, and could not include the Kantian thought that it is a rational autonomy alone that underlies the capacity to form ends or adopt life plans or embark on meaning-giving projects.

For James, what we owe each other (morality) does not rest on agreement about the outcomes of chains of moral reasoning. It rests on a capacity for shared understandings of who and where we are, understandings negotiated from the heart, involving a kind of concerned imaginative discernment-and-response nourished in intimate encounters among mutually caring persons.

---

[6] Ibid., 176.

Of course if persons are to attain "lives of their own" and the capacity to reciprocate moral recognition and concern, we must assume political, social, and economic structures that embody protective rules with incentives and sanctions to support them. But James is after something deeper that such political and legal protections (and their moral counterparts). He finds the roots of morality in conditions of mutual vulnerability and open acknowledgment of the other, where a "movement of consciousness" or a "gestural–conversational exchange" occurs—when something like a founding promise of mutual trust occurs. Mutual trust will underlie humane social contracts.[7]

This is a primordial moment of mutual entrusting of each to the other's care, sealed, as it were, by a recognition that each is morally bound by a promise to the other. And this moment precedes and for the time being bypasses the formulation of specifically moral imperatives, rights, goals, or rules. Furthermore, it can only happen under conditions of mutual understanding that are themselves problematic, fragile, and elusive. It is not abstract persons who entrust themselves to each other, recognize something owed to each other, but particular complex and mobile individuals whose identify is shifting and at risk. Yet for mutual acknowledgment to occur, we must each "know" each other in each other's light.

Can this be a version of Hume's picture of morality as resting on relations of personal sympathy? It might seem that the view Pippin finds in James could be located within a philosophical tradition that stresses native sympathy for others. On this view, the content of the recognition each owes the other, or the content brought about by such mutual recognition, is the principle that we must acknowledge that the other can suffer, and that the response demanded of moral agents is fitting compassion or concern. But from a Jamesean point of view, such a characterization of moral recognition fails to bring out what is central to "modern moral life," in at least two broad respects.

V. The Art of Receptive Response

The necessity of persons to cultivate an ever-more refined attention to each other, to attain a "better" moral vision of a shared circumstance, reminds one of the picture Iris Murdoch and Simone Weil develop of

---

[7] See chapter 3, 39. Contracts signed under threat or duress are another matter; let's say they're "inhumane".

moral consciousness requiring the cultivation of a more loving, accurate, and delicate perception. When James is dealing with his better moral characters (not his villains), he seems to locate their moral shortfalls in a lack of a sufficiently refined consciousness more than in a lack of native sympathy toward others. Their moral flaws seem not just familiar failures of the will to muster adequate response but failures to *see*, or to see enough of the relevantly complex *aspects* of, the suffering of others close at hand. In addition, their moral flaws involve failure to engage a repertoire of response adequately modulated to the contours of the case at hand.

Both seeing more and cultivating a more apt response depend on a subtle expansion of consciousness and imagination. We might say that our moral challenge is in part to activate sympathy, but just as much, to perceive where sympathy is needed, especially where suffering is hidden or disguised or counterfeit. And we might take the other, responsive half of our challenge as not so much to remember *that* compassion is required, as to know *how*, and in what dose, it is to be delivered.

Hardheartedness in disregarding what one could not fail to notice—evident poverty or ill-health or grief—is easy to latch onto and condemn. Less easy to grasp and judge is failure that arises by overlooking or only half-seeing ambiguous or occluded suffering in the labyrinths of subjectivity—including the half-seeing, half-refusing of a "fellow-sufferer" (as Schopenhauer would put it) that is linked to, or a consequence of, a loss of the sense that one inhabits a subjectivity one could call one's own. It may take an exceptionally cultivated eye to see suffering in another, and an exceptionally imaginative person to orchestrate an apt, sensitive, compassionate response. And at times, there may be no compassionate response available beyond the bare acknowledgment that such suffering exists.

VI. CULTIVATING SUBJECTIVITY

We've been considering an important limitation to attributing to James the familiar moral proposition that what we owe each other is simply a concerned response to suffering. The familiar proposition gives insufficient attention to the difficult arts of seeing and responding sympathetically. And there is a second broad limitation to consider. The proposition that we owe each other compassionate response as "fellow sufferers" does not bring out the important presupposition that there must exist a "we"—better, an "I"—of sufficient moral weight to support or embody the art of seeing and responding to another's hurt. As we've already indirectly noted, it is persons of some subjective self-trust, certitude, and courage who alone have hope of developing eyes to see the often cloistered sufferings of others in close quarters, and the skill to respond aptly. But how could I lose subjectivity, fail to see my life as *mine*?

I may acknowledge an "identity of record"—acknowledge this month and day and year as my birthday, that as my graduation date, this job as the source of my income, that child as my son. But even after establishing such a lengthy record, I might sense that in a deeper sense, none of these "facts" coheres in a narrative of a life that has meaning to me. The open question remains after that identity of record is established: what does that life mean to *me*? And that "open question" highlights the possibility that the life others take as mine is to me not felt as mine—not, perhaps, felt as a life worth living, not, perhaps, felt as a life with any hold on me.

How could I lose the sense that I have a life that I can call my own? It could happen because the life "staged" is not one felt to correspond to anything I could identity with, as if God (or "fate," or "society") had assigned me roles I could only passably play, or roles I resented having to play, or because I yearned for an off-stage role, as well as those exposed, public roles that I'd been assigned. It could happen because I sensed that another was living out the life that was properly mine (Salieri seeing Mozart), or because I thought that each and every role offered, by the very nature of the case, was mere "play-acting," and that "having a life of one's own" was in general a grand illusion, fraud, or fantasy.

A capacity to see others and respond caringly waxes and wanes with a capacity to see one's life as one's own. If I lose a felt sense of meaning or center or cohesion in my experience, if the life I lead seems *not* my own, or not *sufficiently* my own, then I suffer loss of soul but also loss of any site from which to launch discernments of another's suffering or start gestures of compassionate response. In order to *see* sufferings in the labyrinth of another's subjectivity (or to muster apt response), I must already have attained a life possessed of sufficient subjective weight and complexity to be owned as the life I lead, and hence the life from which I can acknowledge another's pain. Pippin captures this view in his remarks on Strether's, efforts, in *The Ambassadors*, to be truer both to others and to himself. "It is in exploring the possibilities of this sort of awareness and so of an expanded and more powerful subjectivity, that the Jamesean question of morality—the nature of our affirmative, meaning-constituting dependence on others, and what we owe them in the light of that link—arises."[8]

Pippin calls this responsive movement of acknowledgment an "expanded and more powerful subjectivity" (or understanding) that is, as we've seen earlier, "so subtle, so delicate, that it has no real content, no real new thing one learns, no straightforward moral truth." This "movement" is subtle because there are no—or no clearly explicit—things to do, as a "matter of public record" or principle, in order to enact this acknowledgment. I can seem to acknowledge another, yet not have my heart in it. I can seem to be responsive to another, as if she mattered, yet in fact be taking something else to matter. A classic swamp of Jamesean perplexity arises as an ensemble of characters try to sift through a mix of base attachments to another's status or money or aesthetic allure in search of some more worthy basis of attachment, say love or friendship, if these in fact exist.

Due to the complexity of moral engagements, and due to endless doubts about what my own motives and desires are, and what those of my close associates are, there is often nothing like a convincing account, from either the first or third personal perspective, of what would count as such a requisite acknowledgment. For that reason (its invisibility or elusiveness from a third person standpoint), such acknowledgment, if it exists, might seem irrelevant philosophically. But that would hold only if philosophy could never point beyond third-person pictures of "the real." We rely here on literature's capacity to awaken our first personal resonances with testimony and insight.

I "get what it means" not to have had "my heart in it," or not to have a clear perception of my shifting moral entanglements, or to sense that the life I lead is "not my own" but only the performance of a public or family script, in a way that is extremely hard to spell out conceptually. It's like the difficulty of giving a detailed account of the difference between a flat, indifferent understanding of something and the "eureka" gestalt experience where nothing new is learned, but suddenly my understanding snaps alive. I see an aspect (as in a reversible "duck-rabbit") that I was previously blind to. I can lack, or be blind to, a connection to my life and its entanglements, and then, through a "subtle expansion of consciousness," suddenly "get" what it means "existentially" to "own" my life—even as I stammer to say what exactly I've gained.

---

[8] Ibid., 175.

In addition, as we've seen, this expansion of consciousness can be subtle because my self-conception is shifting, fragile, incomplete, and sometimes in abeyance. When *who* I am depends so much, as it does under conditions of modernity, on the unreliable and shifting sense of who others take me to be, grasping "my life as my own" will be indeed a subtle, hidden, movement, and not at all an explicitly public, and thus easily identifiable exercise of self-recognition.

VII. UNCERTAIN RECOGNITIONS: ANCIENTS VERSUS MODERNS

Considering what is at stake in forming selves capable of moral regard brings into focus what we could call the "start-up" dilemma of modern moral self-formation: 1) only a person properly recognized, acknowledged by another, has the resources in imagination and secure subjectivity for proper moral response to another's need; 2) modern society is precisely the place where conditions for self-certitude or stable subjectivity, and for imaginative insight into the subjectivity of others, are at risk, fragile at best, and in no case assuredly reliable.[9]

This dilemma accounts for the pervasive sense in James' novels and stories that even the most insightful characters continually "get each other wrong," fail in their capacity to see each other truthfully, yet do not by that failure fail utterly as moral agents. Moral agents, it seems, must in some sense strive for the impossible, a reasonably untarnished moral bill of health, knowing full well the futility of the project, yet continuing to so strive, nonetheless.

A sense of pervasive moral failure is coupled in James to an equally pervasive sense that his characters live, as Pippin has it, in "stalled time," waiting for something to happen, waiting for some decisive event or encounter or revelation that will mark their release from what seems to be but a shadow of life, a theatrical shell scripted by others. They suffer the subtle bondage of lacking a subjectivity worthy of the name.

In "modernity" the urgency of mutual recognition becomes especially salient because there is so little else on which to base our sense that to ourselves, the life we lead is in fact our own. God's will,

---

[9] The "start-up" conundrum is conflict among (1) "the unsatisfactoriness of many modern forms of dependence, which makes having a one's own life impossible"; (2) "the impossibility of any final independence"; and (3) the acknowledgment of "forms of dependence that realize rather than qualify one's freedom," 157.

Tradition, the Moral Law, My Station and its Duties, Love of Neighbor, Rational Self-Interest, seem insufficient to dispel a sense of moral ambiguity or absence. Yet skepticism, cynicism, or resignation—or reversion to pre-modern Revelations of Truth—seem unattractive alternatives (to say the least).

A modern need for mutual recognition has a distinct cast that distinguishes it, for example, from our oldest tales of recognition and mutual acknowledgment, say, as central to homecoming, to finding, or renewing one's life. The story of Odysseus's return, the story of who Odysseus *is* unfolds as a series of mutual recognitions. There is the poignant scene where Odysseus' glance of recognition is reciprocated in the glance of Argos, the master's dog, who now can die at peace, their relationship complete, its aspects of loyalty, care, and mutual protection now renewed. In the arbor at the outskirts of the palace Odysseus encounters his father; each is solidified, affirmed, completed in mutual recognition. Odysseus' childhood nurse recognizes the old scar on his thigh, enacting yet another moment of mutual recognition. Odysseus and Telemachus secure their identities through ceremonies of recognition, and there is the culminating instance of mutual recognition when Penelope tests him (perhaps cruelly) by spinning a tale about their marriage bed having been moved to another room, while all along Odysseus knows its headboard is carved from an earth-rooted oak, and so can't have been moved. In his rage she knows finally that this is her husband who knows her as only one who shares a marriage bed can know her. With each ceremony of mutual recognition, Odysseus becomes specifically defined, as father to his son, son to his father, ruler to his household, husband to his wife. Yet these are not modern, Jamesian recognitions.

Through repeated recognitions Odysseus is reestablishing a stature formerly securely held, and hence renewing an established identity that (though measured in decades) is in merely temporary abeyance. On his return, his identity must be meticulously confirmed. But *what* the identity is that needs confirmation is not in question. In James, the ceremonies of mutual recognition are much more subtle, problematic, and fragile, for they do not confirm established identities but attempt to articulate uncertain identities whose shape is tentative, underway, in transit. There is, for them, no solid self to return to, only a less fragile or fragmented or alienated self to hope for, to fleetingly glimpse, to momentarily and only partially, only problematically, attain.

There is a recurrent fear in James of a void, a "black hole" sucking in all meaning, of being not just troubled or conflicted in one's identity, but of being literally nothing, or no one. There is almost a hint that experiencing the loss of any sense of self (a kind of Kierkegaardian despair) might be a prerequisite or prelude to coming for the first time to see others, and feel oneself that one had an identity to call one's own. Odysseus may be wounded, even defeated, but the experience of becoming a void, in a Kierkegaardian, Kafkaesque, or Sartrean sense, is not on his horizon of dangerous risks or misadventures.

The scope of "modernity" seems relatively unexplored in Pippin's book. Clearly James' characters are meant to be modernity's exemplars. But that does not address the wider issues. Pippin claims, for example, that alienation is the paradigmatic *modern* form of unfreedom. But who will qualify as "modern"? Christian or Islamic or Israeli Jewish fundamentalists can despise the achievements of western modernism. At what point do the communitarian, secessionist, and linguistically exclusivist aims of the Quebecois place them outside the camp of "modern morals"? Do third-generation rural Montana farm families (subject to one of the highest suicide rates in the states) count among modernism's alienated—or count instead as alienated precisely because they *refuse to submit* to specifically modern life (and its alienations)? To what extent are the alienations of Californian "cybertechs" or adolescent "goths" comparable to the alienations faced by James' "upper-crust" protagonists? No doubt it asks too much to have Pippin's account of *Jamesean* modern moral life illuminate those parts of contemporary life that lie outside the Jamesean frame.

That canvas, as we've seen evokes a much more fragile world with characters largely unanchored, or about to slip their anchors. It evokes the loss of the world Odysseus enjoyed, and the loss of unnumbered other worlds outside the vortices of modernity. As Pippin puts it, the novels and stories articulate a "figure of loss, the loss of those forms of social hierarchy, predictability, and expectation that made interpretation, meaning, and some psychological stability and determinacy possible."[10]

VIII. Freedoms, Dependence, and Finitude

In Pippin's account of James there is a tension between claiming freedom as the reigning modern good and giving pride of place to the

---

[10] Ibid., 28.

inescapable and valuable dependencies that both enable our lives to be our own and that underlie the personal acknowledgments that we owe each other. If freedom is our reigning modern ideal, such freedom cannot mean, for James, a self-sufficient, unencumbered autonomy; it must include acknowledging essential dependencies and insufficiencies.

Pippin acknowledges these problematic tensions in the context of *The Portrait of a Lady*:

> Madame Merle's eloquent defense of social forms and mutually reflecting dependencies might turn out not just to be a corrective to any exaggerated hope for "one's own private self" but to be the last word, a Rousseauean nightmare . . . the general problem so often at issue in James [is] the possibility of independence at all.[11]

Yet if James does not resolve this problem decisively, if he leaves the tension powerfully in place as something always, or nearly always, irresolvable—a condition of our finitude and human incompleteness—then what is left of the ideal of freedom? James runs the risk of

> letting the great adventures in endless indeterminacy, hesitation, even retrospective reconstitution of psychological and moral meaning raise a . . . threat that whatever heart is left in the moral importance of such autonomy seems, in the light of such adventures, too weak to do much pumping, too endlessly qualifiable, to serve any real moral . . . purpose.[12]

Perhaps this is just a "modern fate" to live with, not to deny or decry or despair about. It is not nihilism, or moral skepticism, in Pippin's view, to hold both that a moral ideal (such as freedom) "has no unambiguous realization" and also that "the moral dimensions of mutual understanding and appreciation should remain so unresolved and unresolvable."[13] Straddling these tensions can itself amount to a moral achievement, rather than defeat. Acknowledging these

---

[11] Ibid., 127.

[12] Ibid. In the full text, Jamesian autonomy threatens to become "too endlessly qualifiable to serve any real moral judgmental purpose." I've deleted the qualifier "judgment" because for Pippin (as well as for James) the emphasis seems always more on the shared conditions that make judgment possible than directly on the detail of judgments with their justifications.

[13] Ibid., 157.

difficult-to-swallow facts can, in Pippin's words, "already amount to an appropriate moral stance."[14]

We seek freedom from want, fear, threat to life, limb and property, and seek the more elusive freedom to be ourselves. The conditions presupposed by a freedom to be ourselves would include possessing enough capital and leisure to consider more than survival needs, to consider and to explore the meaning our lives might have for us. And these conditions would include access to cultural resources—in the case of James' characters, art, travel, libraries, parks—resources sufficient to allow life more nourishment than the minimal needed for survival.

But for James, these freedoms are backdrop assumptions, part of the essential stage setting, not the drama center-stage.

> The acknowledgment of the necessary role of material independence and the acceptance of the benefits of chance does not amount to a profound answer on James' part to the question [of the conditions of having a life of one's own]. It accepts the injustices of luck quickly, almost indifferently, and moves on . . .[15]

The central drama concerns the contrasting freedom to be ourselves, to have, in Pippin's phrase, a life of our own. Thus a case for freedom as the reigning modern ideal rests largely on linking freedoms from poverty, affliction, or alienation, to the freedom to lead a life of our own. This raises several issues.

IX. FREEDOM A REIGNING IDEAL

The broad deployment of freedom as a reigning ideal exposes a puzzle—not an intractable one, but a puzzle nonetheless—at the heart of the James–Pippin account. Consider the idea that acknowledging dependencies is an expression of freedom, or an instantiation of at least part of the ideal of freedom. Will this make freedom (paradoxically) an achievement of *dependence*, rather than an achievement of independence? How can these apparently opposing factors be reconciled?

Perhaps dependence is the *ground* of independence—or heteronomy, the ground of autonomy. A case for this position might start

---

[14] Ibid.

[15] Ibid., 175.

from the observation that the ground of autonomous adulthood is satisfactory childhood relationships of dependency; so in that sense dependence might be seen as the developmental ground of freedom or autonomy. Hegel has been seen as advancing such a view on the grandest historical scale.[16] One reading of enlightenment traditions takes moral maturity to be an unambiguous development away from the dominance or tutelage of others toward a state of autonomy: we give the moral law to ourselves, rather than rest in dependence on others to give it to us.[17] Yet a theological ethics—to take one example of a pre-modern position—can provide clues for the non-theistic position James unfolds. Finding ourselves dependent on God highlights the human virtues of trust, accepting guidance, patience to listen to and await cues from another, non-aggrandizing service. Jamesean dependence might be explored in relation to this Augustinian sense that we are derivative creatures, or the Kierkegaardian sense that our "self-relation" is "grounded in another." This is far from the American notion of freedom as solitary independence.

The tension between dependence and freedom can be approached from another angle, one that brings us closer to the sorts of cases James is concerned with. Take the case of romantic love. It might seem (1) that I am most free to be myself (a Jamesian ideal) when, (2) in the midst of love, I yield my freedom to another (a romantic ideal).[18] In Pippin's idiom, I might say that in enacting a dependence on the one I love, I achieve a kind of freedom to be myself. This example can diminish the puzzle about freedom being grounded in dependence (though hardly any thoughtful person supposes that the phenomena of dependence and freedom and love can ever be rendered perfectly transparent). Softening the puzzle of "dependence/independence" in these ways lessens one objection to deploying freedom broadly as the reigning modern ideal, but it simultaneously exposes a second focus of contention.

---

[16] See essays by Alan Wood, Kenneth Westphal, and Pippin in *The Cambridge Companion to German Idealism*, ed. Karl Ameriks, Cambridge, Cambridge University Press, 2000.

[17] See, most famously, Kant's "What is Enlightenment?" in *Kant's Political Writings*.

[18] Pippin suggests that the overall shape of the novels might be summarized as a search both for freedom and for love, and the recognition that these ends might be incompatible. Ibid., 29.

X. THE DEPTH OF DEPENDENCE

If the James–Pippin view is that modernity is marked by aspirations to freedom that can be achieved only in acknowledgments and enactments of dependencies, why conclude that the reigning modern ideal is freedom? The major reality we must struggle to recognize, or at least cease trying to dodge, is not freedom but dependence. This is a need for intimate relations, for nourishing the self, and also for nourishing a "moral dimension" contained in those revelatory conversations that uphold whatever sense of moral worth we can muster.

> While much of this moral dimension involves the importance of the possibility of one's action being justifiable to those whom such actions effect, . . . the criteria for such acceptance or mutual recognition have nothing to do with natural law, the wisdom of tradition, the approval of the community, religious scripture or religious feeling, pure practical reason, the resolution of class conflict, or some benchmark like a *phronimos*, an experienced man of practical wisdom. In effect, all the major characters are walking a high wire with lots of normative turbulence but without any safety net, *dependent wholly on each other and their own talk and negotiations and perceptions* for balance.[19]

If the power of the Pippin–James notion of dependence can be developed in a way that for the most part *sidesteps* the issue of freedom, this fact should give us pause—especially in the present case where the apparent project is to make freedom and dependency conceptually interdependent. The centrality of dependence rests on the insight that to lead a life that is ours requires an ongoing process of mutual suggestion, exploration, and confirmation, conducted, in large part, in intimate relationships. In addition, the meanings that can make our lives something we can endorse are not pieces of private manufacture but "common property" shaped or left to lie fallow or decay by their placement within a social field of practices.

The meaning of a handshake (among friends) or a comma (within a sentence) emerges not from a single individual's solitary, self-legislating intentions, but from that person's participation in a practice that will secure this meaning, or deny it, or ambiguate it. For me to meaningfully shake another's hand or mark a clause by commas requires that I acknowledge the matrix of social practices that give these "gestures" meaning, and hence allow them to have meaning *for me*. Of course not all handshakes or commas need to have much meaning. But the

---

[19] Ibid., 35; my emphasis.

possibility of their having *any* meaning requires a dependence on others, and the field of mutual endeavor. If the handshake registers my sadness in departing a dear friend, or if the comma lets the poem to my friend become more apt, then we can begin to see how meanings for our lives are not self-crafted but, as it were, borrowed from a common store of meanings not of my making and not at all my private property. Thus the life that unfolds as having meaning of a sort I can recognize as the story of my life, and potentially, of my freedom, rests not on my primal independence but on my dependencies.

Meaning bestowed, made available as what can make my life my own, is not delivered precisely as a title or honor might be ceremonially bestowed. But the analogy can help. I can receive an honor ceremonially only if I recognize the power of such ceremony to in fact bestow meaning and honor. That means acknowledging my *dependence* both on those who occupy the key roles in honor-bestowal and on the powers of the ceremony itself. If my hunch is correct, Pippin–James see conversations of intimacy as the informal but profoundly crucial sites for meaning-exchange and renewal, and our participation in exchange of word and affect in those sites become engagements in ceremonies of mutual acknowledgment and subtle shifts in consciousness. These exchanges are close to what Stanley Cavell calls "passionate speech"—"improvisations in the disorders of desire."[20]

In an effort to highlight the positive role that can be accorded to dependence, Pippin (following James) does not dwell on the dangerous distortions to which such an ideal is vulnerable. A positive acknowledgment of dependence must be distinguished from regression to childlike forms of dependence, including acquiescence to those whose power enables them to enforce such infantilizing dependence. The positive forms of dependence brought to the surface by a Pippin–James account is compatible with the ideal of liberation for those marginalized, "constructed" others, whether they be the poor, the "uncivilized," women, persons of color, or non-heterosexuals. To *seek out* a position of dependence—electing to be a ward of the state or indentured, servile or thoroughly beholden to others, to seek out self-abasement or -humiliation, would also be clear perversions of the legitimate need to acknowledge dependence. Exactly how to work out this distinction between legitimate dependence and its multiple distortions remains (understandably) unexplored.

---

[20] See Cavell, *Philosophy the Day after Tomorrow*, Cambridge, MA: Harvard University Press, 2005, 185.

The upshot is that because meaning is shared we are dependent on meaning-sharers and negotiators, on meaning-exemplifiers and-amplifiers, as well as on the meanings themselves that emerge and solidify, "become actualized," in a social give and take. There is no escaping a primal dependency. Pippin puts this partially in terms of James' view of language as "a social practice among selves, . . . and the Jamesian 'I' is most definitely always and everywhere 'limited,' and radically dependent—on other such selves in a constant enactment of a struggle for mutuality that resonates with moral claims . . ."[21] So, it seems, unless I acknowledge such dependence on others for meaning-exchange, for meaning *recognition* (call it, perhaps, conversational, or gestural, dependence), I will have no life to lead that is my own, and hence no self. And now we have the option of supplementing this description of loss or gain of meaning with a further claim, that to achieve a self through such exchanges of significance is to achieve the highest freedom, the freedom to be who we are.

There is a third issue for anyone attempting to make freedom the reigning value of modernity. We could label this the general problem of "conceptual over-extension" and blurring of difference. If freedom is stretched to cover too diverse a field of phenomena, it begins to weaken at the center. It loses force as a signature ideal as it is held out to mean too much.

XI. A Parliament of Ideals

Apart from the familiar contrast between negative and positive freedom, Pippin seems too willing to take several quite separate phenomena as convergent forms of a single ideal. James and Pippin see intimate connections among freedom from alienation, freedom to be oneself, and freely acknowledging dependence on others. But are essential differences blurred when we steer these diverse phenomena down a single track?

We might ask in a general way if it is wise to seek a *single* reigning ideal, for this age or any other? Perhaps freedom founders as an all-encompassing ideal because human lives are just too diverse in aspiration and satisfaction to hope that any *single* ideal could be both

---

[21] Ibid., 83–84.

differentiating and all-encompassing. For clarity's sake, we might want to say that freedom is one prominent and perhaps preeminent modern ideal, but not the reining ideal, for the simple reason that we are ruled by several separate but roughly interlocking ideals, more like the rule of a triumvirate or parliament than of a single head of state.

Take the James–Pippin ideal of having a life of my own. We've granted that this can be described as achieving a kind of freedom, but it might also be described, as we've seen, as enacting a kind of dependence, and as overcoming a kind of alienation. We might describe having a life of one's own from a third angle as achieving a kind of contentment, or ease with oneself, a sense of not having to flee or to do anything to "prove oneself," or simply enjoying peace of mind. Or it might amount, fourth, to achieving a kind of rich subjectivity and awareness of my world and others, or fifth, achieving a capacity to love, or sixth, a capacity to commit more deeply to my work. By yielding to the hope for a single, integrating ideal to mark the epoch of modernity, perhaps we do a disservice to the variety of our aspirations and the variety of ways we can describe their satisfaction. We owe ourselves a rich account of the ideals that activate our lives and give them weight. If having a life of my own permits me to love, perhaps the emphasis should fall more on love than on freedom. Or if having a life of my own arises from and allows me to acknowledge familial relations, perhaps I should honor an ideal of nourishing familial relations more than an ideal of freedom.

How does it come to seem that freedom trumps alternative candidates for "our reigning ideal"? One factor is our preference for simplicity and convergence. Another is our assumption that freedom and unfreedom face off such that the *escape* from constraint, alienation, and unfreedom is straightforwardly equivalent to the *embrace* of a nurturing, positive freedom. However it's much more likely that the "freedom/unfreedom" contrast resembles the contrasts "savory/unsavory," or "friend/enemy." To escape the unsavory is not to have attained the savory; to escape the clutches of an enemy is not to have won the comfort of a friend. Accordingly, to escape unfreedom or alienation is not to have attained a fulfilling freedom.

To escape modernity's constraints is a worthy aspiration quite apart from whether that escape delivers other moral local goods that might give one's life meaning—say, a capacity for love, work, friendship, or rich familial relations. Becoming "locked into" one or more of these ideals is more than release from the irons of alienation, despair, emptiness, or fear. So what exactly is gained by claiming freedom as *the* reigning ideal, the ideal that focuses and captures the aspirations of modern moral life? Freedom, we could say, cries to be completed in specific lives informed by specific passions, commitments, yearnings, and cares—lives animated by as varied an array of ideals as the variety of persons we find remarkable, exemplary, or worthy, whether encountered in fiction, in the family past, in history, or in the local landscapes of our lives.

XII. The Obscure Tone of a Life of One's Own

Perhaps to have a life of my own is no more (and no less) than the continued capacity and opportunity to review its details and enact those ceremonies of dependence specific to its uniqueness, and to live out more of it, as best one can, with hope for the best. It could include an experience of peace both mobile and fragile, the contentment of resting in a community of friends and intimates mutually dependent and reciprocally acknowledging each other. And perhaps that intimation of contentment might permit me not just to seek a further freedom but to seek paths of exploration, wonder, and vital contact within and beyond a circle of my necessary others, paths whose substance and satisfactions will be forever fragile, faulted, finite. I would find myself living within and out from a community in which I, or any one of its members, might seek a panoply of goods beyond whatever the bare noun "freedom" can begin to suggest.

There will be, as we've seen, a predictable difficulty in giving content to *any* such extensive ideal, be it freedom, dependence, love, or otherwise. However, if asked to characterize what seems to draw out and consolidate the best of James' characters (other than the proclaimed value of freedom), I'd gesture toward a hoped-for tranquility that in fact can seem to suffuse the mood of such characters even through their self-sacrifice, and even through their embrace of conflicts unresolved—as in the almost peaceful melancholy floating not only above Milly, ferried to her burial in Venice, but also above Kate and Densher, who have collaborated against her to their own disgrace, and who both do and do not survive her, so intertwined are these three lives.

Pippin finds "tranquility" as a more fitting description of the tone of the later novels than such alternatives as "resignation, pessimism, or skepticism"—or "tragedy."[22] But he also concedes that James seems to favor letting the "overarching tone" remain "deliberately undefined."[23] Of course in this particular novel, we're meant to hear the Psalmist: "Fear and trembling are come upon me; oh, that I had wings like a dove," a verse that combines anxiety with a mitigating hope. Yet its image and tone will not finally do, for the line takes freedom as flight, as if one could escape one's entanglements, deny one's dependencies. And so it seems to turn us back to our restless, shared beginnings.

---

[22] Ibid., 36.
[23] Ibid., 144.

Chapter 10

PRESERVATIVE CARE:
Saving Intimate Voice in the Humanities

> *our whole lives may have the character of finding that anthem*
> *which would be native to our own tongue*
> —*Henry Bugbee,* The Inward Morning

If I were asked two decades ago if Salmon Rushdie were a dangerous man, I would immediately place him as the author of *The Satanic Verses,* a book that brought a death threat down on his life, drove him into hiding for a number of years, and brought bomb threats to quiet Berkeley bookshops. Is Salmon Rushdie *still* a dangerous man? Yes and no. It's true that years ago he planted political dynamite at the base of our cultural bridges. But if he's a danger today, or at least a source of anxiety, it's because he suggests that the world is *more* than bombs and politics, that there is a forgotten, nonpolitical *intimate* world well worth voicing. Given the persuasiveness of his prose he presents a threat, in schools of humanities, because his magically intimate voice, when it appears in its power, runs counter to the interests of reigning monitors. He might be entertaining, but his unabashed celebrations of mystery and song and love seem to mock the disciplinary frames of Marxian class analysis, Lacanian desire, Neo-Colonial critique, and so forth. His danger today lies in his pure delight in an immediacy that taunts academic reductions of a familiar sort. I'll display two passages that unabashedly sing the allure of "mysteries", that sing the promise of intimate transfigurations, that evoke worlds we can't manage. In the academy, these passages make him an object of anxiety.

Thanks to an anonymous reader for invaluable suggestions on an earlier draft.

Take the striking exaltation bursting from the pages of *The Ground Beneath Her Feet*.[1]

> Five mysteries hold the keys to the unseen: the act of love, and the birth of a baby, and the contemplation of great art, and being in the presence of death or disaster, and hearing the human voice lifted in song. These are the occasions when the bolts of the universe fly open and we are given a glimpse of what is hidden; an eff of the ineffable. Glory bursts upon us in such hours: the dark glory of earthquakes, the slippery wonder of new life, the radiance of Vina's singing.[2]

If our hermeneutics of suspicion or deconstructive tactics have deflated all mysteries, then we'll have little to praise in an evocation like this. Yet I think there is much to praise, embrace, and welcome in this passage, much to preserve—to enact, as it were, by reading aloud in a classroom. But have we lost the knack for passing on, reenacting, the visceral drive of sentences like these? I'll try to say why it's so hard to hear, and rehear these words. And that will involve a rather polemical account of the settings of teaching that discount such exercises in hearing the affective-cognitive flow of words as they unfold. Let me caution, however, that I have nothing to say about Rushdie's *oeuvre*, nor about how to teach *The Satanic Verses*, nor even whether, all things considered, one should. And I'll have nothing to say about *The Ground Beneath Her Feet* and its connections with Rushdie's fugitive life with Bono and U2. I won't even glance at the deadly business of a world-class writer with a price on his head.

We who teach in the humanities may take infinite private pleasure in prose and poetry that evokes things that under the harsh interrogating lights of the academy we'd hide discretely under our desks, or disown, for "political" purposes, as passé or sophomoric. Hold Rushdie's "an eff of the ineffable" in an ungenerous light, and we have something cute, but too like meringue to get one's professional teeth in. I call this passage "iconic" and revert to it often (among many others) in my classes. Do my colleagues have similar iconic passages they introduce to establish a mood in "English Lit," "Religious Studies," or "Intro to Humanities"?

Here is another wonderful Rushdie passage that I suspect we'd disown under professional lights. In our professorial moods, it may only make us blush. It's about singing. Reading too much of this sort

---

[1] Salman Rushdie, *The Ground Beneath Her Feet*, London: Picador, 2000, 19.

[2] Ibid., 20.

of thing, from Rushdie or elsewhere, will seem if not dangerous, then beyond the pale.

> Why do we care about singers? Wherein lies the power of songs? Maybe it derives from the sheer strangeness of there being singing in the world. The note, the scale, the chords; melodies, harmonies, arrangements, symphonies, ragas, Chinese operas, jazz, the blues: that such things should exist, that we should have discovered the magical intervals and distances that yield the poor cluster of notes, all within the span of a human hand, from which we can build our cathedrals of sound, is as alchemical a mystery as mathematics, or wine, or love. Maybe the birds taught us. Maybe not. Maybe we are just creatures in search of exaltation. We don't have much of it. Our lives are not what we deserve; they are, let us agree, in many painful ways deficient. Song turns them into something else. Song shows us a world that is worthy of our yearning, it shows us our selves as they might be, if we were worthy of the world.

The discursive space we enter as teachers in a university or college seems uncongenial to the musical or rhetorical moment of reading these Rushdie passages aloud.[3] There's no argument, and if there are truths, they are not truths of fact or theory. Professors are skilled at sorting method from fact, and both from theory, but what skills have we learned—methodological skills—for tracing the cognitive-imaginative-affective impacts that drive these words one to the next, word-by-word, sentence-by-sentence, through aural and heartfelt space? Perhaps "bursts of glory," or the thought that "our lives are not what we deserve" ring true (or not) in a way that defies our professional expertise, that mocks academic sophistication. We cringe or chuckle dismissively. Doesn't that hard-earned PhD certify that we've outgrown citations of mystery or death, or intimations that we are "creatures in search of exaltation"?

There's a quasi-religious or "spiritual" tonality in these passages that can easily put off. But "the religious" is not just a domain of bombs and power, dogma and rhetorical excess. It's also a register of the heart and imagination. Evocations of wonders and tremors of love and birth, of song and death, arriving often as ineffable epiphanies or revelations, are too valuable a root of our humanity to be dismissed as part of a *dangerous* "religious" sensibility. And that sensibility is not so ineffable (or sophomoric) as to defy generous classroom exploration. A "vital center" of songs, love, or birth, as these are undergone experientially,

---

[3] Schleiermacher builds the requirement of a melodic, rhythmic element into any interpretation of a text—an interpretation is empty until read aloud. See ch 7, note 14.

can be tentatively explored, impressionistic as that exploration may well be. There is no need to flinch at letting "dark glory" or "an eff of the ineffable" burst in on our classrooms.

We spend our lives *knowing* texts, critiquing them, being good exegetes. But Rushdie in his passages offers a love or birth, art or death, poetry or song that is not propositional. They are not, in their immediacy, moments of objective knowledge or stiff critique. Nor can their immediate experiential impacts survive long under an onslaught from critical theory, deconstruction, hermeneutical suspicion, or various styles of cultural study. We are given epiphanies, moments of vision. These are irreducible *Augenblicken,* "occasions when the bolts of the universe fly open." Even an extended thought, like the reminder that "Our lives are not what we deserve; they are, let us agree, in many painful ways deficient. Song turns them into something else." They function more as a glimpse of truth to ponder as a proposition to test or break down. And speaking of what "we deserve" or the transformative power of song, can sound uncomfortably close to a religious moralist, someone pointing to our flaws and touting a singing salvation. Better toss *that*! All that astonishment, tremor, or transport, that sense of "being unworthy of the world," can seem extracurricular well outside classroom sobrieties. Does Rushdie (at least in these passages) force us to set aside the orderly arrangement of our intellectual loves— set Plato's *Diotima* aside—in favor of a drunken Alcibiades who forces a descent into riotous, dangerous, desire?

* * *

We need information about cultures, their histories, and the heroines who inhabit them, and we need to hone skills of reading, analysis, and interpretation. Classrooms are sites for knowledge and analysis, both carried by the flow of our affections and troubled by the flow of our fears and anxieties. As well as preserving the glories that burst upon us, preservative care flows as grief for disasters that befall us, care for things lost. Departments in the humanities articulate and reanimate things worthy of replication and dissemination—good arguments, good historical accounts, fine poetry, fine art, fine philosophy, necessary novels, and striking aberrations or degradations of any of these. Our preservative care can take the shape of salvations.

Ortega Y Gassett tells us in the preface to his *Meditations on Quixote* to expect "essays in intellectual love"— essays, he says, that provide "no informative value whatever; they are not summaries, either—they are rather what a humanist of the seventeenth century would have called 'salvations.'"[4] These "salvations" display a preservative care, a love for *Quixote* that saves *Quixote* for us. And if that battling comic genius, both fool and knight and saint, comes alive through Ortega's "salvations," it is we, along with *Quixote*, who are healed.

Ortega says his essays will take up "a man, a book, a picture, a landscape, an error, a sorrow" and then seek "to carry it by the shortest route to its fullest significance." This might describe the vocation of scholars in any century (not just seventeenth-century Spanish humanists, or their twentieth- or twenty-first-century incarnations). Teaching religion or the birth of the novel or the healing of comedy and laughter might be preserving "a man, a picture, a book, a sorrow" against the ravages of neglect and time. *Quixote* is both special and one of many. Exemplary figures and texts are legion and yet each, in its own way, is exceptional. Rushdie has us attend to and preserve the wonder of birth or the radiance of song. I hope in my class to evoke and preserve the radiance of his singer, allow that radiance to *happen,* then and there. I can set a stage, listen for subtle, perhaps shy responsiveness in the look and awkward or eloquent words of this student or that, and get out of the way, *letting* it happen.

The familiar techniques of criticism or theory are fine in their place. We become expert in teaching and applying them. I could run through their virtues, but my interest is not in their relative strengths or differences, what each can accomplish, but in what gets forgotten as we strive to refine our use of Freud or Derrida, Durkheim or Feuerbach, Eagleton or Adorno. An open response to wonder or dread, to moral horror or the primal mystery of birth, is hard to teach or evoke and emerges at an experiential, pre-theoretical or pre-disciplinary level. Yet to abandon this is to lose intimacy with the world and ourselves.[5]

---

[3] Ortega, *Meditations on Quixote,* trans. Evelyn Rugg and Diego Marín, Urbana: University of Illinois Press, 2000, 3f.

[4] Social science can give me descriptions, even "thick" ones, of how death can be handled—by *them* (by that society over *there*). It can't give me the visceral feel of how *I* might experience deaths around me, or the *feel* of *my* disowning any such experience, or the elusiveness of an image of my death. Deconstruction or a hermeneutics of suspicion may get me to see the way death is a cover for this or that, or how our writing of death is deeply incoherent, an *aporia,* or "impossibility," perhaps. But such analysis holds death at arm's length, at a safe distance, forbidding visceral contact. Rushdie wants to *instill* the mystery of death or the wonder of song—not just report on another's experience of it, or a theoretician's unmasking or deconstruction. If we frame the wonder of song in the theories of Lacan or Nietzsche, we'd learn something, surely, but also break the thread Rushdie spins; we must strive to keep Lacan *and* Rushdie alive.

Garrett Stewart, speaking as the head of a renowned department of English, avers quite astonishingly that literary scholars have lost the "skills and taste and aspiration" for literature. By this he means that focus has shifted from riding a line of writing where "argument and articulation grow indissoluble at the level of affect—and hence of conviction" to a focus on handling the polemics of theory, where literature is evidence for one theory or another.[6] The appeals of Rushdie's sentences go well beyond, or sidestep completely, a love of theoretical assessment. The wonder of love or song, as Rushdie conveys it, sidesteps any theory meant to corral it. (And what goes for wonder applies equally to the terrifyingly evil or forbiddingly uncanny.)

Wonders precisely defy domestication by science, critical theories, or hermeneutical suspicions. A wonder explained is a wonder no longer. A wonder reenacted, read along the surface of its affect, is a wonder sustained. Of course, preserving experiential deliverances (wonder- or terror- or hope-preserving readings, e.g.) can require preliminary critique. I deflate puffery to create space for more viable growth, reduce error to allow broader significance to surface, theorize the brain or political life or "nature writing" to highlight infirmities and cracks in depictions. All this can open up a more lively range of experience and life.[7] We clean out the shoddy for the revelations and delights—or for the acknowledgments of bottomless pain—that await us in Cervantes or Rushdie or Brahms. Preliminary critique can open a place for preservative care, for an ever-widening generosity, sensitivity, and love. As Ortega puts it, such care brings a theme or person or object, into "its fullest significance."

Attaining such preservative care, letting oneself be immersed in those arts of reception and listening it presupposes, does not happen once for all, and is as mysterious and method-defying as any adventure of love is. It's hard to be taught to fall in love. Falling in and out of love is hardly something we accomplish by good study habits or research skills or critical analysis. But denying ventures of love in the academy, especially in the humanities, is not an attractive alternative. Retreat to an enclosure of reductive readings, disciplined by method and theory,

---

[6] Gareth Stewart, "The Avoidance of Stanley Cavell," in *Contending with Stanley Cavell*, ed. Russell B. Goodman, Oxford: Oxford University Press, 2005, 153.

[7] Explanatory and deflationary schematic analysis, powerful in its own right, works at a price. It brackets my experienced affections or anxieties, and suspends experiential absorption. I assume these points can strike home without a detailed and no doubt contentious assessment of the variety of critical-theoretical approaches in play in departments of English, art history, comparative literature, or religious studies (for example).

may give me control and gradable, handleable results—that's self-evident! But that retreat also leaves me bereft of those unmanageable deliverances that it is the genius of the humanities to preserve and pass on.

Love facilitates the fullest significance of *the next step*, we might say: Hamlet, Quixote, or Brahms are unfinished and keep growing (under our care), always one step ahead of our cognitive grasp. An infant's exuberant chortle can step forward and expand through a decade or two toward the soaring power of an unexpected aria—and there are numerous steps of ever-fuller significance along the way. Who knows where our childrens' responsiveness will take them? We don't. But the answer is "*nowhere*" if a faltering care lets fields of significance fall into decay, wilting under the dehydrations of non-stop problematizing and critique. Like ill-treated living things, they will slowly die. The appreciative teacher is an appreciative critic. As curators of invaluable goods, we are charged to practice a hermeneutics of preservation. Texts, paintings, or figures from our pasts hide untapped plenitudes awaiting our care.

An abiding love for the lineaments of passion, imagination, and intelligence that inhere in our texts and traditions and their embedded themes is a love I'm sure others share. But it has become the unspeakable love of our calling, the love that cannot be named. Long before I wrote on them, Thoreau or Melville, Plato or *The Book of Job* fed wide ranges of my imagination and passion. These were moments that saved me from spiritual immiseration. Years later as a fledgling professor I was to pass on just those glories and trials of sympathy, outrage, intellect, and imagination that I had found (or that had found me) in great texts, works of art, and music.

A technical university devoted to the accumulation, reproduction, and dissemination of objective knowledge cannot acknowledge such love. It is wild and untoward, against the grain in systems of discipline, evincing a devotion that borders on the religious, a faith-like enabling passion, a faith-like promise of salvation in terms that exceed those of strict knowledge. That saving impulse of love, preservative care, is what Robert Pogue Harrison, a Stanford professor of comparative literature, describes as the yearning to raise life from the dead.[8] To acknowledge it is to remember the dead, to let their glory burst upon us—that we may live with both the living and the dead.

* * *

---

[8] See his extraordinary *The Dominion of the Dead*, Chicago: University of Chicago Press, 2003.

Duke's president welcomes freshmen with these thoughts. First, they should find in the university a place that is responsive to "the beauty of excellence in its many forms and the pleasure of striving to attain it." Second, a university is pulled by love of open-ended inquiry: "nothing is yet the whole of the truth," he warns, and so "nothing is so true that it is not susceptible to expansion, challenge, revision, and deeper realization."[9] He frames learning as an aesthetic and moral project. Fact, theory, and method are framed in terms of a pursuit of beauty and virtue—good things to preserve. To recognize beauty or virtue, like recognizing those truths that burst through in Rushdie's evocations, means having ready heart and imagination. Yet no simple method prepares that inner citadel of receptivity.

It is a truth of beauty and excellence (not of brute fact nor complex theory) that mathematics can be *elegant,* that good mapping is *alluring,* that a simple but powerful experimental design has *great beauty,* that poetry, dance, and philosophical argument have their own *breath and rhythm,* that a good story in history, biography, theater, or film is (or is not) *irresistible.*[10] These are *revealed* truths, for no method can lead us to them (though good midwives can). Good teachers learn to let them surge up on their own. Unlike a discovery of new facts or the exercise of theories, in moments of revelation we can find our being in question (or renewed), as new experiential frames drop into place. To allow these shifts is to allow a passage from Rushdie to be subversive and saving.

I know in my bones that loss can renew love (as well as renew hurt). This is too close a truth to set out for public confirmation (though I can try to poetically evoke it or give it weight through the weight of my testimony, or that of the poets or otherwise inspired). I know with raw intimacy that power betrays all promise when unhinged from the good, that vengeance is poison, that children are innocent, that we are defeated by time, and that piety resides in attention to art, birth, death, voice, and love. These truths reflect my aesthetic and moral education, and can be passed on by exposing others to the worlds and words they animate, as often as not, congealed in the art, literature,

---

[9] Richard H. Brodhead, *The Good of This Place: Values and Challenges in College Education,* quoted in Stanley Hauerwas, *The State of the University: Academic Knowledges and the Knowledge of God* (Malden, MA: Blackwell, 2007), 202.

[10] For and account of the forgotten moment of wonder and terror in the practice of the physical sciences, see "Real Presences: Two Scientists' Response to George Steiner", Wilson Poon and Tom McLeish, *Theology* Vol. 102 (1999) 169–176.

and philosophy we husband in the humanities. Confirmation does not arrive from the well-oiled machinery of scholarly proofs. Their confirming impact can be whispered—or arrive with the compelling thunder of Job's Voice from the Whirlwind, or strike with the simple aesthetic power of the Watson–Crick double-helix, or transfigure with the opening bars of Bach's Mass in B-minor. And not all truths are pleasant or welcome; we wince painfully at bitter truths; among them the bitter truth that we forever *fall* from excellence and beauty, strike slippery bottoms, and become implicated in evil. There are truths to mourn.

* * *

To evoke hopes—possibilities—for renewal and repair might mean to imagine a cave and then imagine exiting it, to imagine what traps us there, to feel in one's bones the *need* to get light, and to grasp, with no little chagrin, the multiplicities that conspire to *shut down* hopes or possibilities and so keep us trapped. To evoke these variations in imagination requires intimacy with a range of affect, aspiration, self-punishment, and self-deception. Insofar as we move beyond social scientific or theoretical unmasking accounts, humanities open the past as a repository of yearning and desire, and open a wide range of aspiration and affect, imagination and tact, tainted love and rash conceit. Poetry and its allies lead us to imagine requited and unrequited love, betrayal and steadfast courage, fluid grace and tempestuous disorder, arrogance and single-minded vengeance, innocent delight and deep despair. In our texts, we find grief or anger, halting tenderness or baffled confusion, spiteful vengeance or surpassing compassion.

Modeling love of the discipline is modeling these quite specific modes of communion (or alienation) in the world—through pace and pitch of reading and exposition, through facial and bodily gesture. To win these moments of halting tenderness or cruel vengeance requires intimate touch with the contours of a mood or passion, and it requires daring to model that intimacy in gesture and speech and apt analogy. If that moment ripples through a class, we adjust our speech and gesture to acknowledge the hard-won receptivity and assimilation exhibited just then. This is warm engagement, not aloof detachment, the work of a coach or attentive companion, not of a handbook or of a drill master.

Academics are wary of professing, of exercising the subtle arts of witness, testimony, or confession, of imaginative intimacy or affective provocation. Rant or ideological mind-bending (moralistic, religious, political, or otherwise) can be crude and more than a peripheral threat. But it is no solution, certainly not a humane solution, to duck that threat through a retreat to detached critique, dispassion and indifference or protective silence, which so easily clone a cynicism and despair. The subtle arts of witness and evocation of affect invite into one's pedagogy a willingness to allow others so briefly in our charge a well-timed glimpse of whatever sensibilities we may have won from texts, won from what we call experience, and that students can win for themselves.

* * *

Not long ago, an Amish schoolhouse was invaded mid-morning, the children terrorized and several shot by a local deliveryman. The next day, the grandfather of one of the girls killed, from within his inconsolable grief, reminded his family, "We must not think evil of this man." I relayed these words to my class the following day, letting them sink in. Then, quietly alluded to the biblical injunction to love one's enemies. I paused and moved on. This was not preaching. Any agnostic or anti-Christian might have grasped the point. The hush said that something had happened: perhaps someone was struck by a forgiveness that is inconceivable.

Each moment of insight is unique. On *that* day, and with *those* faces, I speak, pause, and move on. On another day I might not try for a connection at all. On a third, I might spend the hour on forgiveness, mentioning the reconciliation movement in South Africa, or traditions of pacifism or the assurance that God loves especially the least. There is no end to pedagogical possibility here, but it all presupposes alertness to moments where minor revelations, small-scale awakenings, occur, or may be waiting, if only we hear.[11]

The Amish murders are but one point of entry to the terrains we inhabit as instructors in humanities, where affect, art, and imagination abide, if we're willing. The portals are innumerable: Hamlet's doubts, Mozart's grace, Tolstoy's accounts of war and the birth of a child, the terror of unexpected death, the defilements of murder, inconceivable compassion. We have barely scratched the surface of the spiritual,

---

[11] Heidegger and Kierkegaard both stress "the moment of vision," "glance" or *Augenblick*, when, as they'd put it, time starts anew in a moment of truth. See my *On Søren Kierkegaard*, Chapter 6.

humanistic, and anti-humanistic resonances of 9/11. These sites of passion, affect, undergoing, and resolve beg to be *tendered out* to the midst of others, launched as the doubt, grace, or terror that they are—tendered out and on to receptive selves. Words awaken affect and wisdom, the wonder of eloquence and love, and the pain of affliction—realities not to be denied.

* * *

To awaken affect is not to dislodge knowledge but to transform the register of its appearance and reception. Knowledge that emerges from care for the words that are "the life of the world"[12] would aspire to a fine-grained sense of things that we can call "tactile" or "visceral" knowing, the sort of acquired, practiced intimacy that a rock climber has with her granite wall, or the fleshly knowledge Jacob has in wrestling his angel, or the knowledge Thoreau has of his Concord paths and ponds. It might be the intimate knowing, painful and joyful, attendant on giving birth, or attendant on a readiness for the next step, grip, or moment as one enters one's impending future. This sort of knowing resists propositional formulation (hence Socratic ignorance is its ally).

I had passed out a short passage on how a Kantian sublime pulls the rug from under routine presumptions of cognitive supremacy and grip. When I received this responsive note from an undergraduate, I knew we were engaged in the most valuable venture. Let me give the full texture and weave of his response.

> I like the idea that the sublime is the final challenge to dreamers of the grandiose. It requires release of control, at least temporarily. It demands laying down whatever weapons are most familiar to our hands. There's a reason why people wave. It's to show that they hold no weapon, that they are non-threatening and it's okay to let down some of our guard. Some people never wave. Others only wave to those like themselves. We all need to learn to wave to each other, in a sense. Fear is a killer, a stifler of openness to deeper things. It closes every door and window, hence puts one in darkness.[13]

---

[12] Simon Critchley avers, speaking with Wallace Stevens, that "Words of the world are the life of the world, and poetry is the highest use of those words." Critchley, *Things Merely Are*, London: Routledge, 2005, 10.

[13] These are the words of a quite exceptional sophomore, not yet in a major.

One cannot know when (if ever) one's words strike home; when they do, we're out of the dark.

* * *

The University of Malta is geared towards the infrastructural and industrial needs of the country so as to provide expertise in crucial fields.[14] This headline sounds a death-knell for humanistic ideals of refining moral, aesthetic, or literary passions, for imaginative inflections or transformative perceptions. This frankly macabre blurb declares the death of learning from a once-vibrant site of exchange among Muslim, Roman, and Christian traditions. The demise of the humanities, so shamelessly abandoned, is the demise of "useless" imaginative variation and the withering of lyrical or memorial perception.

When a university is instrumentally linked exclusively to economic and political needs, it is no longer a site for recuperative visions, for curates of past lives and forgotten cities and resonant texts, curates who attend critically and generously to them, bringing them up from the dead into presence. In such a pedagogical desert there is no place for fleeting dialogue with *this* companionable figure, *this* striking line, *this* image, *this* chord sequence. Nor does this tolling declaration from Malta leave sites for imagining futures that might flow in as dark or lifting winds, for imagining souls taking their next tremulous step into unknowns where questions are so much more than answers and even silence has a place. There is no space for *this* Van Gogh crow, *this* line from Rilke or the Psalms, *this* Socratic exchange; no room for Emersonian invocations or Hepburn moments; no space for the felt-texture of King Lear's rage, Bonhoeffer's courage, or Kierkegaard's plea for knowledge that will "*come alive in me.*"[15]

Whatever comes alive through the humanities arrives through intimacy and openness to texts, dance, and cities as these carry the arts of conversation, gesture, or praise, the habits of attentiveness, gratitude, or compassion, the contours of grieving or outrage; and as these carry the arts of seeing and coping with affliction, injustice, and estrangement (religious, existential, or otherwise). As these arts of coping and conversation and habits of attention gradually disappear

---

[14] Mission statement, University of Malta, fall 2006: http://www.um.edu.mt/about/uom.

[15] *Kierkegaard's Papers and Journals*, trans. Alastair Hannay, New York: Penguin, 1996, 33 (Gilleleje, August 1, 35). See *On Søren Kierkegaard*, 71–86; emphasis in the original.

from the university they do not take up residence elsewhere (at least not in a *healthy* elsewhere). The lives and imaginations and hearts of its students are less for their disappearance. If departments in the humanities husband these varied sensibilities, proto-religious or not, sensibilities at least in *search* of a heart (and mourning its absence), then they keep alive these disappearing locales where the arts of humane expression are cared for and revived.

As we've said, truths of sensibility and the heart are not propositions to test at arm's length or pocket as a creed but words that afford intimate touch with deep conviction. "Fear is a killer, a stifler of openness to deeper things. It closes every door and window, hence puts one in darkness." Such thoughts animate worlds we inherit and inhabit, inform, and abandon. We seek loves or paths that are worthy, and seek truths in art or living. We want contact with Hamlet as he enacts and suffers truths of the most capacious consciousness we've had the fortune to know (and not to know). These truths are embodied as apt attunements to varied worlds and embodied in the lives of aptly beckoning exemplars that in our brief time afoot we marvel to uncover or meet in moments of illumination.

We share a beauty, an excellence, and also share horrifying violations of these—a cry of despair, a desecration, an unspeakable cruelty. And we share the quiet violence of indifference—a ghost that hangs us halfway between good and evil. We undergo these lights and darks in an unending exploration in and around this place called a university whose ambit can indeed welcome Rushdie's "keys to the unseen," his moments of "dark glory"—and yes, those alluring "effs of the ineffable."

Chapter 11

J. GLENN GRAY AND HANNAH ARENDT— SQUIRES IN THIS VALE OF TEARS:
Poetry in a Time of War

> *Parting is all we know of heaven*
> *and all we need of hell.*
> —*Emily Dickinson*

> *Keep your mind in hell*
> *And despair not.*
> —*Staretz Silouan*

I

There's an ancient view that philosophy begins in wonder, amazement, or astonishment. That view holds its own against its opposite, that philosophy begins in disappointment or a sense of loss—say, the sense of unrequited love, or the sense that the world just doesn't meet our expectations. Either view grants philosophy a wide ambit. Its meditations might ally it with poetry and lyric prose, ways of writing that also often have their root in wonder, or a sense of loss. I'll ask if poetry or philosophy have power against the brutal exigencies of war, and that would seem to presuppose that philosophy or poetry will start in disappointment or even mourning. But as we'll see, the shock of wonder and the shock of loss may interlock. As I begin to think of J. Glenn Gray, I circle back not in disappointment but in wonder. I circle back to events beginning close to forty years ago. To think of it, I've been part of several wonderful, astonishing circles.

175

In 1969, I came across Glenn Gray's reflections in the book he titled *The Warriors*.[1] My copy had a foreword written by Hannah Arendt, the Chicago émigré philosopher, student of Heidegger and Jaspers, and fast friend of Glenn Gray. The book astonished me, and I wrote to Professor Gray to tell him so. I signed off saying, in an offhand way, "Well, if you're ever in the Bay Area . . ." It turned out he would be, so eight months later he flew in from Colorado to speak at Cal State Sonoma where I was just beginning my career.

His flight information and self-description were typed on an old manual on a postcard with an eight-cent stamp. I picked him up at San Francisco Airport, pipe, beret, and briefcase. Now I find myself returning the favor, returning to his Colorado haunts and topics— minus pipe and beret, but happy that history gives us such circles, such "happenings," as Heidegger might call them (his word is *Ereignis*).[2] Our present can be sprinkled by such upsurges of meaning that gather up the past in utterly unanticipated ways; in turn, one's sense of possibility is recast. We're constantly reborn through such events. This suggests another happy circle, a conversation circling around the questions of whether love's wisdom—its hope and warmth and wonder— can mitigate war's folly, how poetry's music can push back against dark times. Perhaps the richness of life lies in such circling retrievals, remembrances, and retellings. Though I know that richness in life lies in such circles, I also know that not all of them are happy. Some are wrenching.

II

It was a terrible time in America when Glenn Gray's book came out— it's easy to forget. It was the time of daily Vietnam body counts on the TV news, of no less than six highly visible assassinations of American political leaders, starting with Martin King and two Kennedys, Medgar Evers, Malcolm X, and the Oakland, California, superintendent of schools. There were several murders of young civil rights workers,

---

[1] J. Glenn Gray, *The Warriors: Reflections on Men in Battle*, Lincoln Nebraska: Bison Books, 1998. First Published, Harcourt and Brace, 1959.

[2] Letting Heidegger's *Ereignis* be "happening" (as in "Wow, *what's happening!?*") lets in the element of surprise and suddenness, of being *taken*, and of taking *in*—an improvement on the rather cool "Event," or the shady grasping of "appropriation," or Stambaugh's "Enownment."

including Chaney, Schwerner, and Goodman.³ Detroit, Los Angeles, and other cities were burning. Protesting students at Kent State, in Mexico City and Paris were shot. The details of those times come back with a vengeance. Of course there were bright things then, as well—in music, for example. And the rolling surf of the Sonoma Coast was strangely indifferent to politics. But Glenn's book was a response to war, not to Bob Dylan or to Red Woods.

The Warriors was based on Glenn Gray's World War II experiences in Europe. He was an intelligence officer close to the front lines interviewing German spies and French collaborators. The book served as a kind of therapy in my classes while Vietnam was underway. A fair number of my students were returned vets, often dressed out in fatigues and boots. Some of my other students were subject to the draft and to being shipped off. Still others were draft resisters. Nearly everyone worried for friends, siblings, loved ones. Violent tumult was euphemistically called "the movement"—a volatile mix of civil rights and antiwar protests; of communes and "summers of love"; of the Beetles and free speech confrontations. There were prison breakouts, courtroom shootouts, and political kidnappings. Ronald Reagan, then governor of California, deployed the National Guard against Berkeley students, tear-gassing the campus by helicopter. The relatively recent Twin Tower attacks in 2001 have delivered months of indistinct anxiety as one expects more down the road. The late 1960s and early 1970s were darker, with the daily *reality* of violence, next door, downtown, at school, and through the nation and in foreign capitols.

Revisiting those times would be difficult under any circumstances, but distress is compounded in the realization that war continues in 2009. Vietnam returned to make news during the 2004 Kerry/Bush campaign with images of swift boats and protesting vets returning combat medals, but there's been little comment on the fact that apart from its obvious toll in combat death and disablement, Vietnam derailed the country from a surging campaign against poverty and from seeing the civil rights struggle through to what could have been a far better end. The present version of Vietnam, Iraq-Afghanistan, also takes its toll in combat death and disablement, in the polarization of those countries and ours, and takes money and attention away from domestic security, better health care, and rebuilding an all-but

---

³ The deaths of Chaney, Schwerner, and Goodman are depicted in the 1988 film *Mississippi Burning.*

destroyed New Orleans. I've read Glenn Gray's letters to Hannah Arendt during the late 1960s. He'd be making these comparisons. The present wars will carry untold scars aching deep into our future, and distracting us from famine and genocide in Africa, nuclear proliferation in India, Pakistan, North Korea, and Iran, shrinking ice caps, and Katrina. *The Warriors,* a work of healing, seems to have had little effect at the level of the body politic. Yet I recall these wounds on the eve of an inauguration, listening to a president whose eloquence seems to herald steps toward a better world.

III

Skies aren't always Colorado cloudless. Glenn Gray's appeals to poetry and philosophy were after and during times of war, and—sadly—*our* appeals today are made against such background, too. The telling point is that the poetry of wonder, love, gratitude, and other timbres *can* push back against the dark. The terrible is not crushingly triumphant. How does poetry help? I want to look for clues in several spots: in the Auden quote that Glenn Gray cites, "*We must love one another or die,*" in a poetic phrase from Hannah Arendt, *For Love of the World,* in Rilke's meditation on the archaic Apollo, and in a poetic evocation of a soaring Hawk from *The Book of Job.* These exhibits, and others, track the power of poetic articulation to push back against dark times.

Arendt wanted to call her first book in English, *For Love of the World.* The title is a wonderfully affirmative witness for one who had lived through so much.[4] She had every reason *not* to live or write for love of the world. She had escaped to America—just barely—first from a Nazi noose in Germany, and then from a collaborationist France, sneaking over the border with the papers of Walter Benjamin, who didn't make it. I mentioned the ancient view that philosophy begins in wonder, but it might also begin in disappointment or despair—despair that war comes so easily, or that tyranny reigns, or that innocents are hanged. Plato, who cites wonder as a source for philosophy, also writes under the shadow of his teacher's death, mourning it.

---

[4] François de Menthon characterized war crimes in the context of the Nuremberg Trials as crimes against "*la condition humaine.*" "The Human Condition" has since acquired an abstract tonality that does not serve Arendt well. Some years later she published *Men in Dark Times.* Conjoining them, we have *for love of the world and of men—in dark times.*

Arendt's title suggests that wonder or despair may be intermixed in another impulse for philosophy, or poetry, a tempered love of the world. The challenge is to nourish that love while refusing to cover-over the realities of evil and suffering. Staretz Silouan, a Russian monk writing a bit later than Dostoevsky and through the Revolution, put the challenge this way: "Keep your mind in Hell, and despair not."[5] Silouan's advice is both heartening and depressing. It asks us to expand passionate imagination to encompass, impossibly, suicide bombs and the smile of an innocent child, our demons and a bountiful sunset. We admire Hannah Arendt and Glenn Gray, at least I do, because they live and write *from and for a love of the world.* They *keep their minds in Hell, and despair not.*

Take Auden's words, the words that Glenn Gray quotes in the first pages of *The Warriors*, "*We must love one another or die.*" He opens his book with a letter from the front to a friend at home in which he confides his near despair. These Auden words are his push against the dark. They also establish a mood or tenor, a tone that sends a needed shaft of light. Linking Arendt's title to Auden's words yields a sustaining mood for *The Warriors: for love of the world and each other* (lest we die).

Philosophy often tries to fix a single cognitive or affective template onto the world; poetry gives more latitude to multiple and mixed perspectives. This can set philosophy and poetry at odds, and has done so, from before Plato to the present.[6] The complaint of philosophy is that the single lines we might remember as touchstones for life—say, the lines of Auden or Silouan's "Keep your mind in Hell and despair not" —float free of argument, and are proposals rather than assertions. And they often open perspectives that pull in opposite directions. Poetry might reasonably retort that its multiple and mixed perspectives can deepen our appreciation of experience and introduce us to dimensions of it not otherwise available. Words open into moods, attunements, orientations that are not reducible to a set of assertions

---

[5] Staretz Silouan (1866–1938), "the Monk of Mount Athos," quoted in Gillian Rose's now sadly neglected philosophical memoir, *Love's Work.*

[6] Arendt and Gray loved Greek philosophy, and post-Kantian German thought. Romantics, phenomenologists, and existentialists write about love and know the importance of poetry to life and to philosophy. With the notable exception of Iris Murdoch, their British counterparts remain "properly reserved" about love, leaving its praise to poets and parsons.

about the way the world really is or to arguments on behalf of those assertions. They appeal to our varied and often convoluted sensibilities.

Arendt suggested that a particular tone or timbre held *The Warriors* together. It was a tone—let's say, a poetic tone—of steady affirmation, or stillness.[7] The tone seems akin to Eckhart's (or Heidegger's) *Gelassenheit*—"letting be." Gray was just beginning to translate Heidegger and certainly knew Eckhart, and perhaps found the mood congenial. But other attuning lines weave through *The Warriors*. Perhaps we're not forced to choose between *love for the world and others,* and a serenity called "*letting be.*" They might be linked. And a third mood weaves through the book: a sustaining gratitude and mourning. Now if there are such multiple interpretative tonalities, the job of philosophy, or of poetry, might be to picture how love and gratitude, wonder and mourning, stillness and terror might hang together—or fall apart—in writing or in life.

Let me linger with Auden's words. As Gray writes out, "*we must love one another or die,*" he voices a kind of liturgy, a ceremony of spirit and sustenance, a prayer in impossible straits. We might hear a plea for sustenance, directed not toward God but toward an indefinite assembly of humanity. In his extremity, Gray repeats Auden's injunction. It lacks the authority of the Gospel, "You shall love!" but carries only the authority of the poet, taken up by the philosopher, both speaking in the first person plural. The words call on an indefinite assembly, not the "we" of only Christian believers, but a *we* of indefinitely many others, clearly not an exclusionary pair, me speaking to you. This makes it a kind of neighbor love rather than romantic love or special friendship. It marks the unattainable ideal of an all-expansive assembly. Therein, loving one another means not an imperative, but a heartfelt imaginative *openness* to love *any* other, each and *every* other. Our humanity depends on it. The stark news is that without love, we die. That's no hyperbole, of course. We're utterly dependent on parental love from the start, someone who feeds us and tucks us in. From there we learn love's wider reaches and reciprocities. Love for parents transfers to attachments to stuffed bears, and proceeds, we hope, to embrace classmates, cousins, projects, and amorous others.

---

[7] Arendt hears an absence of fervor, of one-sided indignation, or of sentimentality. Gray doesn't soft-pedal atrocity, betrayal, or danger but he relays it with a kind of composure, a stoic serenity.

Of course, we'll all die *anyway*—love can't prevent that! But there's more than one way to die. Kierkegaard explored a sickness unto death called despair, and Auden would have known this, having edited an early Kierkegaard anthology. So the issue is not just biological demise.[8] *That* death will fell us whether we love, hate, or are coolly indifferent. The death that can be defeated is death of spirit. Sickness of the heart need not be unto death. We can call on love's therapy.

IV

The Warriors opens with poetry's slant. The Auden appeal keeps Gray alive. Arendt finds a quiet stillness in the book, no doubt linked to steady love. I hear this too, but I also hear an oscillating timbre of gratitude and mourning. *The Warriors* takes in that twofold tone. We sense the author's gratitude for the life that has opened up for him, despite its pain and devastation; we sense the author's mourning as he trudges through desolation. He suffers and rues the weakness of the poet's or philosopher's voice. Humane words falter, don't they, against brute power?

Plato often writes from that mixed sensibility. His great middle dialogues came from grief or mourning in the loss of a friend and teacher, Socrates, put to death by an Athens they both wanted to love. That grief grew alongside a gratitude that Socrates had been there. Love, gratitude, and grief mix in writing in anticipation of future readers. Gratitude and mourning complement wonder and disappointment as anchors for philosophy—and poetry.

* * *

Looking out on new snow, before much sun has risen, gratitude and wonder can mix as praise and celebration.[9] Yet attunements to such worlds can be just a hair's breadth from disaster. Great music can bring us from one to the other in a matter of a few chords, the elevating followed quickly by the disturbing. We feel gratitude in the allure of

---

[8] See my "Transfigurations: The Intimate Agency of Death," in *Kierkegaard and Death*, ed Patrick Stokes and Adam Buben, Bloomington: University of Indiana Press, 2011.

[9] See chapter three in this volume; and *On Søren Kierkegaard*, Chapters 1 and 2.

beauty, and when it's interrupted, as it will be, we mourn. Mourning can then bring us back to beauties, goods, or wonders just lost.

V

An achingly difficult poetic photograph from 9/11 shows that access to beauty, wonder, compassion, and to the deepest terror and anxiety can come tied in a single package singed by disaster. You probably remember the falling silhouettes, the two pencil-thin figures arm in arm, diaphanous, falling from the Towers, caught gently in the air like falling leaves. In this vein, Rilke writes that Beauty is just the beginning of terror.[10]

Can we be that clear exactly what we're feeling in that image? It's art, so we have time to contemplate, time to veer away from too much pain. I sense an alternating rush of beauty and terror, terror and compassion, compassion and fear in that floating and falling. I sense serenity, the surreal, and the awful, all at once, rapid fire, stock-still.

Rilke might have said not beauty but the sublime is the beginning of terror, but I suspect he means to elide the two, as this photo does. Kant linked the sublime to a sense of overwhelming vastness or energy, reminding us of finitude or death. This sense is linked, in his view, to a simultaneous sense of elevation or exaltation brought on by the real-ization that we've survived, and live on as freedom present to whatever scene unfolds. But in that 9/11 image I think there's less exaltation than agony, pity, compassion. The image is lines and shadows that in but a tiny way resist the end of the world. It instills fear and paralysis—and a great awe and agony marking our powerless *distance* from others we cherish, especial in this moment—and thus marks an inexpugnable *closeness* to them, however distant. Not every glimpse of beauty or the sublime is so extremely hard to hold in focus. Not all art, thankfully, is as difficult as that 9/11 photo. But it confirms that poetry sends light. We'd be less without it.

Poetry sends different slants of light toward different scenes of trouble. A line from Auden is not quite a line from Hannah Arendt,

---

[10] In *Reading Rilke: Reflections on the Problems of Translation*, New York: Basic Books, 1999, William Gass renders the First *Duino Elegy*, "For Beauty is nothing but the approach of a Terror we're only just able to bear, and we worship it so because it serenely distains to destroy us," 63–67, and 189.

and the photo from 9/11 is something else again. Generalities get no traction here. Particulars are eloquent, and I have two or three more to introduce on behalf of poetry's resistance to despair. Teasing out what particulars might say—so eloquently say—is not laying out a traditional philosophical argument that moves from premise to conclusion. It's not advancing propositions that might be proved. It's making proposals with appeal.

When something eloquent speaks, phenomena resonate—or as Wittgenstein would say, become perspicuous. That's not to throw away all discipline in our writing and attention. If two proposals vie for our attention, that plurality does not declare a general "relativism." Nor does it open floodgates to a veritable thousand of interpretative possibilities.[11] When a line from Auden or Rilke, or an image from 9/11, speaks poetically, that line or image does not say just *anything*. Nietzsche, Pascal, or Kierkegaard give us *proposals with appeal*; give us *possibilities* for hearing. Thus we might read Glenn Gray's resonant, perspicuous accounts of war.

That 9/11 photo is an instance of a poet speaking to disaster, yet disaster does not always condense into a single vivid moment. Poetic images can get stretched into a miniature narration as it does in certain passages from *The Book of Job*.

VI

As I fly in, the crest of the Front Range still laced in snow, I sense vast and unmixed beauty. It's not the start of terror. This could be the way it looks to soaring hawks: "Do you show the Hawk to fly / to stretch her wings upon the wind?"[12] The mood, etched out in *Job*, so far does not intimate war or trouble. Yet we know these lines are linked to the story of Job's afflictions, so shadows can't be too far away: this isn't simple bird-watching. The poet quickly makes this quite explicit:

> Do you show the Hawk to fly
> to stretch her wings upon the wind?

---

[11] The charge of relativism is a conversation stopper, a way of retreating to impregnable fortresses where "*my* opinion rules"—and since "that's just *your* opinion," you can retreat to yours. Dogmatism replaces cordiality. We are no longer exploring "proposals with appeal."

[12] Job 39:26. The rendering is mine.

> Or the Vulture how to soar
> whose nest is in the clouds?
> Look! His home is on a mountaintop
> a fierce, forbidding craig

The tone becomes more ominous still:

> There he sits and scans for prey
> his eye grasps sound for miles
> His young drink blood
> from taloned flesh
> He rules the haunted acres
> of unburied dead

That's the kind of poetic transformation Rilke could cite as Beauty at the beginning of terror. What starts as an almost innocent wonder of a hawk in flight shifts to the soaring of vultures and then to a vulture looking for prey, on to the macabre scene of the young, drinking from the newly dead.

And the final lines, "*He rules the haunted acres of unburied dead.*" We're invited not just to fresh kills. The haunted acres might just include the acres of unburied dead at Gettysburg, Baghdad, or the 9th District of New Orleans. Once this somber music is laid out before us, we can hear it in reverse, from bloody killing fields to the serene soaring of a hawk. That way of hearing can push back against the dark. Or hearing it top down reminds us of strange comfort conveyed by the lofty indifference of the world.[13] That must come close to the comfort Job was taught as he melts before the vast indifference of the whirling blizzard, before which his daily worries, self-importance, and even great afflictions do not have final word.[14]

If the whirlwind speaks we're speechless—we're a quiet openness to otherness, pure readiness to listen. Remember the Homeric poet, "*Sing in me, Muse, of that man of twists and turns . . .*" From the side of the gods, a poet sings through our emptiness. In this regard, a deep environmental ethic has a poet's ear for hearing things that are just radiantly, resonantly *there*—not for our use or pleasure, not because our survival depends on listening up to them, but because their splendor *is*—and fills us.

---

[13] Camus, in the last pages of *The Stranger*, calls it "the benign indifference of the universe."

[14] For "I melt away" as a translation of Job's last words, see chapter three.

Poetry can defeat our self-importance, and that can downsize the estimation of our afflictions, as well slow our dominating impulses. The world's indifference to us can be frightening but also can awaken our appreciation of that which we can't control—as in our reverence for great music; or in our appreciation of things less grand than blizzards, hawks, or mountain crags. The poetry of things defies an impulse to possess or frame things always in terms of usefulness or prudence.

Observing prudence is not falling in love with the world, or writing or living for love of the world, in which mood we cede to things their inestimable worth. Our natural inclination to self-importance is subdued, and recognition of our smallness in the scheme of things seems to occur at the very moment (and because) we yield to a poetic eye that lets the world disable any impulse we might have to possess it. Or better, the particulars that arrive for our attention arrive irresistibly and quell both self-importance and the urge to map or calculate or grasp.

To be so attuned is not to hold a theory of environmental value but to have theory swept aside in this radiance of particulars and their capacity to speak. It's prudent not to cloud skies with soot, or weaken human survival chances by inattention to species-extinction and diminished biodiversity, but attention to clouds and small bits of life can speak otherwise than to survival. As can things in our domestic worlds that also elicit our concern—even through their indifference to our concerns.

Consider a nineteenth-century hallway clock in a great uncle's house. We might care for it because it's a useful tool to keep us on time. But we might also care for it because we remember decades ago when we were children a favorite uncle's loving hands on winter holidays attentively adjusting its springs and gears. And we might remember its soothing, dependable late night metronomic beats, or the shiny brass of its wheel works, or the fact that it toned on regardless of our moods. Falling in love with the world is to cherish the things of the world—old clocks, rusty wagon wheels, a new Swiss army knife, a German-made violin, meadows, livestock, wildlife, wounded friends, hawks. To so cherish is to desire their preservation, but also to be beyond that thought of preservation, in something like a mood of pure attention to what in its mystery is other.

VII

I have another exhibit. It's Rilke's marvelous "The Archaic Apollo"—a meditation on a torso, head and feet and arms snapped off. It is surely defiled, even desecrated stone is it not?—this "decapitated Apollo"? Perhaps, but yet it speaks, sends out a gaze. This "battered remnant of statue" enthralls us, as it does Rilke's translator, William Gass: "that absent look, that vanquished smile, is bright, and burns your eyes as you perceive its shine, flashing from this broken body to confront your inner incompleteness and condemn it. Are you as real as this ancient, battered remnant of statue?"[15]

The stakes might seem less in facing this broken museum piece than in facing broken Towers and their falling casualties, or in facing scavengers perched on war dead. But still, there's a lesson here for how a caring poetic eye can pierce the shadows of the amputated objects of this broken world. Are we repulsed by such mutilation? Do we want to face a body with no face, or stand by one without feet? Wouldn't it be better to avert our eyes from this defiled Apollo?

But note the exquisite care with which Rilke attends the deity:

> Never will we know his legendary head
> where the eyes' apples slowly ripened. Yet
> his torso glows as if his look were set
> above it in suspended globes that shed
>
> a street's light down. Otherwise the surging breast
> would not thus blind you, nor through the soft turn
> of the loins could you feel his smile pass easily
> into the bright groins where the genitals yearned.
> Otherwise this stone would not be so complete,
> from its shoulder showering body into absent feet,
> or seem as sleek and ripe as the pelt of a beast;
>
> nor would that gaze be gathered up by every surface
> to burst out blazing like a star, for there's no place
> that does not see you. You must change your life.[16]

Wherever eyes alight, Apollo looks back. His loins, shoulder, and breast look back, even burst out blazing, "You must change your life!" You're charged to make your life as complete as this shattered yet radiant stone.

Here the presumed predatory male gaze is turned away. The statue holds sway, returns a look that strips the viewer of self-assertion,

---

[15] In Gass, *Reading Rilke,* 92.
[16] Trans., William Gass, op.cit.

security, or self-possession.[17] And in its gaze it strips away war's bitter harvest—anger or self-pity or desolate despair. Hearing that poem aright, seeing that Apollo through Rilke's caring eye, can realign a soul. Who knows *what* will change, only that one *must* change. And we know uncannily that this transforming call has come from a piece of stone—or from a god—or from a poem about a stone or statue—or from a god who looked out from stone at a poet who then sang. It all began in a loving poetic eye. Such rapt moments reanimate a life. I remember an elderly art history professor, in love with Gothic Cathedrals, who confided years later that in London blackouts he would play Schubert for his huddled family, to let fall a shaft of light.

VIII

Sometimes we find strange beauty mixed with saving comedy or humor, another way that poetry pushes back against the world. Cervantes has his Knight and squire face off against bleak despair. Comedy has its way with melancholy. Conventionally, the Knight was noble and the squire, base, a fool, yet Cervantes unsettles this configuration. Ingmar Bergman, in *The Seventh Seal,* doesn't exactly turn the Knight into a fool (and the squire into a knight). But the squire is bright, full of wit, and care—better endowed in these respects than his Knight. They traverse a bleak and melancholy landscape returning from a crusade. The Knight is locked in a chess game with black-robed Death. You can't get darker than a chess match with Death in the midst of the Black Death after a failed Crusade with village girls burned at the stake. But just as Cervantes knows comedy, so Bergman does—a dark humor, to be sure.

The scene of interest shows that even the darkest moment need not be bereft of humor, bereft of a poetic touch of comedy, humility, humanity.

Imagine: The heath stretches out toward the sea. Seeking a path, the squire, Jöns, approaches a sleeping man covered with flies, watched

---

[17] This is the way icons—as opposed to images—work. They are not copies of anything, in the way a map or travelogue illustration might be. They demand we set aside our instrumental knowledge of our way around the world to accept, on terms not of our making, another world.

faithfully by his hungry whining dog. The squire addresses him politely, but when he gets no answer, he approaches to shake him awake. He bends over. The man stares up, a skull *sans* eyes, a corpse with jutting teeth.

Jöns startles, retreats, and rides up ahead to join the Knight:

Knight: Well, did he show you the way?
Jöns: Not exactly.
Knight: What did he say?
Jöns: Nothing.
Knight: Was he mute?
Jöns: No, sir. I wouldn't say that. As a matter of fact, he was quite eloquent.
Knight: Oh?
Jöns: Yes, eloquent enough. The trouble is that what he had to say was most depressing.[18]

A second scene features not the squire's wit but his capacity for action, which sets a contrast with the Knight's onlooking reflection. The Knight thinks, plays chess with Death, and questions a young girl held captive as a witch. They encounter her, tied, parched, about to be burned. The Knight, weak and disillusioned, asks all the right philosophical and religious questions. He wants to grasp what drives her apparently indomitable faith—perhaps hoping to buoy his own. The squire responds to her need—which is not to give answers to curious knights. The squire offers her water and words of comfort in her distress. Clearly in this instance the squire is the better man—despite lacking the Knight's attractive intellectual intensity.

The Knight and Jöns construe death and suffering quite differently. The Knight wants explanatory answers to the offense of suffering. The squire sees that suffering demands nothing but compassion, steady action. For the Knight death is a mystery that one battles philosophically—keeping nobility and honor intact. For the squire, death is a call for help: one responds.

Too often, a brooding reflection like the Knight's seems to capture the stance of philosophy itself—a lean toward skepticism and disillusionment. The Knight remains self-contained, noble in his melancholy. But skepticism is not always contained or noble. The disillusionment of Ahab or Ivan Karamazov erupts in violent

---

[18] Ingmar Bergman, *The Seventh Seal*, Halifax, NS: Lorrimer Books, 1968.

self-assertion. In contrast, the squire's steadiness and concern never veers toward brooding or madness. He resembles Ivan's brother Alyosha, and Ahab's squires, Starbuck and Stubb, who manifest steady compassion.

Of course Melville calls Starbuck and Stubb knights, and their harpooners, Queequeg and Tashtego, squires—there to do the bidding of their Quixotic knights. But once out of their longboats, Starbuck and Stubb become squires to Ahab in Melville's story of the pursuit of a whale. Starbuck and Stubb have a love of the world that Ahab lacks. So in commending squires I'm commending those who, while in Ahab's unyielding grip, nevertheless salvage the remnants of their humanity.

Ahab has an intense and perverse philosophical desire, to corner death and learn its secrets. Starbuck and Stubb have none of this philosophical compulsion and are clearly the better men—not that philosophical questions *create* monsters. And Jöns—the squire to Bergman's Knight—in the instances we've witnessed, also is the better man (though he lacks the attractive brooding, reflective intensity of the Knight). Ahab is a *thinker's* existentialist. I don't conclude that melancholy, because prone to violence or despair, is illegitimate for poetry or philosophy. I conclude that it's best tempered by a companion mood, something like the squire's readiness to respond simply, compassionately, to the vulnerabilities of another. Both reflection and melancholy can delay compassionate response, so both must know their bounds. Here, I praise squires in this vale of tears.

Of course in the best of worlds, we'd transcend the need for a choice between Knights *or* squires, High *or* low, Commander *or* commanded. We'd welcome a world without armor or harpoons, without attack and counter-thrust.

IX

I take Glenn Gray to be more squire than brooding knight, though he's certainly a philosopher. This just reminds us that philosophers need not be melancholy. Arendt certainly wasn't. She was the resourceful émigré who escaped the Gestapo by the skin of her teeth—first in Germany, then in France. She was Heidegger's lover and student. Gray was drafted the day he received his Columbia PhD. He shared with Arendt a love of philosophy, and shared the trauma of German descent into militarism, hatred, and destruction.[19] Philosophers can be patricians, aristrocrats, or knights. They can also live for a squire's love of the world and of others.

In dark times love and poetry can resist skepticism, the melancholy and despair of Bergman's Knight or Melville's Ahab, a suspicion of the world, a doubt that there is anything that really matters in one's attachments to the world and others. Skepticism of this sort is defeated, if it is—or is contained, if it is—by love of the world, by gratitude, by wonder, and by mourning. Philosophy, like poetry, can push back in dark times, cast a ray of light through doubt and despair.

Skepticism might take a classical Cartesian form ("How do I know that the world exists?"). Or it might be allied with unmasking social or psychological certainties, the sort of skepticism that Marx, Nietzsche, and Freud ply, earning them the title "masters of suspicion." Would you say Marx or Nietzsche or Freud lived their suspicions? Yes and no. They saw through illusions and helped others see through them. But they also *lived* straightforwardly immersed in the worlds they suspected. On the other hand, Bergman's Knight, Ivan Karamazov, or Captain Ahab clearly do live out their skepticism, in ways cruel, or satanic.

Stanley Cavell holds the provocative view that even skepticism Cartesian style has analogies to a refusal of others and the world: it's of a piece with tragedy and pride, even violence. In the life of Ivan Karamazov, skepticism is a refusal of others linked to cruelty and finally murder. The cruelty may not be immediately evident: "I'm returning the ticket," Ivan confesses to his brother, the ticket to life, to creation. He has no love of the world. But it's clear that Ivan speaks to pull his brother Alyosha *away* from creation, away from his love for others, and most especially, from his attachment to the revered Zossima. In that, his skepticism becomes cruel. Cavell would frame the impasse between Ivan and Alyosha as a failure not of knowledge or reason (as if there were a neutral spot from which one could decide that the world was or wasn't worthy of love). It's a failure, rather, of affirmation, or acknowledgment—a failure of love. The one thing needed is to *fall in love with the world.* For Cavell, though he doesn't address the Karamazov's directly, there is only one way that Ivan's

---

[19] When I saw Arendt's name on the cover of *The Warriors* (in 1960), I wondered, naively, what a woman philosopher would find to praise in a war book; and I wondered what a college philosophy professor (in tweeds?) would say on that unlikely subject. I learned soon enough.

doubt and world denial can be answered (as we've seen in an earlier chapter).

> To live in the face of doubt, eyes happily shut, would be to fall in love with the world. For if there is a correct blindness, only love has it. And if you find that you have fallen in love with the world, then you would be ill-advised to offer an argument of its worth.[20]

This might be a diagnosis of what Ivan lacks, and so a hope for what might save him—a hope in the event, disappointed. It has a familiar ring for those who read Kierkegaard, as well. Wittgenstein had asked "Do I doubt?" and answered, "My eyes are shut." Cavell's elaboration is that skeptical doubt, though beyond refutation, can lose its grip—as when we close our eyes before a kiss. A fearful mutual vulnerability is for a moment shelved. This is the blindness of love, the only blindness that can be "correct." It's living *happily* in the face of doubt—impossible all the time for anyone, and impossible any of the time for some unfortunate few. Yet for life it seems a necessity.

Cavell says that if we are to "fall in love with the world," we must sometimes avert our eyes. But this closing of eyes for love is the opposite of Oedipus' self-blinding. It's a startling thought—that blinding can open a place for love, but it seems right. It's good that love can blind doubt, that gratitude can blind melancholy, that beauty can blind terror. It's good that wonder can muffle despair, and that simple care can derail excessive roils of reflection. The Whirlwind from *The Book of Job* delivers wonders of such extent, that one by one they avert Job's eyes from his suffering. Before beauties and terrors, his anger and self-assertion subside. He finds space for affirmation of the world. The skeptical doubts about *why* there should be suffering, the doubts that fueled his rebellion, are set aside—not refuted. Job melts before the wonders of creation. This conversion, this revelation and transformation, is poetically effected. The whirlwind is pure, sublime poetry.[21] The wedding of doubt, affirmation, and poetry is no more fragile (and

---

[20] *The Claim of Reason*, 431. The passage continues, "you would be ill-advised to offer an argument of its worth by praising its Design. Because you are bound to fall out of love with your argument, and you may thereupon forget that the world is wonder enough, as it stands. Or not." There is no guarantee that you will find the world "wonder enough." Perhaps since the Holocaust we have lost much of what Arendt calls the capacity to write or act "for love of the world." See chapter seven in this volume.

[21] Anthony Rudd defends the co-presence of doubt and poetic attunement in *Expressing the World: Skepticism, Wittgenstein, Heidegger*, Chicago: OpenCourt, 2003.

just as fragile) as love itself. One thinks here of Levinas, who builds the acceptance of the other into the very basis of any responsible philosophy, long before epistemological compunctions can surface.

Cruelty drives Ivan. He returns to his family from Paris because he smells his father's blood. He wants to be there for the murder he will slyly instigate. He enjoys unleashing his Paris-trained intelligence against his younger brother's love and faith. His cool Euclidian understanding culminates in violence. He sets up the elder Karamazov's death, and sets out to kill Alyosha's spirit and his devotion to the holy Zossima. Ivan's famous poem of the Grand Inquisitor is in the service of despair, and it is conveyed to his brother on the very evening Alyosha heads to the monastery to comfort the dying Patriarch. The poem is meant to derail Alyosha's devotion.

The scene is the sixteenth-century Spanish Inquisition with its immolations overseen by a wizened Cardinal. He turns suddenly to see Christ among the throng. The Cardinal jails Him, and in an evening visit, accuses Christ of placing an impossible burden on his people. They cannot cope with freedom, he argues. Out of a far greater compassion than Christ can ever know, the Church, so the Cardinal avers, removes this impossible burden. The inquisitorial fires will claim this Jesus. Ivan's skeptical invention is brilliant and strangely resistant to conclusive philosophical refutation, and just as important, it's deployed sadistically. Skepticism becomes refusal of one's brother, and a hatred of the world. Incapable of love, Ivan dies.

X

In 1963, when Arendt's *The Banality of Evil* appeared, Cavell interrupted his Berkeley lectures on *Moby Dick* to take up evil in a different guise. In many ways, Eichmann has nothing in common with Ahab, yet if there is evil, they are each instances.[22] I like to think that both Cavell and Arendt were not just asking, as the Knight might, *Why is there evil, banal or demonic?*, but also enacting the squire's response, and Alyosha's: *Let me help!*

---

[22] Arendt's book on Eichmann does not sing with a love of the world. *How could it!* But her dispassionate take on the proceedings infuriated many readers. She lacked righteous indignation.

If there must be realism about pain, there must also be room for hope and the steadiness of care. Both are fueled when poetry taps its powers to push back against the worst. Pushing back poetically is not pushing with argument or doctrine but with simple lines and longer narratives. In the last pages of his *Postscript,* Kierkegaard's Johannes Climacus revokes arguments and doctrine in favor of falling in love with a certain way of life, Socratic and Christian.[23] I think Glenn Gray worked for a kind of writing about war that, by maintaining a tonality of love and steady action, pushed back against its horror. Perhaps he is best figured as a squire (though in the company, as perhaps most of us are, of a Knight).

I've said poetry might veer toward prayer, that Glenn Gray's invocation of Auden's "*We must love one another or die*" might echo as liturgy, perhaps part of a service of gratitude and mourning responsive to the call of the world and others, an invocation to see the world as worthy of love, an invitation to fall in love with the world. Whether from Rilke, Auden, or *Job,* poetry often resonates as prayer: words strangely quiet and weak, yet bracing, sustaining and resilient.

This brings to mind a haunting story, darkly poetic, from Eli Wiesel. From the midst of a concentration camp, a group of rabbis argues noisily, putting God on trial. The charges are impeccable. How could He mete such affliction on his people! They deliberate vigorously, and find God guilty. And then pray.

I hear in that story a shift from the perplexed and melancholy disillusionment of the Knight to the outright rebellion of Job as he battles Yahweh, claiming his innocence (rightly, as it turns out), and insisting loudly for an account. The rabbis battle with God for an answer. They push forward with their arguments. They utterly *fail.* And from depths we can't fathom, they muster strength for prayer: open their hearts for a moment, close their eyes, as it were, awaiting a touch. Their God is terribly absent, perhaps even broken. Unfathomably, their hearts do not die, do not block hope for light that yet—even yet—might glimmer—even blaze—from their abyss. Prayer, then, is hope that even broken Gods might yet look (or murmur), that even broken souls listen, that even broken worlds, from their shattered beauty, can captivate a caring eye, can call alluringly, poetically, and plead: Behold, all around you! *you must change your life!* Thus affirming, *we matter in affliction.*

---

[23] See *On Søren Kierkegaard,* Ch. 12.

Chapter 12

THOREAU'S TRANSLATIONS:
John Brown, Apples, Lilies

Thoreau's evocations of wilderness and his piercing political essays are unified expressions of a single impulse, a love of the world, a world that must continually be raised from desolation, shadows, decline, and death. He delivers the serenity of Walden Pond with one hand, and with the other, a defense of civil disobedience in protest of the invasion of Mexico. We share his climb up Maine's austere Ktaadn and then share "Slavery in Massachusetts" delivered at a rally after the re-enslavement of Anthony Burns. We may remember "Walking" or "Wild Apples," redolent of woods or meadow, and we remember equally his impassioned "Plea for Captain John Brown." Brown's raid on Harpers Ferry appears today as the opening skirmish of a bloody uncivil War, a skirmish won by the South who had him hanged. Thoreau's full-throated defense was as much against the local grain as his "retreat" to Walden. His vivid accounts and evocations work from an impulse to save what's best in Brown and what's best in the land and terrain we inhabit together.

Through varied phases of his life, Thoreau sought fullness in becoming, recounted, composed, passed on to us by words. They're words we savor, save, and reenact in speech and deed, continuing thereby continuous creation marked by cycles of grief and celebration, of perishing (tender or cruel), and of unfailing advent of new days. His song enacts an instinctive love, a passion to save what's worth saving, whether it's the eternal sound of the sea saved for our ears, the taste of wild apples saved as the elixir of the gods, the testament

Thanks to Marcia Robinson and Clark West who each in their way made this reading possible.

of John Brown saved for our humanity, or the scent of a lily saved as the hope of creation.

I. SENSING THE LIFE OF THE WORLD

Thoreau is a philosopher of the senses: "*We need pray for no higher heaven than the pure senses can furnish . . .*"[1] Sensing the world from new angles brings it alive anew. His paths toward the rocky heights of Ktaadn cut through varied wilderness. He sees and takes note of the detail along the way, beholding a mobile, evanescent surround that alters as he moves and sees anew. There are lakes, dense forests, dangerous rapids, and the sense that few humans have marked the terrain, perhaps none with the poetic renderings he will afford. Approaching the summit, he's stopped dead in his tracks, for the top is invisible, shrouded in mist, unnerving, forbidding. There is no sense of the human or even of life—only boulders, precariously balanced, as if cast away and ready to plummet. A mile into clouds, he's struck down by the sight of "some undone extremity of the globe."[2] This is no longer the forested approach. It seems to Thoreau that "some vital part" of him "escape[s] through the loose grating of his ribs."[3] Ktaadn gives him an inhospitable, unfinished creation, quite unlike the creations, the dawns, he recounts by Walden Pond. This sight doesn't so much bring the world alive as remind him that the world can be *drained.*

Worlds otherwise drained can be filled by Thoreau's ample poetic approach. Here he seeks the shipwrecked remains of his friend, Margaret Fuller:

> I expected that I should have to look very narrowly at the sand to find so small an object, but so completely smooth and bare was the beach . . . that when I was half a mile distant the insignificant stick or sliver which marked the spot looked like a broken spar in the sand. There lay the relics in a certain state, rendered perfectly inoffensive to both bodily and spiritual eye by the surrounding scenery, a slight inequality in the sweep of the shore . . . It was as conspicuous on that

[1] Henry David Thoreau, *A Week on the Concord and Merrimack Rivers*, ed. Carl F. Hove, William L. Howarth, and Elizabeth Hall Witherell, intro. John McPhee, Princeton: Princeton University Press, 1980, 382; italics mine.
[2] "Ktaadn," originally, "Ktaadn, and the *Maine Woods*," Lewis Hyde, *The Collected Essays of Henry D Thoreau*, 108.
[3] Ibid.

sandy plain as if a generation had labored to pile up a cairn there . . . It reigned over the shore. That dead body possessed the shore as no living one could.[4]

The place of Fuller's bones is at first of dark mourning or grief; yet a sprig rises to become a ship's spar and then a rugged cairn, holding her reign and majesty. A place otherwise redolent of death is transformed toward radiance and dawn. "Her bones were alone with the beach and the sea, whose roar seemed to address them . . . as if there were an understanding between them and the ocean that necessarily left me out."[5] So her communion with the endless surf lengthens the time she inhabits. Thoreau witnesses communion too vast, long lasting, and impersonal to include him. Nevertheless, the beach cradles a fellow-writer and activist, and he has time to *give witness* to her majesty. On Ktaadn, in contrast, he is affronted by the impossibility of anything *like* communion, personal or impersonal, the impossibility even of contact with the terrain. It repels his presence, his view goes blank and spirit flees, as if before a terror that cannot afford to be seen.

II. TASTES AND SAUNTERING

Sight of the world is one path of access. Taste of the world strikes us differently. Thoreau is wise in the taste of wild apples, the taste of a breeze. But even here, matters of angle, scale, and placement obtrude. The refreshing taste of wild apples expands toward the gods and eternal youth. Wild apples "*pierce* and *sting* and *permeate* us with their spirit,"[6] and hold the elixirs "that keep the gods forever young."[7] To taste is to know spirit, to enjoy and suffer an immediacy of contact that brings moments of fulfillment. The world provides a sting that answers desire for impact. "What a healthy out-of-door appetite it takes to relish the apple of life, the apple of the world!"[8] The life of the

---

[4] Thoreau, *Cape Cod*, 123, worked up from *Journal*, vol. 3, 1848–51 ed. R. Sattelmeyer, M.R. Patterson, W. Rossi, Princeton, 1990, 127. Fuller is not named here, but it's clear that he alludes to his search for Fuller in the sands of Fire Island where he was sent from Concord to retrieve her effects and body. The bones that he found there were too decomposed to be identified as hers; only some of her clothing was found, and none of her writing.

[5] Ibid.

[6] Thoreau, *Essays*, 305; emphasis added.

[7] Ibid., 295.

[8] Ibid., 306.

world is the life of our tastes for apples or sharp winds, for damp earth beneath our feet or a stream's curling eddy around blistered toes. The world's life is the flickering of our mobile senses and visceral responses, and also the life of our words. The contacts Thoreau transmits are conveyed through words that reenact his primordial contacts—with the world, but also with the words of the *Gita*, of the *Gospels*, of Milton, and of endless others.

Thoreau is a saunterer. Seeing, hearing, and tasting, and a sense of breath and body in motion, and then stilled, converge in his tramping. Walking is an art, he says, that very few have mastered.[9] (A parallel thought is that few know how to die.) To leave the enigma hanging— the rather offensive provocation that I may not know how to walk— leaves his words strange, and the world strange and wonderful. If we give our heart to that wonder, if we yield to the thought that we might yet learn to walk, we acknowledge the world as a holy place we have yet to enter. Henry Bugbee, a philosopher deeply indebted to Thoreau, characterizes philosophy as a "walking meditation of the place."[10] This fits Thoreau's practice exactly. He is a prodigious tramper, living the visceral contact with body, earth, and air that walking so wonderfully affords.

Sauntering is a beholding-in-motion, a moving in and toward the wondrous, sacred, or sublime. It uncovers and accepts the world as a place in motion, in unending creation. Sauntering is pilgrimage, but as Thoreau has it, not *away* from the ordinary toward the holy or sacred, but through the *midst* of the ordinary-become-sacred, or the sacred-become-ordinary.[11] It is not passing from A to B but a happening joined to the sacramental act of taking steps steeped in the wilds all around. The holy appears *through,* and *in* walking that is a receptive articulation and consecration. Though we had heard that the sacred is housed just over the horizon, we arrive at the realization that ours is already a special, sacred place, given to our care and attention.

Where earth, sky, and waters, where blossom of trees, sounds of companions, and tastes of apples greet us, are imbibed and transformed, there we have sacred sites. Their sacrality is redeemed in their power to transform as we move therein. Contact is not "raw data" but schooled, thought-seasoned, often toward the bounteous. As Thoreau

---

[9] Thoreau, "Walking," in ibid., 149.

[10] Bugbee, *Inward Morning*, 139.

[11] Ibid. Also, see Andrea Wilson Nightingale, *Spectacles of Truth* and chapter one in this volume.

has it, "We are comparatively deaf and dumb and blind, without smell
or taste or feeling . . . *What is it, then, to educate but to develop these
germs [seeds] called the senses?*"[12] We sense the taste of apples (gifts of
the gods), the meteor flash that is John Brown, the communing of
the sea with Fuller's bones, achievements of sharpened eyes and
ears. The world is not primitively either sacred or unsacred, but awaits
its best advent through our tuned sensibilities. Thoreau helps hone
them toward receiving the bounteous in its ephemeral passing. That
passing is through, and of, unfinished creation, accrued in walking in
the place. The poet–walker *in* and *of* a holy place, is also a singer and
rower, matching breath, limbs, and motion to song. "We rowed by
turns swiftly over the surface [of the lake], singing such boat songs
as we could remember."[13] As all singers must, Thoreau listened—in
expectation of howls answering evening songs from the boat; in expectation of the "droll trill" of a whippoorwill, its "wailing hymns," the
"idiotic hooting" of owls, the "thump" of the frog, the thunder that
even the gods hear with awe.

In a college essay on the sublime, Thoreau holds that it is not triggered by fear, as Burke and Kant would hold. "Contact with the infinite," he says, occurs through wonder and awe, and responds less to
fear and death than delight and birth. What he later calls "dawn"
supervenes on afflictions and dread.[14] Because they were immortal,
Greek gods could have no fear of death, he says, yet the thunder of
Zeus could still bring them to awe as it clears the heavens for dawn.[15]
Thoreau awakens hearingly to the lusty herald of a cock at first light,
and also to godly thunder, yet he would not slight the wonder of
more diminutive sounds. He builds simple walls against the elements,
affording a dry place for sleep, where he's serenaded "by the sound of
raindrops on the cedar splints which covered the roof."[16]

---

[12] Thoreau, *A Week*, 382; emphasis added.

[13] "Ktaadn," in *Essays*, 90.

[14] *Thoreau's Writings, Early Essays and Miscellanies*, ed. Joseph J. Moldenhauer and
Edwin Moser, Princeton, 1975, 94.

[15] Thunder, the top of Ktaadn, or floating alone looking skyward in a boat—these
mark moments of "the sublime" or "infinite" for Thoreau. Rousseau, too, has a reverie,
looking up from a boat's bottom to find a glimpse of "the infinite" (*Reveries of a Solitary
Walker, no. 5*). See chapter four in this volume.

[16] "Ktaadn," in *Essays*, 80.

III. TRANSFORMATIVE CONTACT

To have a love in and for the world is to be alive in and for its preservation, which assumes a knack for contact. Sight, taste, scent, and
hearing are modalities of impact that expand, close down, and transfigure—even as the world they contact expands, contracts, and transfigures. On Ktaadn Thoreau's sense of the world falls away. Somewhere
between desperation and ecstasy, he shouts "rocks, trees, wind on our
cheeks! The *solid* earth! The actual world! The *common sense! Contact!
Contact! Who* are we? *Where* are we?"[17] We get contact and orientation
(we hope), and then rely on our powers of articulation and conveyance. Sometimes a dumb stupor supervenes, but stupor aside, variations of impact (and of monotony or absence) achieve poetic
translation. Words then enact the mobility and evanescence of the
world at hand, across spectrums of importance. We take in importance
from one angle to the next, from a *lack* of touch to vivid sight or hearing, from the corrupt to the redemptive. It's a poet's gift in which we
all take part. When schooled toward the sacred, contact restores bounteous worlds. From Thoreau's pen and capacity for contact, we're
delivered gentle and striking translations as he moves from stench to
sweet lilies, from bare bones to saint's relics, from a noose that kills
to a hanging that launches a meteor, John Brown.[18]

We give and take such translations from one angle to another, one
placement to another, one time scale to another, one sense of verticality to another (reaching toward the gods or the higher law or the
good). Or in moments of dark, things are flat, with no rise or fall, no
verticality at all.[19] Thoreau gives us life through plays of words whose
spring seems inevitable, compelling, like a dawn or thunderclap. We
might shut down, but why should we!

A single passion, a yearning for life's well-springs, makes Thoreau's
political words of a piece with his sauntering or rowing. It's a passion
amidst social desolation—for life to fund protest and moral appraisal;

---

[17] Ibid., 113; emphasis in the original.

[18] Thoreau has Brown's hanging as the day of his "translation" from a man having
his last meal with his wife to "a divine spark," and "a meteor," making him "more alive
than he every was. Brown earns immortality," and is now "in the clearest light that
shines on this land." *Essays*, 288.

[19] Thoreau calls on our knack for *seeing as,* for *hearing as,* for *tasting as.* The classic
discussion of "seeing as" is in Wittgenstein's *Philosophical Investigations.*

for life-springs to stiffen spirit on a climb on Ktaadn, or for waters that sooth in a walk through woods. He has passions to find and deliver life's swirls, to ride them, however wild, to write them as he finds them (and as they find him).

Thoreau takes sources of life to be the wild, untamed, unknown, or sublime. The life of the world means contact with wildness, and contact with the life of our words,[20] words that tap this wildness bringing new angles, new life. In families, tribes, collectivities, and in solitude, we receive and give back articulations, for language is not a private preserve. Thoreau brings us to fields of words (as we read) that in turn sing the fields of Maine (as we hear). He keeps us among lustrous things and things austere: the call of the whippoorwill, the roll of the sea, the mist on Ktaadn, delivering us from shadow and collapse.

How does this happen? For thunder to enter and be in my world, scrubbing it clean with a bang, I must have ears attuned. (I can't be deaf, or too absorbed to notice.) And the heavens must roaringly provide. Thunder is renewing, mobile, and evanescent: *there*—in and of the world. Portals for thunder or the thump of frogs allow sheen or ornament to be *added to* the world, and also allow flow back from the world as sheen or terror that enter *us* become *ours* (or not). The ear gives power to thunder and thunder shapes the ear. Contacts transfigure bi-directionally. *Thoreau* is shaped by the entry of birdsong, and birdsong enters because his ear is so shaped. As his ear is schooled, his *world* is changed, and he marks that change poetically, recapitulating it as a voice of creation, conveyed, for example, in *A Week*, or *Cape Cod*. Sound betokens the world transformed. In learning to listen the world is reborn.

Thoreau is not the same after writing *The Maine Woods* nor is Ktaadn, now misted in ghostly power. He's not the same after "Wild Apples," and the apples around Concord have changed, too, after Thoreau has us taste one frozen, then thawed. As Fuller's bones are transfigured, just so, the body spirited in secret from Harpers Ferry to Manhattan's Battery, and north again by rail to North Elba for burial. John Brown's fugitive, secreted body cannot be the same after being taken up in Thoreau's "Plea" and "The Last Days."

---

[20] Simon Critchley, *Things Merely Are*, London: Routledge, 2005, 10.

IV. APOCALYPSE

It's not just the crow of a barnyard cock that transforms night to day, and not just a slender stick marking Fuller's bones that triggers the change from a cruel site of unnecessary death to the raising of a cairn and a communion of bones with the lap of the sea. On occasion, at issue is the raising up of an entire polity or nation or region—not particulars but a world itself, gripped by desolation and demanding restoration, as if vast suffering were a cosmic and inhuman punishment. Yet even as he addresses the darkness of the nation under slavery, or addresses somewhat more "metaphysical" matters, Thoreau renders life at sites that yield *singularity of contact*: contact with Fuller, contact with John Brown.

There is a coming apocalypse, and John Brown is its prophet and avenging angel. The portal of scent keys Thoreau's presence to slavery's Hell. Corruption has left its inescapable olfactory mark. In "Slavery in Massachusetts," Thoreau recounts the unbearable stench of Daniel Webster's joining slavers in support of the fugitive slave act of 1850. The Massachusetts senator sponsored a bill that strengthened Southern power, and granted license to slavers infiltrating the North to hunt down blacks on the run.

Anthony Burns was the center of one of the more violent and celebrated cases of slave recapture and attempted rescue.[21] He was cornered by Southern hunters and jailed in the Boston courthouse, as the new federal law required. A crowd of several hundred abolitionists and free blacks joined for a rescue attempt, battering a hole in the doors. The crowd grew to at least two thousand. In the assault, shots were fired. A jailer was killed, apparently stabbed. An acquaintance of Thoreau gained entry, but Burns was held inaccessible on the third floor.[22] Federal soldiers moved in, *foreign* soldiers, as it were—or at the least, enforcers of a despised law that was work of a foreign, alien, and

---

[21] "Slavery in Massachusetts" was Thoreau's exasperated, angry, even despairing, but ultimately affirming response to the Burns case, delivered July 4, 1854, at an abolitionist protest and rally in Framingham, MA. It was published in Garrison's *Liberator* July 21, an "affirming response" in light of its closing image of the lily.

[22] Thomas Wentworth Higginson, a friend of Thoreau, gained entry, and was to become a member of The Secret Six who financially supported John Brown's Kansas paramilitary activity and attack at Harpers Ferry. He was also an editorial confidant at the *Atlantic* of the young Emily Dickinson.

corrupt power. Or so it was for Thoreau and a great number of angry and humiliated New Englanders.

Burns was paraded as a captured trophy between columns of cavalry and foot soldiers in full military dress, rifles loaded at the ready, even a horse-drawn cannon, should it be needed. The ceremonial parade was meant to demonstrate regal Federal power and the nullity of the slave. He was made to publicly endure a humiliatingly slow and shackled walk down to a Federal ship that would return him to the South. Fifty thousand citizens lined the streets shouting "shame!" at this spectacle, a second Boston massacre.[23] There was no New England spring that year for Thoreau. He mourns lost fragrance of woods and meadows. Everything offends his keen moral sense. In place of sauntering there is only a joyless slog through stench.

At last, graciously, access to a world-worth-saving is afforded his ever-alert senses. Wondrously, multiple registers of radiance appear. Fuller's bones are bones, but became not only that. The woods were woods, then hell—and now, not only that. After walking us through page after page of moral pollution, he comes finally upon a fragile lily, so slight it is almost overlooked. His keen nose opens this site of surviving heaven—and closes out hell. Or perhaps hell remains, but the lily pushes back with hope. This might be the difficult wisdom of Staretz Silouan: "Keep your mind in hell, and despair not."[24] The sweet scent of a swamp-lily opens to the wondrous.

Thoreau finds purity lodged in the muck of servility and slavery.[25] The flower whose tendrils descend indecorously to a fouled anchorage gives off a fragrance rising from an aeon of accumulated grime. Mud feeds sweet bloom, and Thoreau finds hope in this. More or less permanent pollution may belie a moment of uncorrupted courage and honor. The lily's scent, an aroma of instant transfiguration, cuts through, restoring the promise of a world reborn.

Julia Ward Howe was the wife of one of the undercover Secret Six, men who at great risk provided financial support for John Brown's

---

[23] Burns was made to march alone flanked by four Federal companies in full regalia, two companies of Boston militia, and several artillery companies, including a cannon. It was a ridiculous show meant to ridicule the Abolitionist cause and Burns himself. Soldiers were ordered to shoot into the crowd at any sign of "disturbance"—hence a restaging of the Boston Massacre. Southern slave-catchers gloated. The military intimidation, in their view, was "teaching New Englanders a lesson" (see Austin Willey, ed. Maine's *Portland Inquiry*, June 1, 1854). The headline for Willey's account is "Rubbing it in! Man-Hunting in Boston." I thank Marcia Robinson for this source.

[24] Silouan is quoted on the frontispiece to Gillian Rose, *Love's Work*, Schocken, 1997.

[25] "Slavery," in *Essays*, 193.

paramilitary antislavery work. She invokes the lily in verses published in 1862, too late for Thoreau to have heard them. They were set to the tune of "John Brown's Body." We hear the lily's Gospel roots as the verse pushes hope forward into the coming bloody mess:

> In the beauty of the lilies Christ was born across the sea,
> with a glory in his bosom that transfigures you and me.
> As he died to make men holy,
> let us die to make men free.[26]

Thoreau had no doubt that John Brown died to make men free.

V. RAISING THE DEAD

We've encountered the transfiguration of apples and bones and the stench of the woods and meadows, and we've met the transfiguration of Ktaadn to dark Chaos. Thoreau musters a new response to the death—and life—of John Brown by recalling what he has *heard* of the man and his fate. He offers an angle of *hearing*. On the day of Brown's death, he "heard that he was *hung*" but did not "*hear* that he was *dead*..." and he lets the enigma linger. If he had heard that Brown was hung, why, for heaven's sake, would he *need* to hear that Brown was dead? Crediting Thoreau with sanity and full powers of articulation, we must work with his words as he gives them—not slough them off as confusion, mental lapse, or poetic acrobatics. He leaves time to let this paradox settle in, testing our imaginative patience, as it were. The incongruity is that a life might not perish in hanging, and that hanging might not bring death.

Thoreau intimates that he had not *heard* that John Brown was dead—because he *wasn't*. In being hung, Brown might have been given new life, as martyrs are. Or Brown might live because it's impossible to *believe*, or *comprehend*, that Brown is dead—not because the shock of the news can't be absorbed but because anyone as alive in action, principle, and spirit as John Brown cannot have died *for all the life in him*. It may be that Thoreau's missing the news suggests that Brown survives indefinitely, into an extended future, in just the way the life of a meteor or of a Schubert Sonata outlasts the microscopically small, clocked

---

[26] "John's Brown's Body" was already a popular military camp song. It began, with different words, as a campfire spiritual, sung to the tune of "The Battle Hymn of the Republic."

interval of its entry into, and departure from, the world. My most recent contact with a Schubert Sonata, in one sense ended when my CD player stopped, and I paused before moving on. Yet I know simultaneously that the music has not ceased but extends sempiternally. Taking the long view, we might say that John Brown's origin is as old and dateless as Old Testament prophets or angels, and that his life extends forward from his hanging to our time and into an indeterminate beyond. The eloquence of his life outlasts the interval between his census-recorded life-and-death in much the same way as the radiance of a meteor outlasts the momentary flash of its light or the echoing rebounds of a Sonata outlasts my most recent hearing.

Life and death are anomalous phenomena in that they follow no single law of determination. My recording of Sonata 960 has stopped playing but that does not determine that it is not still alive—as ever. The gloaming shifts imperceptibly toward night but that does determine that the day is not still alive—as ever. The threshold of my door belongs to the beckoning outside as I stride out to the backyard from the kitchen but that does not determine that the threshold does not also belong to the inside of the house. The anomalous location of thresholds may matter less than the anomalous extent of the life of a Schubert Sonata, and both may matter less than the anomaly of Brown's death. He was hung yet perhaps is not definitively dead.

Thoreau calls tidal creatures, belonging to sea and to land and to neither and both, "anomalous creatures."[27] Something anomalous escapes a law or pattern of expected and well-defined action or status, belonging only problematically to them. Brown is outside Federal law, but more to the point, he's anomalous taxonomically, ontologically. There's something deeply troubling about whether this celebrated hanging gives or takes life. Brown's status is anomalous, for a medic's rule-bound conventions for determining its place and time are not absolutely determinative; he belongs to a mysterious wild.[28]

---

[27] That tidal strip (that held Fuller's bones) seems more important to Thoreau than either land or sea. Those who inhabit it—clams and jellyfish, for instance—he calls "anomalous creatures." See *Cape Cod*, Chapter IV, 81.

[28] Thoreau belongs to the anomalous wild, as does John Brown. Anomalous creatures can both survive and not survive, both die and not die; such alteration transpires both "inside" ("in consciousness") and "outside" ("objectively in the world"). For the possibility of both living on and not living on (inside and outside consciousness) see Kristeva's discussions of abjection and death, discussed in Ludger H. Viefhues-Baily, *Beyond the Philosopher's Fear: A Cavellian Reading of Gender, Origin and Religion in Modern Skepticism*, Aldershot: Ashgate, 2007, Chapter 5.

Thoreau has yet another sense in which John Brown slips out of the noose, this one keyed to the *opposite* of life-beyond-hanging. Daniel Webster miserably *failed* to survive hanging. Webster's vote for a strengthened fugitive slave law was his noose. He died even though census-takers found him living a year later. He is now in an anomalous zone because the laws of physiological death are not the laws of *moral* death. For a previously admired Northern Senator to promote a law that strengthened the powers of slavers to roam the New England countryside armed in pursuit of escaped slaves marked his moral death. Thoreau and Bronson Alcott each allude to gunshots in the woods signaling recapture or killing or terrorizing of a man, woman, or child on the way to Canada. On pain of federal arrest, the law forced citizens of Concord and Boston to assist in and not impede the capture of escaped slaves. In 1850 Theodore Parker preached in Boston that Webster "takes back his [previous anti-slavery] words and comes himself to be slavery's slave." Webster is an anomaly, a slave, despite appearances. Webster died despite appearances.[29]

In 1852, on the occasion of Webster's physiological departure, Parker asks if he can now mourn the man who two years earlier had signed the hated bill. He answers that he cannot, for the good reason that Webster died and was mourned *two years earlier.* John Greenleaf Whittier reinforced the point: "When faith is lost, when honor dies, the man is dead!"[30] Webster dies when he disavows his antislavery position; despite hanging, John Brown lives on as his avowed word lives on. When faith is secure and honor alive, the man is alive. Long before clerks mark him dead, Webster dies. Long after clerks stamp him "dead," John Brown lives.

VI. MEMENTO MORI!

If we credit Plato, to abandon the thought of death is to abandon philosophy. Court records list the living and dead, but those records do not reveal who really lives and dies. Thoreau cites the inscription, *Memento mori!*—Think of your death!—worrying that we hear this in only a "groveling" sense. We grovel before death rather than seek that angle from which life defeats death. An exultant life passes through death to add more to life, to *complete* it. Thoreau claims, "we've wholly

[29] See Edward J. Renehan, Jr., *The Secret Six, The True Tale of the Men who Conspired with John Brown,* Columbia: University of South Carolina Press, 1997, 47.
[30] See *Secret Six,* 47–48.

forgotten how to die," abandoning life by letting death be merely life that is "rotted or sloughed off."[31] Overseers at one end of a line of judges will have death declared as medics or census-takers might; those at the other end will have death declared in the fashion of those who would measure loss of character, radiance, or honor. The upshot? Brown's hanging does not lessen or kill his character, radiance or honor, but enhances these. Thoreau "fails to hear" that Brown is dead—because he *lives*.[32]

Cultures we inherit keep moral moments alive, keep persons of principle or great character alive through their display in texts or theater, in stories passed on by kin or by community action. Such moral moments are magnetic foci of admiration that fuel worthy aspirations and are fulfilled in worthy deeds and dispositions. Ideals of character, action, or bearing provide tacit or explicit models to measure life's worth: frankness or honor, courage or great kindness, dedication to justice or to the needs of kin. In no obvious order, these pictures of worth embed as relatively inescapable parts of lived reality. An ideal, or sets of them and their components, are sustained through our praising judgments of them, and through their continued affirmation by admired others. Aversions also play a role. A despised or disfavored action or temperament reinforces its converse. Dispraise or mocking distance keeps the unworthy at bay.

An ideal's strength can rest on self-mustered conviction, and also on affirmation by significant others. We affirm in concert, a fact hidden in a North-Atlantic ideological regime that would valorize absolute autonomy.[33] However, "*No man is an Island*," and no woman either. We grow up in families and they never abandon us, even as we trade some members for others, even distant others. Conviction grows amidst parents, neighbors, friends, and adopted next-of-kin. Thoreau might be one such adopted next-of-kin, one who becomes our conscience.[34]

---

[31] "A Plea," in *Essays*, 277.

[32] Kierkegaard suggests that Socrates escapes death at the moment of his sentence, for from that moment on no threats can coerce him. See *Fear and Trembling*, trans. Alastair Hannay, New York: Penguin, 1985, 141. Thoreau may see Brown's hanging against the death of Socrates.

[33] See chapter nine in this volume.

[34] On conscience, see James Conant, "Nietzsche's Perfectionism: A Reading of Schopenhauer as Educator," in *Nietzsche's Postmoralism*, ed. Richard Schacht, Cambridge: Cambridge University Press, 2001, 208. See also my "Wonder and Affliction: Thoreau's Dionysian World," *Thoreau as Philosopher*, ed. Rick Anthony Furtak, Stanford, 2010.

When an ideal takes on life, we depend on its successful conveyance through word and deed among a "we" of indefinite and changing extension and affinity. Exemplars are found and maintained through depiction, song, and direct face-to-face exchange. In contact, we soak in their traits, bearing, and deeds. John Brown is an exemplar for Thoreau, and perhaps through praise, he becomes one for us. Thoreau works to convey Brown's immortal worth; he says, in effect, "*Here is Life! Behold!*"

Brown's sixty-year life marks a successful if sometimes floundering biological achievement, the survival of a physically discrete body in time. As an animated *physiology,* Brown ceases with his hanging; yet his story, his life, his ensoulment does not stop there. In the words of the Civil War camp song, Thoreau keeps him from "amoulderin' in his grave."[35] Thoreau preserves Brown through writing, and as important, through resistance to slavery, both in the company he keeps and in his work escorting ex-captives on the underground railroad, acts kept alive in his writing and in the writing of others.

Beyond physiology, humans enter a cultural life that links sisters, mothers, brothers, friends, teachers, mayors, musicians, whose souls richly mix and are receptively porous to each other in the moment and over time. And we enter the abundance of Plato, Shakespeare, Christ, the Buddha, and endless others, an abundance that continues indefinitely past the demise of single physiologies. This flow of exchange over indefinitely expanding time and space constitutes what I call "infinite culture" and shapes what it is to be among the living.

What separates life from death? Remembering his accounts of walking, rowing, and seeking wild apples, we'd say that to be alive is to be immersed in taste, sound, touch, listening, sight—to behold—to be in contact with one's mobile surround. To be alive is also to nourish such contact in stride and song, in words and reenactments. This can be focused at three overlapping levels of resolution. We exercise *poetic* capacities of reception and transformation at the level of perception. A splinter appears as a spar. We exercise *moral* capacities of perception, deed, and character in styles of living that carry life beyond the confines of its merely physiological expression. (To risk bodily harm or social acceptability for an ideal is to let character trump physiological-only or conformist-only considerations.) And we exercise

---

[35] The Union civil war song begins, "John Brown's body lies a-mouldering in the grave/ But his soul goes marching on." To moulder is to turn to dust; making mouldings translates lumber to dust.

hermeneutical, interpretive capacities, engaging, altering, and repro-
ducing the cultures we inherit and inhabit. Powers of cultural articulation and conveyance let us articulate and reproduce our inherited
poetic and moral surround, passed on in texts, folklore, and endless
conversation. We imbibe and pass on ways of understanding of, and of
comportment toward, kin and strangers and those exemplary characters we praise and admire. To engage at this level of hermeneutical
transmission includes exercising expressive forms of politics, family
life, the arts, schooling, and ever-so-many other strands of our complex cultural identities.

Ktaadn becomes an outpost of the gods, Fuller's sandy remains
become relics, John Brown becomes a meteor: these radical rejuvena-
tions or animations of Ktaadn, Fuller, and Brown speak to Thoreau's
powers of imaginative transposition, his capacity for lyric transfigurations of others that in turn transfigure our own imaginations. A moral–
religious dimension is in play: he delivers "essays in intellectual love,"
Ortega-like "salvations," of Fuller, wild apples, or Walden. In the event,
his moral character and poetic–hermeneutic skills give *their* character
immortality. Transposed slightly, *their* character, as he absorbs it, gives
him power to *render* their immortality, which in turn underwrites *his*
character (and immortality). Rendering Fuller's capacity to rise above
her mangled body, or Ktaadn as the shrouded place where the gods
attend unfinished business, or John Brown as a serene and terrible
judge, tests our capacity to be alive. And we must not shut down
with the further test that asks us to acknowledge that only a half-dozen
persons have truly lived since the world began.

The bulk of villagers and citizens who have entered the census tables
in and about Concord have *neither lived nor died,* in the configuration
of those notions of interest to Thoreau. Can neighbors be dispossessed
so easily, with a stroke of the pen? Thoreau raises the bar for having
lived and places it out of reach, which might be perverse, but then
again, might snap his neighbors—*us*—awake. In "Walking," he raises
the bar for simply *walking,* saying that in his experience, only one
or two persons have learned that art. How many have been alive to
the taste of the evanescent world in all its poetic variety and intensity, the world of the saunterer, a world that is always already on the
way to the holy? His installing impossible, humbling, or frankly exclusionary standards can seem impertinent. For the moment (I'll return
to this issue) we might say that these upward revisions of what it takes
to be walking or living appear frivolous mainly for those mired in
merely village wisdom. For Thoreau, these startling reformulations are
neither passing fancy nor conceptual tinkering.

One way or another, Thoreau's poetic translations are intended to be *moves into reality*, into contact that completes it and so also transfigures. His translations are from one register of reality to its successor. By the light of the first, the successor may seem improbable. Yet with the right touch, the successor will seem mysteriously inevitable. Thoreau gives us contact with our not knowing how to walk or live or die—with the strange reality of our having *neither* lived nor died, even as Washington and Franklin have neither lived nor died.

VII. Behold!

Thoreau meets John Brown for an evening some months before Harpers Ferry. Later, after his civilly certified death, he beholds John Brown transfigured. Brown would be ill-served by having the interval of his life recorded only as the clerk's notes on his birth and burial, or the astronomer's timing of the few seconds of a meteor-flash. A photographic plate can't pick up the extended cultural impact of a meteor, nor can it catch the meteor that is John Brown. The interval of Thoreau's beholding is much longer, for it is repeated again and again, with each reading generation, like my hearing and rehearing of Schubert's 960. And Meteors are portents, as timeless as John Brown is timeless. He is revived yet again—as a portent now a full century and a half later. Thoreau notes the dates for Brown leaving Concord, for his battle at Harpers Ferry, and for the day he mounts the gallows or is buried in North Elba. But these dates do not answer—in any deep sense—whether Brown is alive or dead. As a philosopher, Thoreau wonders how one can die if one has never lived, and how one can live if one's death does not echo through the tissues of one's life, making it add to, rather than deplete, the life.

The fullness of Brown's life casts a shadow on the so-called lives of earlier notables. Washington and Franklin, for instance, did not really die, for Thoreau holds that their death failed to speak, failed to echo back through their life. Theirs was nothing like a *sacrificial* death, a death *for* something of importance. Brown dies for *freedom,* his death *speaks* for it, enriching the life devoted to it. This cannot be said of the death of Franklin or of Washington. "It seems," Thoreau writes, "as if no man had ever died in American before, for in order to die you must first have lived."[36]

---

[36] "A Plea," in *Essays*, 277.

Tracing Brown's life from a plateau like that beneath Ktaadn's cloud-shrouded summit (the place of the gods, the place of creation), a census-keeper's tally of life and death dwindles precipitously in significance. An apotheosis brings John Brown into view, and diminishes Franklin and Washington enough that their life-and-death is no more than a *mechanical tick.* As Thoreau wryly puts it, they merely "ran down like a clock"; they "were let off with out dying." Released from the ranks, "they were merely missing one day."[37]

To rise to Ktaadn is to reign from the place where the world began. The fathers of the Republic do not so rise. The press noted funerals, dates, and accomplishments. Family and friends will miss them. But from the summit of Ktaadn where gods forge worlds, give life, and take it—from that height, these were minor deaths, or no deaths at all. "No temple's *vail* was rent," Thoreau protests, "only a hole dug somewhere." Why should a vail be rent? Well, we want to *learn* something, not only from a life, but in a death. Thoreau finds no shattering revelation in commonplace demise. Brown's death rends a vail; it conveys—*is*—a revelation, an apocalypse. To die on a gallows for the *best* of things throws light back on life, affirmatively. Gallows shimmer as a cross, and a death sheds radiant light. To listen to Brown's words from jail, Thoreau says, is to hear a new testament, and he confronts his countrymen with scathing irony, "You don't know your testament when you see it."[38]

VIII. IMPOSSIBLE MEASURES

Thoreau has installed a standard for life-and-death that will seem harsh and ungenerous to those who hope to have lived, and hope that their deaths are fitting and instructive. Only he who fully lives can really die, and only he who really dies can have fully lived. In a loose sense this seems fair enough. But for Thoreau, Brown is not just one of a number who share the widely distributed characteristic of fully living (and dying). For Thoreau, he embodies a *measure* of living. He is not an example of something we would recognize without him, but an exemplar by means of whom we know an excellence, and without whom we would be ignorant. Everest is not an example of high alpine terrain; it is *exemplary,* the *measure,* of snowcapped majesty. Brown is not *an*

[37] Ibid.
[38] Ibid., 280.

example of moral heroism, any more than the "yard stick" at the Bureau of Standards is an *example* of something a yard long. Brown is *exemplary*, the uncontestable *measure* and *standard* of what heroism *will be*. In his apotheosis of John Brown, Thoreau drives the bar for *fully* living up and out of reach. Brown is placed in a select company that includes Socrates and Christ and but one or two others. Is the rest of humanity thus dispossessed? For an ordinary mortal aspiring to *realize* virtue or excellence, this standard might seem useless, or even brutally dismissive. Thoreau is disheartening and candid: "Only a half dozen or so have died [hence *lived*] since the world began."[39]

I am not asking whether, all things considered, John Brown is a good man, or his actions, justifiable, or whether Thoreau is correct to extol him. I ask how Thoreau's position can be *intelligible in its own terms*, in a *charitable reconstruction*. To ask whether John Brown was justified in his actions, or whether Thoreau was justified in praising them, would involve asking, for example, whether our moral landscape can accommodate "moral terrorists," as it were; and second, whether Brown might be less a terrorist than a prematurely enlisted Union Army officer (he jumped the gun); and also whether he is a reincarnation of the farmers and villagers of Concord who opened fire on those surely legitimate defenders of civic order and the law, the British Army; and finally whether his action was one in a sequence of earlier battles, a tactical response, say, to the slavers' sack of Lawrence, Kansas— these are questions I only mention here.

I set aside these questions of justification in favor of seeking intelligibility. I ask why, in general, we should pay attention to men or women held up as exemplary—say, as Thoreau holds up John Brown as a radiant, immortal figure—when they install a dismally *unrealizable* standard. Thoreau says only a few have learned to live, which puts *life* dismally out of reach. He also says that only a few have learned to *walk*. The exemplary tramper is equally out of reach. Does it make sense for Thoreau to valorize exemplary moral virtue (in the life of John Brown or Socrates) and valorize exemplary walking (in the stride of a saunterer) when that seems to deflate the aspirations of those who know that the exemplary is hopelessly out of reach?

Yet, a standard hopelessly out of reach still shows us something *other* than the uninspired standards of passable life, or passable death. Something other than the conventional life exists—*somewhere—somehow*.

---

[39] Ibid., 277.

To give leeway to a higher requirement can *by itself* pull us out of complacency (at least for a moment). That would be ecstasy, for to be ecstatic just *is* to be pulled outside of oneself. A glimpse of the best in the person of the exceptional Socrates or John Brown makes the standards of the merely passable no longer the only game in town. Excellence can be exultingly wonderful to view. In art, we admire genius in performance or composition. Yet showing us a skill or life that could never be ours should not end in belittling us or depriving us of life. Thoreau gives us a measure for living that's set at the highest notch. Should we therefore discredit it? That could seem like sour grapes, or *resentment.*

A standard we can never fully attain, or even hope to attain, can nevertheless sharpen our perceptions of excellence. Listening to a performer we could never become, we learn something special about musical depth. And hearing Brown's life as Thoreau does, we can hope to learn more about full life and death, despite our having no hope of scaling the heights Brown attains. From this angle, an exemplar does not so much give us a goal to attain as a new light that alters the landscape we traverse. We are given the glitter of new possibilities and the impossibility of old options. We get no new action-guide but a new orientation. We are awakened to a sensibility previously unknown. Our perceptions are translated to a new register. Perhaps slavery is more impossible than it was. The world after Brown is not the same as the world before Brown. He does not give us the specific *telos* of our action but casts his light over the space in which our specific actions will occur.

By the dim light of those who graze in a good-enough, passable pasture, Brown will be found mad, a fanatic, fantasy-driven killer, subject to delusions of grandeur, an irresponsible man leading the naïve to disaster and threatening all civil order. Thoreau based his high assessment of Brown on first-hand acquaintance. Some months before Harpers Ferry, Brown had approached both Thoreau and Emerson for funds—without being terribly specific about his plans. Talking with him over dinner, both men were impressed by Brown's demeanor, courage, and character. In their view—and they were sharp observers of character—it was no fanatic or bungler that they faced. In his apotheosis, Thoreau saves Brown from the denigration and abuse he otherwise attracts, and saves Concord and its surrounds from their indifference to his testament. And for those who were already indignant at the debasement of government in enforcing slave practices, Thoreau's writing stiffens the spirit of resistance to evil and affirmation of good.

Finally, as we've seen, there's more than one standard to pit against the complacency of only passable living. In Thoreau's hands, John Brown is pitched to apocalyptic intensity. More gentle and perhaps more attainable are the standards wafting through "Walking," "Wild Apples," and *Walden*. So the choice, at last, is not, or need not be, solely between the party of Brown and the party of men of quiet desperation. Our ideals of full living are many and varied. We may fail at the demands John Brown exacts, and if Thoreau's practice sets the bar, we may also fail at truly walking. We can nevertheless sharpen our sensibilities in the light of their lives.

Thoreau also holds, beyond walking and living and dying well, that we might inhabit a paradise in the taste of a late December apple, newly thawed, picked some months after freezing, when its fermentation makes it the favorite of the gods. Need we fall short here, as well? Perhaps we can exalt in knowing wild apples, and that, for a moment, will be achievement enough.

IX. PORUS SOULS

When John Thoreau, Henry's brother, died of lockjaw, Henry nearly died with him. It was as if the bodies, their very physiologies, were porous, as disease, and near death passed from one to the other. John died in Henry's arms, and Henry took on all the symptoms of John's disease. Their souls, too, became porous. John's death entered Henry's spirit, killing part of him, causing a psychic trauma. John's spirit entered also in the form of an impulse to write a long account of their time together. This resuscitation of John's spirit came out quite a bit later in *A Week on the Concord and Merrimack Rivers*. Henry takes in John's spirit, and sends it out in writing. Then later still, he takes in John Brown's spirit, and sends it out in writing. Or we could reverse the directionality: John Thoreau and John Brown each enter Henry's spirit to transform it, enter through the porous membrane that is his soul. Henry suffers Brown's affliction, and having allowed it entry, keeps it from the dead in writing two of his most eloquent and topical essays: "A Plea for Captain John Brown," written after Brown's arrest, and its companion, "The Last Days of John Brown," written for his burial. Writing becomes consecration as Brown's spirit enters Henry's and is returned blessed, to be received by waiting others.

Brown is not ordinarily, passably good. As Thoreau puts it, he is a transcendentalist in virtue of transcending garden-variety goodness. He risks his life escorting a dozen hunted strangers to a Canadian freedom through hostile and armed territory. His life, the life of his family, and the lives of those he escorted were at risk. He pursues a heroic vocation. He would bring captives from captivity. He aroused a dread among the Missourians through whose territory he passed, Thoreau said, for it was known they confronted a man who would not be taken. As news of Harpers Ferry traveled north, he became a meteor, an avenging angel, a portent and first taste of apocalypse ahead. "He has a spark of divinity in him," Thoreau says, and attests, "Of all the men who were my contemporaries, it seemed to me that John Brown was the only one who *had not died.*"[40]

Thoreau is not pleading for Brown's life, as if it were something physiological to prolong or steal away under cover of night. Crito offered Socrates an escape from certain execution; an ex-Kansas soldier offered Brown an escape, which he refused.[41] Brown's character, like Socrates' secures his "immortal life." Thoreau writes of life that can't be lost, immortal life. Thoreau saves Brown as Paul saves Jesus and as Plato saves Socrates. Each figure is a place within a field of spirit, a porous place of mutual openness to others open to us. Soul or spirit is that open field of possibility, spread temporally forward and back, and spatially in every direction. To take place within the flows that constitute this field is to let saving words arc through it, to receive such words, reanimate them, and pass on their salvations to endless unknown others. Souls open as spirit—take in, give back.

X. Infinite Culture

We are biological creatures who are also essentially cultural, creatures that exercise power and undergo powerlessness in the reception, sustenance, and reproduction of a second nature, cultural spirit, as it were. We work in and under lasting institutions that are more than physiological inheritance: music, politics, and schooling; ways of burial, birth, and war; ways of painting, poetry, and sports; of raising kids and marrying them; of writing out lives. These forms are supra-personal or institutional and also intensely personal, forming the persons we are, our second natures, in play as a culture's practices and its varied exemplars of them take residence as our inheritance.

---

[40] "A Plea" (278) and "Last Days" (288) in *Essays.*

[41] Silas Soule offered a rescue attempt after Brown was captured and jailed.

Thoreau is invaded by his brother's suffering in a physiological transmission of symptoms, brother to brother.[42] By simple accounting, John had lockjaw and Henry didn't, Henry survives and John doesn't. But it's also clear that Henry is translated into a new somatic-psychic configuration (call him Henry-J, or John-H), whose spirit translates forward in the living (cultural) words of *A Week on the Concord*, and translated still further afield as *A Week* finds its living breath in my classroom. Thus a many-times-translated Concord spirit is active in our present, having flowed forward from lives robust 150 years ago.

Thoreau travels mysteriously from sister to sister, from brother to speech, from words to books, from books to new spirit, growing in animation and momentum (when robust). Perhaps in his present incarnation as *A Week*, *Walden*, and "Civil Disobedience" (or "Resistance"), Thoreau is as robust as he ever was. In a world in and of anomalous spirit, declarations of what life-or-death amounts to are not definitive. To acknowledge the liveliness of Thoreau, or Henry-John, confirms the efficacy of cumulative generations of cultural reproduction, and confirms porous boundaries between Henry and *A Week*, between *A Week* and us, and between us and those to come.

Porous membranes are gates that open or shut to another's somatic-psychic presence. We are reciprocally dependent in that when I shut down a gate to you, I kill part of you and part of myself. If enough souls shut down to a style of music, that style dies, ceases to be translated into ever-new life. If I shut down to the brothers-Thoreau, part of *A Week* will die. If collectively we die to the spirit of *A Week*, culturally we die a small (or large) death. Imagine if *A Week* goes unread and dies, and after it "Resistance to Civil Government" and *Walden*. Henry will have suffered a death and a dimension of global interconnectedness will have died, as well. The death of "Resistance" or "Disobedience" will take with it a part of Gandhi and Martin Luther King, and lessen the punch of the idea and practice of resistance that underlie parts of American and Modern Indian history.[43] Happily, Thoreau and Gandhi survive as we read "Civil Disobedience" attentively. We die in solitude, to be sure, but also in community, collectively. A reader letting

---

[42] See Wai Chee Dimock's brilliant discussion in *Through Other Continents: American Literature Across Deep Time*, Princeton: Princeton University Press, 2008, Chapter 1, "Global Civil Society: Thoreau on Three Continents." She has John and Henry linked like Siamese twins: the somatic-psychic border, porous.

[43] Dimock describes what I call "infinite culture" in *Through Other Continents*.

Thoreau's life have impact can occlude the Concord town hall record of his death.

Thoreau does not write to pass on data but to dramatize, restage, relive, so that in reading we can restage, relive, live. Reliving Thoreau's "Resistance" or *A Week on the Concord* resuscitates a part of cultural life that stretches back to Thoreau's Concord, and rebounds forward through Gandhi and King and bounces back again toward some of the oldest writing on the globe. Thoreau reached back to the *Gita* and over to Greece and Aeschylus and then forward and north to a Milton who in turn reaches back to Biblical time and space. To relive *A Week* in reading is to intercept and then relive a river trip, let's say a *mere* century and a half ago, for it's also to relive passages on death and war that Thoreau culls and transmutes from the *Bhagavad Gita.* How can we picture this longevity?

We might think of rippling circles radiating from a stone tossed in the middle of a quiet lake, the spatial extensions from a center read as temporal extensions, as well. Or we might think of carbon radiating from an ancient bone, still sending out its powerful signals from a distant past, say the past of the *Gita,* or the more recent past of *A Week.* But the images of widening ripples and of radiation from a shard of ancient life predict steady disintegration of signal, yet some cultural texts seem to show only *expanding* strength in their circles of signal. Their energy is dispersed in strengths that far exceed the power of their initial signals. Cultural dispersion, it seems, is more like the spread of an ancient species of forest life, a dispersion or broadcast marked by multiple advances and declines, adaptations and transmutations. The *Gita* in the woods outside Concord is not exactly the *Gita* in third-century Bombay or in nineteenth-century London. Nevertheless, despite endless translation-mistranslation, "A Plea" or "Slavery in Massachusetts" reanimates our present second nature. Those Concord essays only gain strength as we hear beneath their surface *Aeschylus* or the *Book of Joel* or the *Gita,* as their resonance confirms an infinite culture.

In preparing his transmissions, at once literary, religious, and philosophical, Thoreau hopes for readers. He envisions them as the next step in the ever-emerging reality of his writing. As his spirit and the spirit of John Brown intertwine, so both intertwine with the interanimations that lie ahead.[44] The burden of Thoreau's writing rests

---

[44] Thoreau's walking and politics converge. He delivered "Wild Apples" in February 1860, less than three months after Brown was hanged. He died on May 6, 1862. It was published in November 1862, and so might be considered Thoreau's "Amen."

with him, but not with him alone, and at the present, we might hazard that his hopes are somewhat requited. If not everywhere, he yet has his attentive circle of readers keeping him alive. And we can hope for more of them ahead. The day after Brown's death, no doubt under immunological stress from the event, Thoreau caught the cold that led to the bronchitis and tuberculosis that would kill him, by coroner's accounts—but by other accounts, it was just the beginning of his translations.

XI. NOT MERELY MATTER

Cultural events spring out of their underlying material contexts. Catgut and varnish, wood and steel, are the material underlay for the sweet sound of a violin. But the spread of a new concerto around the globe is a transmission that springs free from a plane of catgut and steel. John's material life-and-death can spring into Henry's. The *Gita*, as a material book, can pass into the spirit of *A Week*. As we read *A Week*, we absorb a Henry animated by John and the *Gita*. Who knows the boundless material underlay of the *Gita* or Henry or John? For *A Week on the Concord*, we need at least lumber, paper, water, and pencils— and the institutions of publishing and libraries—and then cultural ceremonies of schooling in history and verse, and ears that can hear, all of which allow spirit to spring free.

The powers of bodily expressiveness begin with an underlay of physiology and bodily mobility, but bodily expressions then spring free, say in an Anthony Hopkins performance. The powers of poetic expressiveness begin with an underlay of intelligible, simple speech, but can spring free in the eloquence of a Thoreau. His remark that he had not heard of John Brown's death is a crucial moment in the raising of Brown—from physiological extinction to spiritual perdurance. A spirit plays on the surface of an expressive body, and a spirit plays on the surface of a prose and poetry penned by Thoreau. John Brown is recreated, translated as spirit in "A Plea" and "Last Days."

If we let powers at play in the words of the texts speak to us as our own, we're transformed, transfigured by reading and words. Through openness to eloquence we achieve openness to otherness. We see the other as our own, and ourselves in the other. And we find that our community of words contain and renew the spirit of Thoreau, the spirit of Ktaadn, the spirit of wild apples or lilies, and the spirit of Fuller's bones and John Brown's death. That is enough to keep us alive.

APPENDIX: FURTHER NOTES

On "Translation"

In the last paragraph of "Last Days of John Brown," Thoreau figures
the day of his death as the day of his "translation"—as if Brown's words
and actions now begin lengthy translation, perhaps from an earthly to
a heavenly text, but surely from his words and actions into words that
Thoreau and others will offer to ensure he has not spoken in vain.
Thus Brown is translated from the gallows to new life, and to an indefinitely extending life. In a different instance of translation, the old
body is buried in North Elba, yet a new body appears translated to
canvas, one painted by Thomas Hovenden nearly three decades later,
ca. 1884, now hung in The Philadelphia Museum of Art. Thoreau
foretells this cultural translation days before Brown's demise, predict-
ing that the likeness of Brown will appear as an "ornament in some
future national gallery" (final paragraph, "A Plea"). The man's spirit
was also translated through its rendering by James Redpath (*Echoes of
Harpers Ferry*, 1860), and later by W.E.B. Du Bois (*John Brown*, 1909),
and Russell Banks (*Cloudsplitter: A Novel*, 1998).

The Burns Case and Before

In the Shadrach case (1851), the rescue of a purported slave from
the Boston courthouse was successful: a group of free Blacks stormed
the courtroom, taking the guards by surprise, grabbed Shadrach, and
fled through a large supportive crowd to a waiting carriage. In the
Sims case (1851), a rescue failed. Guards were prepared this time and
in great enough number to keep a large crowd from breaking into
the courthouse. Sims was returned to Georgia where his "master" gave
him a near-fatal public whipping—as a lesson to would-be-rescuers
in the north. Marcia Robinson steered me toward contemporary
newspaper accounts of this failed rescue and the Burns case in
Garrison's *Liberator* and in Austin Willey's *Portland Inquirer*. Burns
was kidnapped (or arrested) on Wednesday, May 24, 1854. Friday,
free blacks and the white abolitions met separately to plan his rescue.
Theodore Parker, Wendell Phillips, Thomas Wentworth Higginson,
and others voted that night to muster a confrontation the next morning. Their black counterparts, who had been meeting separately, had
already come to the streets to storm the courthouse. The attempted

rescue that night became an improvised but concerted effort. There were enough guards within to repel them. Burns was tried under increased guard on May 27–31. The verdict was delayed so that Federal and Boston military and civic authorities had time to orchestrate a show of force. The verdict was delivered on June 2. The militias dressed Burns in silk and brightly colored pantaloons for a showy and humiliating walk to the ship for delivery South.

On Victor Hugo's Plea

Victor Hugo wrote a plea for Brown's life from his Guernsey exile. It was dated December 2, 1859, the day Brown was hung, and was widely published in Europe and America:

> [. . .] Politically speaking, the murder of John Brown would be an irreparable mistake. It would create in the Union a latent fissure that would in the long run break it. Brown's suffering might strengthen slavery in Virginia, but it would upend all American democracy. You save your shame, but you kill your glory. Morally speaking, it seems a part of the human light would put itself out, that the very notion of justice and injustice would hide itself in darkness, on that day where one would see the assassination of Emancipation by Liberty itself. [. . .] Let America know and ponder on this: there is something more frightening than Cain killing Abel, and that is Washington killing Spartacus.

On "an Ethical Sublime"

On the sublime, Thoreau has this to say: "[Death] has all the attributes of sublimity—Mystery, Power, Silence—a sublimity which no one can resist, which may be heightened, but cannot be equaled, by the thunder's roar, or the cannon's peal" (*The Writings of Henry David Thoreau: Early Essays and Miscellanies* ed. Joseph J. Moldenhauer and Edwin Moser, Princeton, NJ: Princeton, 1976, 93). And if the prospect of death, or the cannon's peal, snaps us morally alert, the sublime will have *ethical* import. Thunder, the top of Ktaadn, or floating alone looking skyward in a boat mark moments of "the sublime" or "infinite" for Thoreau, and hearken to the infinity of the soul and its boundless ethical relevance.

The sublime spans an associative field from "brute" physiological impact (the involuntary startle reflex) to forever unfinished hermeneutical interpretations—the continuous translations in "infinite culture"—including its possible "ontological import": a "revelation of the infinite," an "intrusion of the undeconstructible," or the tempering of an appearance of the divine or unknown. The non-moral sublime—a thunderclap across dark skies, the sudden breaching of a whale—breaks up our routine and "ordinary" perceptions and copings. The ethical sublime is an occasion when moral copings and "ordinary" perceptions are broken up by a startling, forbidding, and alluring eruption, perhaps the appearance of one who "rends the veil" of the commonplace, delivering the way he or she *is* in life. This appearance makes an inescapable demand on me to reorient myself, admitting new moral possibilities, and new moral impossibilities, in my moral landscape. I might shift, for instance, from seeing slavery as bad, to seeing it as intolerable. Exemplars can be guides, increasing the depth of our moral sensibilities, even though we would never hope—or wish—to replicate their lives.

On a Plurality of Planes of Moral Evaluation

It would be impossible to rank the importance of the taste of a wild apple, the need to pay one's bills, the necessity to speak for John Brown, the necessity to honor Margaret Fuller. There can be a flow from routine fulfillment of routine obligation (the threshold requirements of a passably not dishonorable life) to the imbibing of apples in ongoing creation that nurtures one's moral-aesthetic attention and responsiveness and then to one's "recognition" of the meteor that is John Brown—or another exalted moral paragon. How one negotiates these shifting terrains is itself an ethical issue, a burden of Dante, Cervantes, Kierkegaard, Levinas . . . Thoreau, to wrestle with or display, as they are able. We live amidst shifting moral landscapes with varying demands that resist systematization.

On the Complex Unity of Thoreau's Production

Thoreau ends his last essay, "Walking," with a long quote from the Old Testament *Book of Joel* that cites the Lord's dissatisfaction with his people and the consequent destruction by plague of all orchards, including life-giving apple orchards. Thoreau's citation of the destructiveness of the Lord should be linked to the presumption, quite common in the years leading up to the Civil War, that the coming bloodshed would be God's vengeance on a sinful slave-holding people. Thoreau is happy to move effortlessly from Hindu to Greek to Hebraic to Christian divinities. The penultimate section of the essay recounts Thoreau's Dionysian joy in drinking a frozen, thawed, and fermented apple. Innocent, pagan, Dionysian delight precedes God's wrath—but surely *not* as punishment for pleasure. Jehovah's wrath, for Thoreau, is reserved for slavery and all those who permit it. It's a credit to Thoreau's genius that unlike the writing of *Walden,* which filled nearly a decade (1844–54), his eloquent political essays are started and completed in a matter of weeks in the heat of unrelenting political skirmishes.

If we pair "Slavery in Massachusetts" with "Wild Apples" we find a chiasmus, a crossing of opposites recurrent in Thoreau's writing. The fundamental movement of "Slavery in Massachusetts" is dark disillusionment with the stench of slavery's corruption—yet it ends with the hope of the lily. The fundamental movement of "Wild Apples" is gentle celebration of the land and its fruits (even though orchards are sadly replacing the wild)—yet it ends with the disillusioned wrath of God. The original impetus to work out the interplay between "John Brown" and "Wild Apples" came from Clark West. He challenged us, in a Thoreau seminar, to see Thoreau whole; I thank him for that.

Paradise and Hell are intertwined, intermixed, perhaps even interanimating. If we are on the verge of apocalypse, perhaps always on the verge, what will be revealed? For Thoreau, at least, I sense it will be something like the rhythms of an endless creation worth praising, where perishing heralds resuscitation and life heralds perishing. This interplay of heaven and hell is as central to Thoreau as his fundamental impulse of love for the world, the affirming and preserving impulse that lets his political writings implicate the preservation of human character and freedom and also the preservation of the expressive animation of nature. Simultaneously, this impulse lets his evocations of nature implicate the preservation of character and freedom among the creatures, human and otherwise, who traverse and inhabit it.

CONCLUSION

The time is past to bring the explorations undertaken here to some grand or not so grand conclusion. At most I can say why I think that is not an option. I think of philosophy often as necessarily piecemeal, and perhaps especially so when its underlying aim is to follow its own roots, its capacity to attract and entrap and inspire, which means living with incompleteness, and proceeding at a rather autobiographical, or at least personal level, as the bulk of these essays do. The German Romantics rediscovered the fragment as a vehicle for philosophy, and Wittgenstein patently avoided "grand conclusions" by calling his explorations "remarks," "investigations," or "scraps," taking a cue from Kierkegaard's *Philosophical Scraps*. It's instructive that the first word in Cavell's most recent philosophical–autobiographical piece is "Excerpts"—he will not, toward the end of his prolific writing career, give us conclusions.

Rather than try to say once more, no doubt failingly, in a general way what seems to underlie these essays, let me share a final sense of disappointment, a moment lost, as I see it. It's a moment lost to Richard Rorty in a late lecture at Columbia on William James' *Varieties of Religious Experience*.[1] This moment of loss betrays a hope I have for James and others, a hope I've tried to realize to some small extent in these essays.

William James is a philosopher who no doubt belongs among the thinkers I've traveled with in this book. His own experience, it's clear, seeps through on nearly every page of *Varieties*, which in no way belittles his striking accomplishment in those lectures. In his recorded talk on those remarkable lectures, Rorty begins by confiding that he has found himself wanting to say new things about James—despite his

---

[1] This lecture was Rorty's contribution to a conference sponsored by Columbia University's Center for the Study of Science, March 24–25, 2002, that focused on William James' *The Varieties of Religious Experience*. A video of the lecture can be found on youtube.

having written on *Varieties* before, and taught it many times. It had come alive in new ways, he says. He tries this way and that to make James' attestations and claims come out right. He clearly enjoys the wit and verve of James' prose, but confesses dismay in the final moments of his talk. Having canvassed all the arguments, he concludes that none pass muster. But not wanting to be utterly deflationary, Rorty adds a note of promise. Despite its failures, the book will continue to be read, and rightly so, he avers. And why should we cherish and pass on to our students a bag of bad arguments? Here's what he says, and what he says is on target: "[*Varieties*] is a portion of the intellectual autobiography of an exceptionally magnanimous man. James' mind was more capacious and his charity more expansive than most of us, and so reading his book may help us become more like James, and so help us become better people." To me this is eloquent and generous. Because it's blurted out as time ran out, it also seems stinting—too little, too late. Rorty has let a moment slip by. He's held back when he might have expanded that wonderful parting thought, on which so much hangs.

The thought is that despite bad arguments, a philosopher can be worth reading because it counts what sort of a person that philosopher is, and further, that good persons teach by example, and by the tenor of their words, by what they reveal in their words as those words meet and engage (or deny) the world, and mirror their contact with it, as persons. Seldom, if ever, do we connect with the worth of the world or our teachers on the basis of argument assessment alone. The power of arguments to pull the train of conviction is indeed great, but they don't pull on their own, and don't need to. I hope I've pitched in on the task that Rorty cut short by showing how philosophy, as it's lived and written with clarity and passion, can deliver conviction. It delivers through a voice that evokes and preserves, that offers things for our glance and our praise, and that warms the fires of imagination and the heart.

I've lingered here with writers who show generosity of spirit, love of the world, and the steep cost of lost intimacy with one's senses; who show us ever-present shadows of affliction, and the importance of language and poetry in expressing a soul; who instill courage and hope and any number of other essential virtues and sensibilities; and who know that personal revelation has a role in showing what philosophy and a better life might be.

Philosophy's lamp shines beyond argument to illuminate the contours of the local, and the penumbras of the poetic or religious. Its beacons sparkle in ever widening disclosures alongside the lights of the arts, religion, and literature, retaining a love for the world, and wonder—retaining the power of poetry, as Plato's myths do. It preserves wisdom and faith that is close to the heart and to the intimate grain of experience.

* * *

Thoreau tracks a slender stick, rising slightly from the sand—then writes close to it, and as it changes, sings all it might mean.

BIBLIOGRAPHY

Alter, Robert, trans. *Genesis*, New York: Norton, 1996.

Ameriks, Karl, ed. *The Cambridge Companion to German Idealism*, Cambridge: Cambridge University Press, 2000.

Antonaccio, Maria, and William Schweiker, eds. *Iris Murdoch and the Search for Human Goodness*, Chicago: University of Chicago Press, 1996.

Arendt, Hannah. *The Human Condition*, Chicago: University of Chicago Press, 1998.

Baier, Annette A. *Progress of Sentiments: A Study of Hume's Treatise*, Cambridge MA: Harvard University Press, 1991.

Basho, *Knapsack Notebook*, in *Basho's Journey*, trans. and intro. David Landis Barnhill, Albany, NY: SUNY Press, 2005.

Beiser, Frederick. *The Romantic Imperative*, Cambridge: Harvard University Press, 2003.

Bergman, Ingemar. *The Seventh Seal*, Halifax, NS: Lorrimer Books, 1968.

Borradori, Giovanna. *The American Philosopher*, Chicago: University of Chicago Press, 1994.

Brodhead, Richard H. *The Good of This Place: Values and Challenges in College Education*, New Haven: Yale University Press, 2004.

Bugbee, Henry. "The Sense and the Conception of Being," PhD diss. 1947, University of California, Berkeley.

—*The Inward Morning, A Philosophical Exploration in Journal Form*, foreword Gabriel Marcel, intro. Edward F. Mooney, Athens, GA: University of Georgia Press, 1999, first published State College, PA: Bald Eagle Press, 1958.

—"The Philosophical Significance of the Sublime," *Philosophy Today*, Spring, 1967.

—"A Way of Reading *The Book of Job*," unpublished.

Burke, Edmund. *On the Sublime and the Beautiful*, Harvard Classics, no 24, ed. Charles W. Eliot, New York: P.F. Collier & Son, 1909–14.

Caputo, John L. *The Prayers and Tears of Jacques Derrida*, Bloomington: Indiana University Press, 1997.

Cavell, Stanley. *Must We Mean What We Say?* New York: Charles Scribners, 1969.

Cavell, Stanley, *Philosophy the Day After Tomorrow*, Cambridge, MA: Harvard University Press, 2005.

—"The Availability of the Philosophy of the Later Wittgenstein," chapter 2 in *Must We Mean What We Say*, New York: Charles Scribner, 1969, 41–72.

—*The Claim of Reason: Wittgenstein, Skepticism, Morality, and Tragedy*, Oxford: Oxford University Press, 1979.

—*The Senses of Walden, an Expanded Edition*, San Francisco: North Point Press, 1981.

—*A Pitch of Philosophy: Autobiographical Exercises*, Cambridge, MA: Harvard University Press, 1994.

—*City of Words, Pedagogical Letters on a Register of the Moral Life*, Cambridge, MA: Harvard University Press, 2004.

—"Excerpts from Memory," *Critical Inquiry* (36), 2006.

Cody, Arthur. "Words, You, and Me," *Inquiry*, September 2002.

Conant, James. "The James/Royce Dispute," in *The Cambridge Companion to William James*, ed. Ruth Anna Putnam, Cambridge: Cambridge University Press, 1997.

—"Nietzsche's Perfectionism: A Reading of Schopenhauer as Educator," in *Nietzsche's Postmoralism*, ed. Richard Schacht, Cambridge: Cambridge University Press, 2001.

Conway, Dan. "Walking with Bugbee and Thoreau," in *Wilderness and the Heart*, ed. Edward F. Mooney, Athens: University of Georgia Press, 1999.

Critchley, Simon. *Things Merely Are*, London: Routledge, 2005.

Davenport, John. *Will as Commitment and Resolve: An Existential Account of Creativity, Love, Virtue, and Happiness*, New York: Fordham University Press, 2007.

Davidson, Donald. *Subjective, Intersubjective, Objective*, Oxford: Oxford University, 2001.

Dimock, Wai Chee. "Global Civil Society: Thoreau on Three Continents," chapter 2 in *Through Other Continents: American Literature Across Deep Time*, Princeton: Princeton University Press, 2008.

Dostoevsky, Feodor. *The Brothers Karamazov*, New York: Bantam, 1984.

Edwards, James. *The Plain Sense of Things: The Fate of Religion in an Age of Normal Nihilism*, College Park: Penn State University Press, 1997.

Eldridge, Richard. *Leading a Human Life: Wittgenstein, Intentionality, and Romanticism,* Chicago: University of Chicago Press, 1997.

Fingarette, Herbert. "The Meaning of Law in The Book of Job," in *Revisions,* eds. A. MacIntyre and S. Hauerwas, Notre Dame: University of Notre Dame Press, 1981.

Fisher, Philip. *The Vehement Passions,* Princeton: Princeton University Press, 2002.

Furtak, Rick Anthony. *Wisdom in Love: Kierkegaard and the Ancient Quest for Emotional Integrity,* Notre Dame: University of Notre Dame, 2005.

Gass, William. *Reading Rilke: Reflections on the Problems of Translation,* New York: Basic Books, 1999.

Glatzner, Nahum, ed. *Dimensions of Job,* New York: Schocken, 1969.

Gray, Glenn. *The Warriors: Reflections on Men in Battle,* Lincoln Nebraska: Bison Books, 1998. (First Published, Harcourt and Brace, 1959.)

Hadot, Pierre. *Philosophy as a Way of Life,* Malden, MA: Blackwell, 1995.

Harrison, Robert Pogue. *The Dominion of the Dead,* Chicago: University of Chicago Press, 2003.

Hauerwas, Stanley. *The State of the University: Academic Knowledges and the Knowledge of God,* Malden, MA: Blackwell, 2007.

Heidegger, Martin. "A Dialogue on Language," chapter 3 in *On the Way To Language,* trans. Peter Hertz, New York: Harper and Row, 1971.

Hitt, Christopher. "Toward an Ecological Sublime," *New Literary History,* 30.3, 1999.

Hocking, William Ernest. *The Meaning of God in Human Experience,* New Haven: Yale University Press, 1911.

—*The Self: Its Body and Freedom,* New Haven: Yale University Press, 1928.

—"Lectures on Religion," unpublished, 1941.

Kant, Immanuel. "Idea for a Universal History from a Cosmopolitan Point of View," *Kant's Political Writings,* ed. Hans Reiss, Cambridge: Cambridge University Press, 1970.

—*Critique of Judgment,* "Analytic of the sublime," New York: Barnes & Noble, 2005.

Kierkegaard, Søren. *Concluding Unscientific Postscript,* trans. Walter Lowrie and David Swenson, Princeton: Princeton University Press, 1941.

—*Concept of Dread,* trans. Walter Lowrie, Princeton: Princeton University Press, 1957.

—*Fear and Trembling*, trans. Alastair Hannay, New York: Penguin, 1985.

—*Either/Or*, vol. 2, trans. Howard V. and Edna H, Princeton: Princeton University Press, 1987.

—*Sickness Unto Death*, trans. Alastair Hannay, New York: Penguin, 1989.

—*Kierkegaard's Papers and Journals*, trans. Alastair Hannay, New York: Penguin, 1996.

Ladinsky, Daniel. *Love Poems from God*, New York: Penguin, 2002.

Lamore, Charles. *The Romantic Legacy*, New York: Columbia University Press, 1996.

Lingis, Alphonso. *The Community of those who have Nothing in Common*, Bloomington: University of Indiana Press, 1994.

Marcel, Gabriel. *The Mystery of Being*, 2 vols. South Bend: St. Augustine's Press, 2001.

McNeil, David N. "Human Discourse, Eros, and Madness in Plato's Republic," *The Review of Metaphysics*, LV.2, December 2001.

Melville, Herman. *Moby Dick*, New York: Penguin, 2001.

Miles, Margaret R. *Reading for Life: Beauty, Pluralism, and Responsibility*, New York, Continuum, 1997.

Mooney, Edward F. "Love, this Lenient Interpreter," chapter 5 in *On Søren Kierkegaard: Dialogue, Polemic, Lost Intimacy, and Time*, Aldershot: Ashgate, 2007.

—*On Søren Kierkegaard: Dialogue, Polemic, Lost Intimacy, and Time*, Aldershot: Ashgate, 2007.

—"Transfigurations: The Intimate Agency of Death," in *Kierkegaard and Death*, ed. Patrick Stokes and Adam Buben, Bloomington, IN: University of Indiana Press, 2011.

Mooney, Edward F., ed. *Wilderness and the Heart: Henry Bugbee's Philosophy of Place, Presence, and Memory*, foreword by Alasdair MacIntyre, Athens, GA: University of Georgia Press, 1999.

Nietzsche, Fredrich. *The Birth of Tragedy*, Cambridge: Cambridge University Press, 1999.

Nightingale, Andrea Wilson. *Spectacles of Truth in Classical Greek Philosophy*, Cambridge: Cambridge University Press, 2004.

Nussbaum, Martha, *Love's Knowledge, Essays on Philosophy and Literature*, Oxford: Oxford University Press, 1990.

Ortega y Gassett, José, *Meditations on Quixote*, trans. Evelyn Rugg and Diego Marín, Urbana: University of Illinois Press, 2000.

Pattison, George L. *"Poor Paris!": Kierkegaard's Critique of the Spectacular City*, Berlin: Walter de Gruyter, 1999.

—*A Short Introduction to the Philosophy of Religion*, London: SCM Press, 2001.

Pippin, Robert B. *Henry James and Modern Moral Life*, Cambridge: Cambridge University Press, 2000.

Pitcher, George. "A Review," *The Journal of Philosophy*, 61. 2, 111–12, 1964.

Poon, Wilson, and McLecish, Tom, "Real Presences: Two Scientists' Response to George Steiner", *Theology* Vol. 102 (1999) 169–176.

Putnam, Hilary, "Jewish Ethics," in *The Blackwell Companion to Religious Ethics*, ed. William Schweiker, Malden, MA: Blackwell, 2005.

Renehan, Jr., Edward J. *The Secret Six, The True Tale of the Men who Conspired with John Brown*, Columbia: University of South Carolina Press, 1997.

Richardson, Robert H. Jr. *Emerson, The Mind on Fire*, Berkeley: University of California Press, 1995.

Roberts, Robert C. "Existence, Emotion, and Virtue: Classical Themes in Kierkegaard," in *Cambridge Companion to Kierkegaard*, ed. A. Hannay and G. Marino, Cambridge: Cambridge University Press, 1998.

—*Emotions*, Cambridge: Cambridge University Press, 2003.

—"Kierkegaard and Ethical Theory," in *Ethics, Love, and Faith in Kierkegaard*, ed. Edward F. Mooney, Bloomington: University of Indiana Press, 2008.

Roberts, Tyler. "Criticism as a Conduct of Gratitude: Stanley Cavell and Radical Theology,". *Post-Secular Encounters: Religious Studies, Humanities and the Politics of the Academy*, New York, Columbia University Press, 2011.

Rose, Gillian. *Love's Work: A Reckoning with Life*, New York: Schocken, 1995.

Rousseau, Jean Jacques. *Reveries of a Solitary Walker*, New York: Penguin, 1980.

Rudd, Anthony. *Expressing the World: Skepticism, Wittgenstein, Heidegger*, Chicago: OpenCourt, 2003.

Rushdie, Salman. *The Ground Beneath Her Feet*, London: Picador, 2000.

Russell, Bertrand. *Autobiography*, London: Routledge, 2000.

Ryle, Gilbert. *The Concept of Mind*, London: Hutchinson, 1949.

Steiner, George. *Real Presences*, Chicago: University of Chicago, 1989.

Stern, David G. *Wittgenstein on Mind and Language*, Oxford: Oxford University Press, 1995.

Stewart, Garrett. "The Avoidance of Stanley Cavell," in *Contending with Stanley Cavell*, ed. Russell B. Goodman, Oxford: Oxford University Press, 2005.

Taylor, Charles. "Heidegger, Language and Ecology," chapter 8 in *Philosophical Arguments*, Cambridge, MA: Harvard University Press, 1995.

Thoreau, Henry David. *Cape Cod,* New York: Thomas Crowell, 1961.

—*Thoreau's Writings, Early Essays and Miscellanies,* ed. Joseph J. Molden-hauer and Edwin Moser, Princeton: Princeton University Press, 1975.

—*A Week on the Concord and Merrimack Rivers,* ed. Carl F. Hove, William L. Howarth, and Elizabeth Hall Witherell, intro John McPhee, Princeton: Princeton University Press, 1980.

—*Thoreau's Writings, Journal,* vol. 3, 1848–51, ed. R. Sattelmeyer, M.R. Patterson, and W. Rossi, Princeton: Princeton University Press, 1990.

—*The Collected Essays of Henry D. Thoreau,* ed. Lewis Hyde, San Francisco: North Point Press, 2002.

Tilley, Terrence. *The Evils of Theodicy,* Washington DC: Georgetown, 1992.

Tolstoy, Leo. *Anna Karenina,* New York: Penguin, 2004.

Unamuno, Miguel de. *Our Lord Don Quixote: The Life of Don Quixote and Sancho,* Princeton: Princeton University Press, Bollingen series, 1976.

—*Mist: A Tragic-comic Novel,* trans. Werner Fite, New York: Alfred A. Knopf, 1928; Chicago: University of Illinois, 2000.

University of Malta mission statement 2006, http://www.um.edu.mt/about/uom.

Viefhues-Baily, Ludger H. *Beyond the Philosopher's Fear: A Cavellian Reading of Gender, Origin and Religion in Modern Skepticism,* Aldershot: Ashgate, 2007.

Wilshire Bruce. *Wild Hunger: The Primal Roots of Modern Addiction,* Lanham, MD: Rowman and Littlefield Publishers, 1998.

Wilshire, Bruce. *The Primal Roots of American Philosophy: Pragmatism, Phenomenology, and Native American Thought* College Park: Penn State University Press, 2000.

Wittgenstein, Ludwig. *Culture and Value,* Chicago: University of Chicago, 1984.

Zimmerman, Michael. "Heidegger, Buddhism, and Deep Ecology," in *The Cambridge Companion to Heidegger,* ed. Charles Guignon, Cambridge: Cambridge University Press, 1993.

INDEX

Adorno, T. 166
Alcibiades 35–7, 51, 96, 165
Alcott, B. 205
Amish elder 38, 171
anomaly/anomalous zone 138,
    204–5, 215
Arendt, H. 15–16, 176–82, 189, 192
argument x, 11–12, 16, 22–3, 30, 40–1,
    50, 96, 101, 113–14, 116–18, 120,
    126, 165–6, 169, 179, 180, 183,
    191, 193, 223
Aristotle/Aristotelian 9, 74, 114,
    123, 133
Auden, W.H. 16, 178–83, 193
Augenblick 74, 165, 171n
Augustine 22, 24, 79, 95–6, 111n, 124

Bach, J.S. 76, 106, 170
Beethoven, L. 61, 76, 112
behold/beholden 8–14, 44, 66, 138,
    157, 193, 195, 197, 207, 209
Benjamin, W. 178
Bergman, I. 187, 188n, 189–90
birth/natality/rebirth 4–5, 32, 35,
    48n, 66, 68–9, 100, 102, 105, 113
    136, 138, 163–4, 166, 169, 171–2,
    198, 209, 214
blessing 12, 58, 104–6, 123, 213
Bloch, E. 99
body-self/ body-spirit 131, 138
Bonhoeffer, D. 173
Brahms, J. 112, 167–8
Brown, J. 16, 194–5, 198–221
Bugbee, H. ix–xi, 7, 9, 11–14, 19–77,
    78–9, 86, 89–92, 93–107, 135,
    137, 197
Buddha 207

Burke, E. 59, 61, 66, 198
Burns, A. 194, 201–2, 218–19

Camus, A. 114
Caputo, J. xiii, 79, 80, 111n
Carnap, R. 98
Cartesian/Descartes 10, 16, 51, 84,
    114, 135, 137–8, 190
Casey, E. 96
Cavell, S. x, xi, xiii, 13, 14, 24, 58, 62n,
    73, 94–107, 111–28, 157, 167n,
    190–2, 222
Cervantes, M./Quixote 3–4, 46, 53,
    165–8, 187, 220
Christ/Jesus 4n, 57, 119, 211, 119–20,
    192, 203, 207, 211, 214
Cixous, H. 96
compassion 147–9, 189
confession 24, 95, 102, 114, 122–3,
    170
Conway, Dan x, xiii, 97n
Critchley, S. 172n, 200n

Davenport, J. xiii
Day, W. xiii
death 4–5, 13–14, 16, 25, 28–9, 37–8,
    44–6, 49, 53–7, 59–63, 65–71,
    74–5, 77, 80, 103–4, 119, 127, 129,
    136, 138, 162–5, 166n, 169, 171,
    173, 177–8, 181–2, 187–9, 192,
    194, 196, 198, 201, 203–7, 209–13,
    215–19
Deleuze, G. 59
delight 11, 24, 68, 81, 83, 89, 162, 167,
    170, 198, 221
dependence/interdependence 36, 63,
    136, 142, 149, 150n, 152, 154–60

231